Women in Latin America and the Caribbean

Women in Latin America and the Caribbean

RESTORING WOMEN TO HISTORY

by Marysa Navarro and
Virginia Sánchez Korrol, with Kecia Ali

*Indiana
University
Press*
BLOOMINGTON AND INDIANAPOLIS

Maps from *Latin American History: A Teaching Atlas,* by Cathryn L. Lombardi and John V. Lombardi, © 1983. Reprinted by permission of the University of Wisconsin Press.

This book is a publication of
Indiana University Press
601 North Morton Street
Bloomington, IN 47404-3797 USA

http://www.indiana.edu/~iupress

Telephone orders 800-842-6796
Fax orders 812-855-7931
Orders by e-mail iuporder@indiana.edu

The paper used in this publication meets the minimum requirements of American National Standard for Information Sciences—Permanence of Paper for Printed Library Materials, ANSI Z39.48-1984.

Manufactured in the United States of America

Library of Congress Cataloging-in-Publication Data

Navarro, Marysa.
Women in Latin America and the Caribbean : restoring women to history /
by Marysa Navarro and Virginia Sánchez Korrol, with Kecia Ali.
p. cm. — (Restoring women to history)
Includes bibliographical references and index.
ISBN 0-253-33479-9 (cl : alk. paper). — ISBN 0-253-21307-X (pa : alk. paper)
1. Women—Latin America—History. 2. Women—Caribbean Area—History.
I. Sánchez Korrol, Virginia. II. Ali, Kecia. III. Title. IV. Series.
HQ1460.5.N38 1999
305.4'09729—dc21   99-10085

1 2 3 4 5 04 03 02 01 00 99

*For Gail Vernazza, Patsy Carter,
Genevieve Williamson, and Virginia Close,
with thanks and affection, from Marysa.*

*For Aura, Pamela, Lauren, and Anelisa,
with love and appreciation for your support,
from Virginia.*

*For our mothers and our daughters,
who for us bridge the past and the future and
encourage us to seek the women of the world.*

MARYSA NAVARRO AND
VIRGINIA SÁNCHEZ KORROL

CONTENTS

SERIES EDITORS' PREFACE

This book is part of a four-volume series entitled "Restoring Women to History": *Women in Sub-Saharan Africa; Women in Asia; Women in Latin America and the Caribbean;* and *Women in the Middle East and North Africa.* The project began in 1984, bringing together scholars to synthesize historical information and interpretation on women outside of Europe and the United States of America. Earlier versions of the volumes were produced and distributed by the Organization of American Historians (OAH) as *Restoring Women to History: Teaching Packets for Integrating Women's History into Courses on Africa, Asia, Latin America, the Caribbean, and the Middle East* (1988; revised, 1990).

These volumes are intended to help teachers who wish to incorporate women into their courses, researchers who wish to identify gaps in the scholarship and/or pursue comparative analysis, and students who wish to have available a broad synthesis of historical materials on women. Although the primary audience is historians, scholars in related fields will find the materials useful as well. Each volume includes a bibliography, in which readings suitable for students are identified with an asterisk. Each volume is preceded by a broad, topical introduction written by Cheryl Johnson-Odim and Margaret Strobel that draws examples from all four volumes.

This project is the culmination of many years' work by many people. Cheryl Johnson-Odim and Margaret Strobel conceived of the original single volume, extending OAH projects published in the 1970s and 1980s on U.S. and European women's history. Joan Hoff (then Joan Hoff-Wilson, Executive Director of the Organization of American Historians), Cheryl Johnson-Odim, and Margaret Strobel wrote proposals that received funding from the National Endowment for the Humanities for a planning meeting of eight other authors, and from the Fund for the Improvement of Postsecondary Education (FIPSE) for the preparation, distribution, and dissemination of the manuscript. Under the leadership of Executive Director Arnita Jones, the OAH took on the responsibility of printing and distributing the single volume. The FIPSE grant enabled us to introduce the project through panels at conferences of the African Studies Association, the Association of Asian Studies, the Latin American Studies Association, the Middle Eastern Studies Association, and the World History Association.

Because of the strong positive response to the single volume, Joan Catapano, Senior Sponsoring Editor at Indiana University Press, encouraged the ten of us to revise and expand the material in four separate volumes. In the decade or so since the inception of this project, the historical literature on women from these regions has grown dramatically. Iris Berger and E. Frances White added important new information to their original contributions. White was assisted by Cathy Skidmore-Hess, who helped revise some of the material on West and Central Africa. Barbara Ramusack and Sharon Sievers found new material for Asia, with certain regions and periods still very unstudied. Marysa Navarro and Virginia Sánchez Korrol, with help from Kecia Ali, reworked their previous essays on Latin America and the Caribbean. Guity Nashat and Judith Tucker developed further their material on the Middle East and North Africa from the earlier volume.

This project is a blend of individual and collective work. In the 1980s, we met twice to discuss ways to divide the material into sections and to obtain consistency and comparability across the units. Each author read widely in order to prepare her section, reworking the piece substantially in response to comments from various readers and published reviews.

Scholars familiar with each region read and commented on various drafts. For this crucial assistance, we wish to thank Edward A. Alpers, Shimwaayi Muntemba, and Kathleen Sheldon for Africa; Marjorie Bingham, Emily Honig, Veena Talwar Oldenberg, Mrinalini Sinha, and Ann Waltner for Asia; Lauren (Robin) Derby, Asunción Lavrin, Susan Schroeder, and Mary Kay Vaughan for Latin America and the Caribbean; and Janet Afary, Margot Badran, Julia Clancy-Smith, Fred Donner, Nancy Gallagher, and Jo Ann Scurlock for the Middle East and North Africa. In revising the introduction, we received useful comments from Janet Afary, Antoinette Burton, Nupur Chaudhuri, Susan Geiger, and Claire Robertson. Anne Mendelson ably copyedited the OAH publication; LuAnne Holladay and Jane Lyle copyedited the Indiana University Press volumes. At various times over the years, undergraduate and graduate students and staff helped with nailing down bibliographic citations and/or preparing the manuscript. These include Mary Lynn Dietsche, Geri Franco, Jill Lessner, Lisa Oppenheim, and Marynel Ryan from the University of Illinois at Chicago, and Carole Emberton, Maryann Spiller, and Esaa Zakee from Loyola University Chicago.

This project owes much both to the Organization of American Historians and to Indiana University Press. We thank the following OAH staff members, past and present, who contributed to the project in various ways: Mary Belding, Jeanette Chafin, Ginger Foutz, Brian Fox, Kara Hamm, Joan Hoff, Arnita A. Jones, Nancy Larsen, Barbara Lewis, Michelle McNamara, and Michael Regoli. Our editor at IUP, Joan Catapano, waited months on end for the completion of our work. Without her prompting, we would probably not have taken the initiative to attempt this revision and publication of separate volumes. We appreciate her patience.

From reviews, citations, and comments at conferences, we know that scholars, teachers, and students have found our efforts valuable. That knowledge has helped sustain us in those moments when each of us, having moved on to other scholarly projects or having assumed demanding administrative positions, questioned the wisdom of having committed ourselves to revising and expanding the original materials. This kind of scholarship, what Ernest Boyer calls the "scholarship of integration," is typically not rewarded in academe as much as is traditional research, what Boyer terms the "scholarship of discovery."* For this reason we are particularly thankful to the authors for their willingness to commit their minds and energies to revising their work. Although our effort to get ten authors simultaneously to complete all four volumes sometimes made us feel like we were herding cats, we appreciate the intellectual exchange and the friendships that have developed over the years of our work together.

Cheryl Johnson-Odim
Chicago, Illinois

Margaret Strobel
Chicago, Illinois

*Ernest L. Boyer, *Scholarship Reconsidered: Priorities of the Professoriate* (Princeton, N.J.: Carnegie Foundation for the Advancement of Teaching, 1990), 16–21.

AUTHORS' PREFACE

In the fifteen years between the publication of these essays in the *Restoring Women to History* teaching packets and the publication of this volume, women's roles in Latin America and the Caribbean have undergone significant transformation. In many countries, women have achieved an unprecedented relevance and visibility. Their contributions to the cultural sphere have multiplied and their participation in the work force and social and political reform movements has increased. In Chile, Argentina, Uruguay, and Brazil, for example, they have played a crucial role in the demise of authoritarian dictatorships. They have also taken part in the process of democratization that has ensued, including the writing of new constitutions, the enactment of legislation to increase their political representation, and the end to centenary discriminatory laws. Unfortunately, too many women still continue to struggle for economic survival, lack education, and have to organize against enormous odds to resist and overcome class and ethno-racial oppression.

This work emerged from our own concern to document the history of women over a broad historical span. Aware of the struggles of a growing Latina population in the United States, we saw connections and recognized the importance of raising their consciousness, not only about their historical antecedents, but also about the similarities and differences among women of color throughout the Americas. Moreover, this volume represents an opportunity to synthesize a growing body of historical and literary scholarship on Latin American and Caribbean women, produced in great measure during the last two decades. It was important to include a critical analysis on gender as well as the intersection of race, class, and ethnicity over time. Our attempt to balance breadth and depth lent itself to comparative overviews and opens the way for new research in a number of areas.

We are deeply indebted to our editors, Margaret Strobel and Cheryl Johnson-Odim, for having the vision to explore women's history on a global scale. Their enthusiasm and commitment to the larger project kept us all on track. Joan Catapano, at Indiana University Press, encouraged us all to revise our work and make it available for broader distribution. We wish to thank Kecia Ali for reading and editing the manuscripts, and for bringing new information to our attention in the revision stages. Our readers—Lauren (Robin) Derby, Susan Schroeder, Asunción Lavrin, and Mary Kay Vaughan—deserve our sincerest appreciation for offering helpful suggestions. We hope that this work signals the beginning of closer collaborative efforts to bring about understanding regarding women's world history.

Marysa Navarro
Hanover, New Hampshire

Virginia Sánchez Korrol
Brooklyn, New York

GLOSSARY

aqllas: Inka "Wives of the Sun."

aqllawasi: Inka nunneries.

ayllu: Basic social unit of the Inka empire, of pre-Inka origin; communal land-owning, endogamous descent group.

B.C.E.: "Before the common era." Used in place of B.C.

cacique, cacica: Male, female chief.

calpullec: Aztec male council of elders.

calpulli: Aztec tribal kinship unit.

campesinas, campesinos: Female, male peasants.

castas: Racially mixed people.

C.E.: "Of the common era." Used in place of A.D.

chicha: Alcoholic beverage used in Inka religious ceremonies.

cihualpilli: Aztec noblewoman.

compañera **(pl. *compañeras*):** Partners, companions.

criada **(pl. *criadas*):** Female domestic servants.

criollas, criollos: Females, males who were American-born Spaniards during the colonial era.

encomienda: Right granted by Spanish crown to collect tribute and labor from Indians, in exchange for which the *encomendero* agreed to protect, Christianize, and "hispanize" the Indians.

encomendero, encomendera: Grant holders; see *encomienda*.

hacendado: Hacienda owner.

hacienda **(pl. *haciendas*):** Large, self-sufficient agricultural estates.

junta: Military rulers (contemporary period).

kurakas: Local male political authorities installed by Inkas to govern the populations they conquered.

mãe de santos **(pl. *mães de santos*):** Priestesses.

mameluco: Individuals of mixed Indian and European/Portuguese parentage.

maquilas, maquiladoras: U.S.–Mexico border factories.

mestizo: Individuals of mixed Indian and European/Spanish parentage.

Pallas: Females of Inka ruling class.

peninsulares: Spanish individuals born in Spain; cf. *criollas.*

pilli (**pl.** *pipiltin*)**:** Member of Aztec ruling class.

quilombos: Communities of runaway slaves.

soldadera (**pl.** *soldaderas*)**:** Woman (or women) accompanying Mexican revolutionary soldiers.

tertulias: Intellectual social gatherings.

veladas: Intellectual social gatherings.

MAPS

Latin America:
Culture Levels
and
Tribal Groups
Prior to Contact with Europeans

1. High Civilization Empires
2. Theocratic and Militaristic Chiefdoms
3. Tropical Forest Farm Villages
4. Desert Farm Villages
5. Nomadic Hunting, Fishing, and
   Gathering Peoples

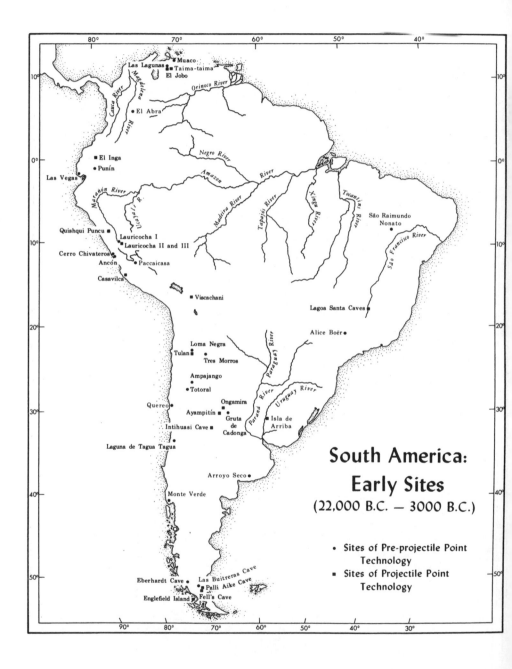

South America:
Early Sites
(22,000 B.C. — 3000 B.C.)

- • Sites of Pre-projectile Point Technology
- ▪ Sites of Projectile Point Technology

Muaco
Las Lagunas   Taima-taima
El Jobo
Orinoco River
El Abra
Negro River
El Inga
Punín
Amazon River
Las Vegas
Marañón River
Ucayali R.
Madeira River
Tapajós River
Xingu River
Tocantins River
São Raimundo Nonato
São Francisco River
Quishqui Puncu
Lauricocha I
Lauricocha II and III
Cerro Chivateros
Ancón   Paccaicasa
Casavilca
Viscachani
Lagoa Santa Caves
Alice Boër
Loma Negra
Tulan   Tres Morros
Paraguay River
Ampajango
Totoral
Quereo   Ongamira
Ayampitín   Paraná River   Uruguay River
Intihuasi Cave   Gruta de Cadonga   Isla de Arriba
Laguna de Tagua Tagua
Arroyo Seco
Monte Verde
Eberhardt Cave   Las Buitreras Cave
Palli Aike Cave
Englefield Island   Fell's Cave

Cauca River
Magdalena River

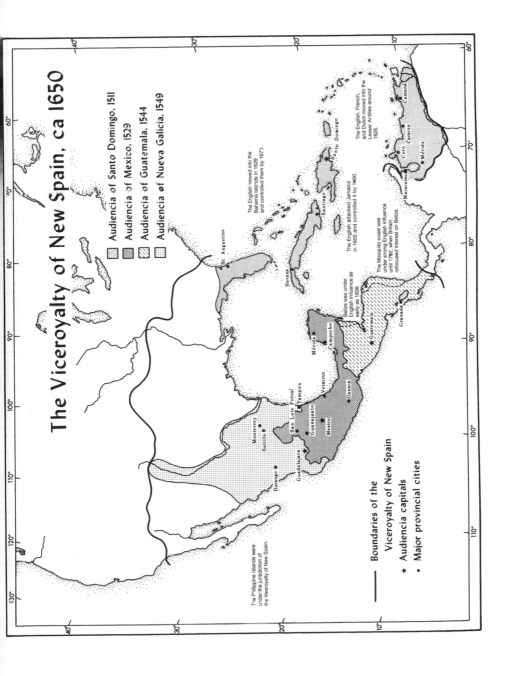

The Viceroyalty of New Spain, ca 1650

Audiencia of Santo Domingo, 1511
Audiencia of Mexico, 1529
Audiencia of Guatemala, 1544
Audiencia of Nueva Galicia, 1549

The English moved into the
Bahama Islands in 1629
and controlled them by 1670.

The English attacked Jamaica
in 1655 and controlled it by 1660.

Belize was under
English influence as
early as 1638.

The Mosquito coast was
under strong English influence
until 1782, when Britain
refocused interest on Belize.

The English, French,
and Dutch moved into the
Lesser Antilles around
1625.

The Philippine Islands were
under the jurisdiction of
the Viceroyalty of New Spain.

Durango
Saltillo
Monterrey
Guadalajara
San Luis Potosí
Guanajuato
Tampico
Veracruz
Mexico
Oaxaca
Mérida
Campeche
Guatemala
Granada
St. Augustine
Havana
Santiago
Santo Domingo
Mérida
Coro
Caracas
Maracaibo
Cumaná

—— Boundaries of the
        Viceroyalty of New Spain
★ Audiencia capitals
• Major provincial cities

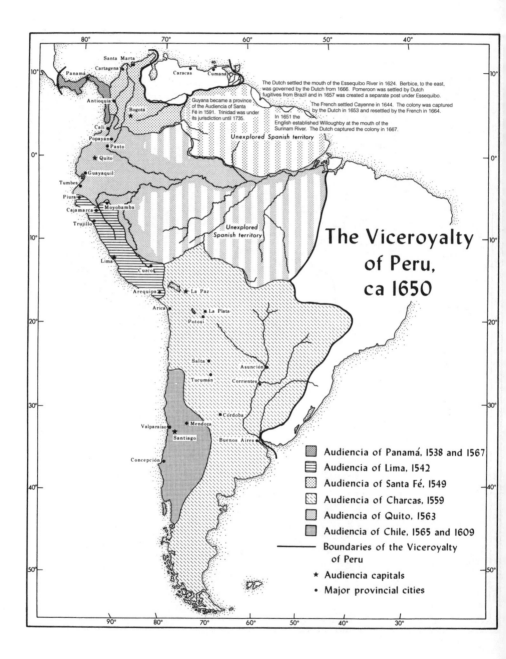

The Viceroyalty
of Peru,
ca 1650

The Dutch settled the mouth of the Essequibo River in 1624. Berbice, to the east, was governed by the Dutch from 1666. Pomeroon was settled by Dutch fugitives from Brazil and in 1657 was created a separate post under Essequibo.

Guyana became a province of the Audiencia of Santa Fé in 1591. Trinidad was under its jurisdiction until 1735.

The French settled Cayenne in 1644. The colony was captured by the Dutch in 1653 and resettled by the French in 1664.

In 1651 the English established Willoughby at the mouth of the Surinam River. The Dutch captured the colony in 1667.

Unexplored Spanish territory

Unexplored Spanish territory

	Audiencia of Panamá, 1538 and 1567
	Audiencia of Lima, 1542
	Audiencia of Santa Fé, 1549
	Audiencia of Charcas, 1559
	Audiencia of Quito, 1563
	Audiencia of Chile, 1565 and 1609
———	Boundaries of the Viceroyalty of Peru
★	Audiencia capitals
•	Major provincial cities

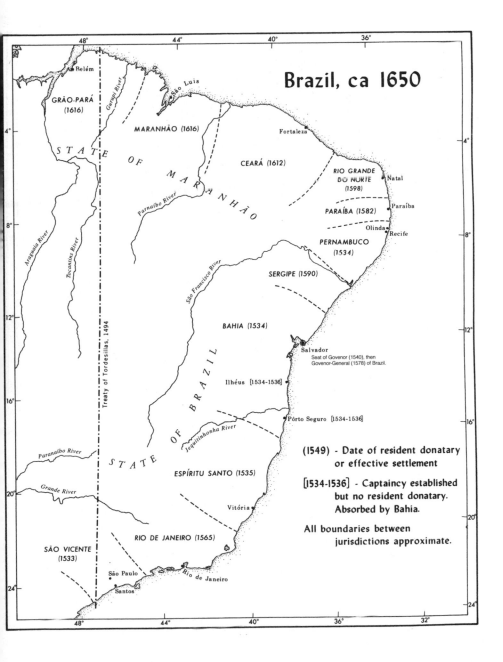

Brazil, ca 1650

GRÃO-PARÁ (1616)
Belém

STATE OF MARANHÃO

MARANHÃO (1616)
São Luis

CEARÁ (1612)
Fortaleza

RIO GRANDE DO NORTE (1598)
Natal

PARAÍBA (1582)
Paraíba

PERNAMBUCO (1534)
Olinda
Recife

SERGIPE (1590)

BAHIA (1534)

Salvador
Seat of Govenor (1540), then
Govenor-General (1578) of Brazil.

Ilhéus [1534-1536]

Pôrto Seguro [1534-1536]

STATE OF BRAZIL

ESPÍRITU SANTO (1535)
Vitória

RIO DE JANEIRO (1565)
Rio de Janeiro

SÃO VICENTE (1533)
São Paulo
Santos

Araguaia River
Tocantins River
Parnaíbo River
São Francisco River
Jequitinhonha River
Paranaíbo River
Grande River
Gurupi River

Treaty of Tordesillas, 1494

(1549) - Date of resident donatary
or effective settlement

[1534-1536] - Captaincy established
but no resident donatary.
Absorbed by Bahia.

All boundaries between
jurisdictions approximate.

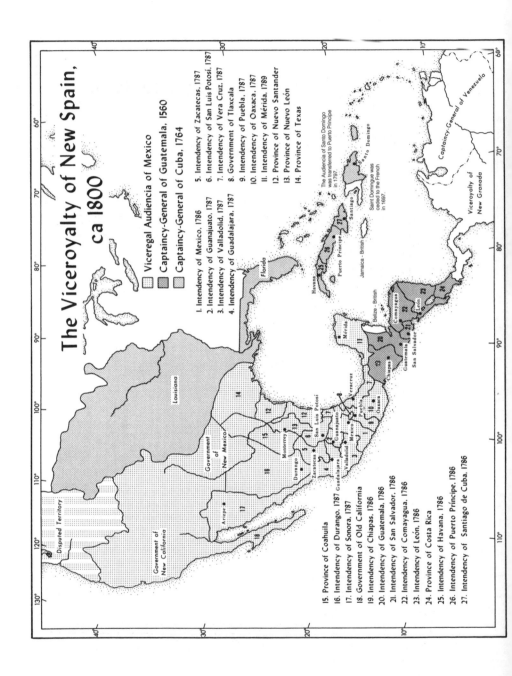

The Viceroyalty of New Spain, ca 1800

Viceregal Audiencia of Mexico
Captaincy-General of Guatemala, 1560
Captaincy-General of Cuba, 1764

1. Intendency of Mexico. 1786
2. Intendency of Guanajuato. 1787
3. Intendency of Valladolid. 1787
4. Intendency of Guadalajara. 1787
5. Intendency of Zacatecas. 1787
6. Intendency of San Luis Potosí. 1787
7. Intendency of Vera Cruz. 1787
8. Government of Tlaxcala
9. Intendency of Puebla. 1787
10. Intendency of Oaxaca. 1787
11. Intendency of Mérida. 1789
12. Province of Nuevo Santander
13. Province of Nuevo León
14. Province of Texas

15. Province of Coahuila
16. Intendency of Durango. 1787
17. Intendency of Sonora. 1787
18. Government of Old California
19. Intendency of Chiapas. 1786
20. Intendency of Guatemala. 1786
21. Intendency of San Salvador. 1786
22. Intendency of Comayagua. 1786
23. Intendency of León. 1786
24. Province of Costa Rica
25. Intendency of Havana. 1786
26. Intendency of Puerto Príncipe. 1786
27. Intendency of Santiago de Cuba. 1786

Disputed Territory

Government of New California

Government of New Mexico

Louisiana

Arizpe

Durango

Monterrey

Zacatecas

Guadalajara

San Luis Potosí

Valladolid

Mexico

Puebla

Veracruz

Oaxaca

Florida

Mérida

Guatemala

San Salvador

Chiapas

Comayagua

León

Belize - British

Havana

Jamaica - British

Puerto Príncipe

Santiago

Santo Domingo

The Audiencia of Santo Domingo was transferred to Puerto Príncipe in 1797.

Saint Domingue was ceded to the French in 1697.

Captaincy-General of Venezuela

Viceroyalty of New Granada

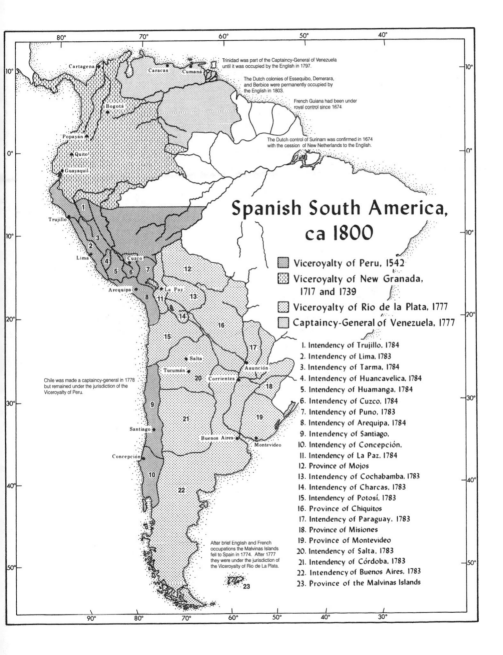

Spanish South America, ca 1800

- ▨ Viceroyalty of Peru, 1542
- ▨ Viceroyalty of New Granada, 1717 and 1739
- ▨ Viceroyalty of Rio de la Plata, 1777
- ▨ Captaincy-General of Venezuela, 1777

1. Intendency of Trujillo, 1784
2. Intendency of Lima, 1783
3. Intendency of Tarma, 1784
4. Intendency of Huancavelica, 1784
5. Intendency of Huamanga, 1784
6. Intendency of Cuzco, 1784
7. Intendency of Puno, 1783
8. Intendency of Arequipa, 1784
9. Intendency of Santiago,
10. Intendency of Concepción,
11. Intendency of La Paz, 1784
12. Province of Mojos
13. Intendency of Cochabamba, 1783
14. Intendency of Charcas, 1783
15. Intendency of Potosí, 1783
16. Province of Chiquitos
17. Intendency of Paraguay, 1783
18. Province of Misiones
19. Province of Montevideo
20. Intendency of Salta, 1783
21. Intendency of Córdoba, 1783
22. Intendency of Buenos Aires, 1783
23. Province of the Malvinas Islands

Trinidad was part of the Captaincy-General of Venezuela until it was occupied by the English in 1797.

The Dutch colonies of Essequibo, Demerara, and Berbice were permanently occupied by the English in 1803.

French Guiana had been under royal control since 1674

The Dutch control of Surinam was confirmed in 1674 with the cession of New Netherlands to the English.

Chile was made a captaincy-general in 1778 but remained under the jurisdiction of the Viceroyalty of Peru.

After brief English and French occupations the Malvinas Islands fell to Spain in 1774. After 1777 they were under the jurisdiction of the Viceroyalty of Rio de La Plata.

Cartagena, Caracas, Cumaná, Bogotá, Popayán, Quito, Guayaquil, Trujillo, Lima, Cuzco, Arequipa, La Paz, Salta, Tucumán, Corrientes, Asunción, Santiago, Buenos Aires, Montevideo, Concepción

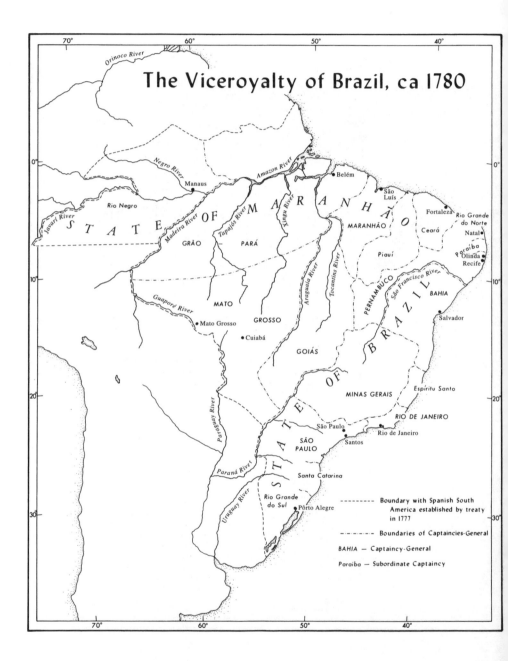

The Viceroyalty of Brazil, ca 1780

70°   60°   50°   40°

Orinoco River

0°

Negro River

Amazon River

Manaus

• Belém

Rio Negro

São Luís

Javari River

Madeira River

Tapajós River

Xingu River

S T A T E   O F   M A R A N H Ã O

Fortaleza

Rio Grande do Norte

MARANHÃO

Ceará

Natal

GRÃO

PARÁ

Piauí

Paraíba

Olinda

Recife

São Francisco River

Araguaia River

Tocantins River

PERNAMBUCO

BAHIA

10°

Guaporé River

MATO

• Mato Grosso

GROSSO

• Cuiabá

GOIÁS

Salvador

S T A T E   O F   B R A Z I L

Paraguay River

MINAS GERAIS

Espíritu Santo

20°

Paraná River

São Paulo

RIO DE JANEIRO

SÃO

PAULO

Santos

Rio de Janeiro

Santa Catarina

Uruguay River

Rio Grande do Sul

Pôrto Alegre

30°

– – – – –   Boundary with Spanish South America established by treaty in 1777

–·–·–   Boundaries of Captaincies-General

BAHIA — Captaincy-General

Paraíba — Subordinate Captaincy

70°   60°   50°   40°

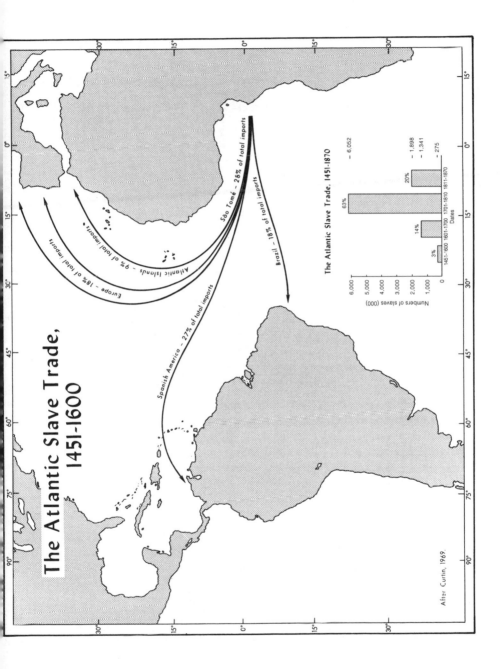

The Atlantic Slave Trade, 1451-1600

Europe – 18% of total imports

Atlantic Islands – 9% of total imports

São Tomé – 26% of total imports

Brazil – 18% of total imports

Spanish America – 27% of total imports

The Atlantic Slave Trade, 1451-1870

Numbers of slaves (000)

Dates	
1451-1600	3%
1601-1700	14%
1701-1810	63% – 6,052
1811-1870	20% – 1,898
	– 1,341
	– 275

After Curtin, 1969.

Latin America in 1830

Santo Domingo gained its independence from Spain in 1821. Occupied by Haiti in 1822, it finally regained its independence in 1844.

The United Provinces of Central America was dissolved by 1839.

British Guiana was founded in 1831 by uniting Berbice, Demerara, and Essequibo.

Cuba-Spanish
Belize-British
Jamaica-British
Puerto Rico-Spanish
Trinidad-British
Guiana-French
Surinam-Dutch

Mexico
Veracruz
Caracas
Bogota
Quito
Lima
Salvador
Rio de Janeiro
São Paulo
Asunción
Santiago
Buenos Aires
Montevideo

Argentine Confederacy 1810-1816
Patagonia

States with date of independence

- Mexico - 1821
- United Provinces of Central America - 1823
- Haiti - 1803
- Gran Colombia - 1819-1830
- Peru - 1821
- Bolivia - 1825
- Brazil - 1822
- Paraguay - 1811
- Uruguay - 1828
- United Provinces of La Plata - 1816
- Chile - 1817

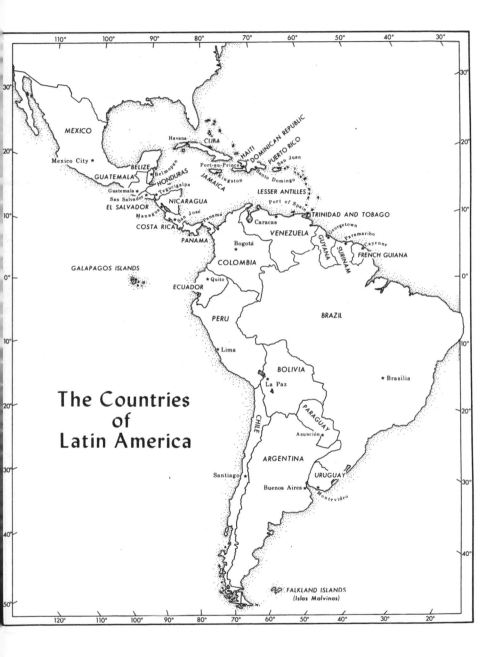

The Countries of Latin America

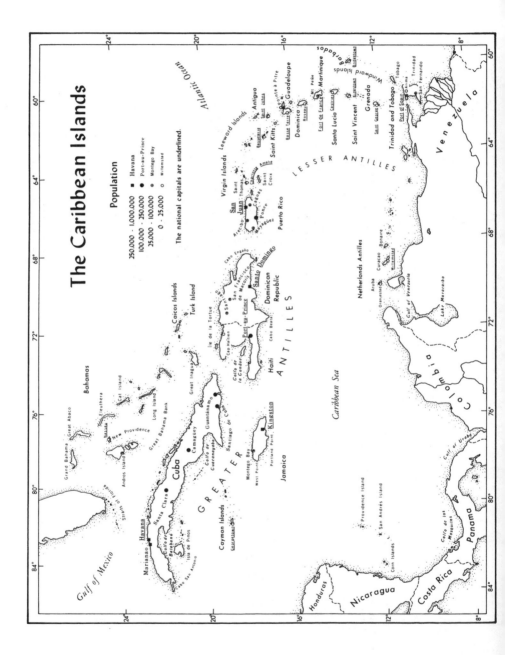

The Caribbean Islands

Population

250,000 - 1,000,000	■ Havana
100,000 - 250,000	● Port-au-Prince
25,000 - 100,000	● Montego Bay
0 - 25,000	○ Willemstad

The national capitals are underlined.

CHRONOLOGY

1804	Haiti declares independence.
1808	Spain and Portugal occupied by French forces. Portuguese Crown takes refuge in Brazil.
1809 to 1812	First Latin American insurrections.
1810 to 1850	Slavery abolished in most countries except Cuba, Puerto Rico, Brazil.
1818	Chilean independence.
1819	Colombian and Venezuelan independence.
1824	Battle of Ayacucho. Independence of Peru.
1828	Banda Oriental province becomes Uruguay.
ca. 1825 to 1855	Era of *caudillos,* civil wars, and political instability.
1830	Gran Colombia partition: Colombia, Venezuela, Ecuador.
1831 to 1889	Reign of Pedro II in Brazil.
1833	Abolition of slavery in British colonies.
1839	Central America partitioned into five republics.
1848	U.S.–Mexican War. Abolition of slavery in French colonies.
ca. 1850	Legal codes adopted in most countries.
1861	Benito Juárez heads Liberal government in Mexico.
1864 to 1870	Triple Alliance War. Paraguay, Brazil, Argentina, Uruguay.
1867 to 1876	Era of reforms, secularization, and modernization in Mexico.
1868 to 1878	Independence movements in Cuba and Puerto Rico. Ten Years' War in Cuba.
1873 to 1886	Slavery abolished in Puerto Rico, Cuba.
1879 to 1883	Pacific War. Chile, Peru, Bolivia.
1880	Indian Wars end in Chile and Argentina.
1880 to 1900	Republic proclaimed in Brazil. Abolition of slavery. Road, rail and communications developed in major Latin American countries.
1876 to 1910	Porfirio Díaz era in Mexico.
1898	End of Cuban War for Independence, known as the Spanish–American War.
1903	Panama secedes from Colombia, under U.S. influence.
1910 to 1917	Revolution in Mexico.
1912 to 1933	U.S. occupies Nicaragua, Haiti, Dominican Republic.
1914	U.S. builds the Panama Canal.
1925 to 1933	Gerardo Machado dictatorship in Cuba.
1929	Women gain franchise—Ecuador.*
ca. 1930	Military governments emerge in Argentina, Brazil, Peru.
1932	Women gain franchise—Brazil, Puerto Rico, Uruguay.

Note regarding dates for enfranchisement of women: In years of political strife when military takeovers suspended the constitutions, no one voted. Also, these are the years women got the right to vote, not necessarily the years when the laws were implemented.

1932 to 1935	Chaco War between Bolivia and Paraguay.
1934	Women gain franchise—Cuba.
1934 to 1940	Lázaro Cárdenas's presidency in Mexico.
1936 to 1979	Somoza era in Nicaragua.
1937 to 1945	Getulio Vargas era begins in Brazil. Ends with military coup.
1939 to 1959	Fulgencio Batista era in Cuba.
1942	Women gain franchise—Dominican Republic.
1945 to 1955	Juan Perón era begins in Argentina; ends with military coup. Gabriela Mistral awarded Nobel Prize in literature. Women gain franchise—Guatemala, Panama.
1947	Women gain franchise—Argentina, Venezuela.
1949	Women gain franchise—Chile, Costa Rica.
1950	Women gain franchise—El Salvador.
1950 to 1954	Jacobo Árbenz's presidency in Guatemala ends with CIA-backed military coup.
1952	Puerto Rico becomes U.S. Commonwealth. Women gain franchise—Bolivia.
1953	Women gain franchise—Mexico.
1954	General Stroessner era begins in Paraguay; ends with military coup.
1954	Women gain franchise—Colombia.
1955	Women gain franchise—Honduras, Nicaragua, Peru.
1957 to 1971	Duvalier era in Haiti.
1959	Triumph of the Cuban Revolution; Fidel Castro era begins.
1960 to 1983	Decolonization in Non-Hispanic Caribbean.
1961	Women gain franchise—Paraguay.
1967	Miguel Ángel Asturias awarded Nobel Prize in literature.
1970 to 1973	Salvador Allende's presidency in Chile; ends with coup d'état led by General Augusto Pinochet and sponsored by CIA.
1971	Pablo Neruda awarded Nobel Prize in literature.
1974 to 1976	Isabel Martínez de Perón assumes presidency of Argentina. Administration ends with military coup.
ca. 1978	Guerrilla warfare spreads throughout Central America.
1979	Triumph of Nicaraguan Revolution.
1982	Malvinas–Falklands War between U.K. and Argentina. Gabriel García Márquez awarded Nobel Prize in literature.
1983	Assassination of Prime Minister Maurice Bishop in Grenada; U.S. invades Granada.
1983 to 1989	Raúl Alfonsín is elected president of Argentina in a democratic process. Military accused of atrocities during the "dirty war" of the seventies is tried under civilian jurisdiction.
1985 to 1988	Democratic governments emerge in Guatemala, Argentina, Brazil.
1986	Democracy returns to Haiti.

SERIES EDITORS' INTRODUCTION

Conceptualizing the History of Women in Africa, Asia, Latin America and the Caribbean, and the Middle East and North Africa

CHERYL JOHNSON-ODIM AND MARGARET STROBEL

In this thematic overview* we hope to do, with beneficial results, what historians are loath to do: dispense with chronology and introduce several themes common to the histories of women in the "non-Western" world. A thematic focus will accomplish several purposes. First, we can discuss the significance of phenomena—for example, the existence of female networks and subcultures—so that the authors' references to such phenomena are given a broader context than the sometimes-scant evidence allows. Second, we can introduce and synthesize approaches and ideas found in feminist scholarship. Third, because regions often develop distinctive sets of research questions and ignore others, our overview may suggest new areas of exploration. Finally, we can suggest possibilities for comparative investigation.

We cannot here do justice to the specificity of the historical tradition in each region; readers may use the indexes of relevant volumes to locate elaborations on the examples cited below. Our themes highlight the similarities in women's experience across these very diverse regions, but the differences, not dealt with here, are equally crucial.

---

*An earlier version of this essay appeared in the *Journal of Women's History* 1, no. 1 (Spring 1989): 31–62.

The intellectual justification for addressing these four regions together rests on the assertion that most of these areas have experienced broadly comparable relationships with Western Europe and the United States in the past five hundred years. Although these volumes examine the long eras in each regional area before the last five hundred years, it is because of their histories of the last five hundred years that they are broadly viewed in the United States as "Third World," or "non-Western." We understand the need to problematize viewing *most* of the world's people, in all their diversity, in such "catch-all" categories and do not mean to claim the commonality of their relationship(s) with the West as the only reason for their appearance here.

It was difficult to decide on a common terminology that allowed us to keep from constantly listing the regions under consideration. "Third World" (despite some controversy) was often appropriate as a geopolitical designation, but it left out places such as Japan that are not generally regarded as Third World due to a high degree of industrialization. "Non-Western" also seemed appropriate, except that after many centuries of contact, Latin American societies cannot legitimately be regarded as entirely non-Western. Although we prefer not to refer to people by a negative term such as "non-Western" and are aware that terms such as "Third World" are problematic, we ended up employing both terms despite sometimes imperfect usage, in addition to the cumbersome listing of all four geographic regions.

A final word about terminology: we distinguish between "sex" as a set of biological (physiological) differences and "gender" as socially constructed roles that may build upon or ignore biological sex. Hence, in place of the common term "sex roles," in this text, we will instead use "gender roles."

THE CHALLENGE OF THIRD WORLD WOMEN'S HISTORY

It is important to avoid three common pitfalls: interpreting women as the exotic, women as victims, and women as anomalies. Stereotypes regarding the non-Western world (particularly those labeling it as "primitive," "backward," or "barbaric") are very prevalent in our society and frequently provide the only knowledge many North Americans have about other cultures. The roles, positions, and statuses of women in non-Western societies are often as central to those stereotypes today as they were when European colonizers first pointed to women's "oppression" in Africa, Asia, Latin America and the Caribbean, and the Middle East and North Africa as partial justification for their own imperialist designs. "Brideprice," women as "beasts of burden" and female genital mutilation (FGM) in Africa, *sati* and footbinding in Asia, *machismo* in Latin America, female hypersexuality in the Caribbean, and the harem and seclusion of women in the Middle East frequently represent the extent of the Western public's exposure to the lives of women in these regions. It is in fact such images of women that help fuel our pictures of these societies as exotic. Feminist historians challenge this notion of the female exotic by placing cultural practices in an appropriate sociocultural framework and by looking at a multitude of women's activities over the broad scope of their lives.

Women, just because they are women, have undeniably been disadvantaged in their access to political and economic power. Where the fact of being a woman intersected with belonging to a racial, ethnic, religious, or other minority, or with poverty or lower-class status, women could be doubly or triply disadvantaged. But women have never been a monolithic group even within the same society; class, race, and/or ethnicity could have consequences as significant for women's opportunity and status as did (does) gender. Women's history, however, is not primarily a history of disadvantage and degradation. Such a "victim analysis" fails to present a picture of the variety of women's multiple statuses and relationships (including those with other women), the dynamism and creativity of their activities, and their importance in various cultures.

Women's agency and initiative, as well as their subordination, must therefore be explored. Integrating the histories of women in Africa, Asia, Latin America and the Caribbean, and the Middle East and North Africa in part poses the same challenge as that of European and U.S. women's history: the expansion and transformation of conceptual categories that, in explaining male, rather than integrated, human experience, have treated women as anomalies. For example, political history has tended to focus on activity in the public sphere and on office holders, both of which highlight male experience. The evidence demonstrates that women also have exercised power. Historically, however, it was most often within gender-segregated settings that ordinary women were able to exercise their greatest degree of power and decision-making. And, when they acted collectively, women could exercise considerable power even within male-dominated societies. Individual women—for example, Eva Perón—were often important political actors and exerted influence, both inside and outside of formal political structures. Because women's political participation did not always appear in obvious places or ways, it has been regarded as peripheral or absent, a view that ignores the complex processes through which power is exerted in societies. An investigation of gender relationships can add a critical element of analysis to our scrutiny of history and to definitions and explanations of the operation of political power and the conceptual category of political activity.

In addition to challenging definitions of what constitutes political history, the study of women can reveal important insights into the study of an entire region. For example, if one looks at the actual impact of Confucianism on women's lives in East Asia, the system of teachings becomes a much less monolithic historical force than it has hitherto been considered.

Similarly, looking at gender clarifies our understanding of Latin American society. Scholars have long studied the development of racial division there, yet gender and class were central to that development in several ways. Sex both opened and closed racial barriers: sexual activity across racial lines was legitimized through the practice of concubinage and was sanctioned because of the unequal sex ratios among the colonizers. But concubinage, while protecting status differences between the colonizers and the colonized, also resulted in a mestizo and mulatto population whose existence undermined racial barriers. Thus the control of (female) sexuality was linked to the control of racial purity.

In the Middle East, aspects of women's position that are at the core of historical and contemporary Islamic society (e.g., seclusion and veiling) have their roots in pre-Islamic practices. Hence, Islam can be seen not only to have introduced important changes in the Middle East, but also to have built upon existing practices; the introduction of Islam does not mark as sharp a break as some scholars have claimed.

In the study of Africa, the recent emphasis on examining gender has transformed our understanding of the Atlantic slave trade, a topic of longstanding importance in African historiography. Scholars had noted that African males outnumbered females on the Middle Passage, but why this was the case received little attention. As scholars began to problematize gender roles within Africa—and noted the extraordinary role women played in agriculture—some came to view the Atlantic slave trade as being partially shaped by the desire of African slave-owning societies to accumulate female labor.

The act of including women in the histories of these regions represents a more profound challenge than the "add women and stir" approach, as it has often been identified. The mere insertion of famous women, like the insertion of only "exotic" and hurtful practices, gives a distorted and inadequate history of the bulk of women's experience in a given society.

Just as adding information about women challenges the existing histories of Africa, Asia, Latin America and the Caribbean, and the Middle East and North Africa, so too does adding information about women from these regions challenge the writing of women's history. Because the oppression of Third World women is the result of both internal sexism and externally induced dynamics (e.g., mercantile capitalism, colonialism, neo-colonialism), being citizens of the Third World is as crucial as gender. Therefore, studying women in the Third World means studying not only a less powerful category within society, but also a category within societies that have often been dominated in the international arena. Thus, some things that oppress(ed) women also oppress men (slavery, indentured labor, alienation of land from indigenous owners or conversion of land to cash crop production, export of raw natural resources and import of finished products made from those resources and even of food), though often in different ways. And many issues that are not obviously gender-related, such as lack of self-sufficiency in producing staple foods and provision of water, bear their heaviest impact on women who are disproportionately charged with providing food and water.

Finding women in the histories of the non-Western, just as in the Western, world requires persistence due to the silence or obliqueness of "traditional" historical sources such as documents written by historical actors themselves. The roles of women in agriculture, health, crafts, religion, politics, the arts, and other arenas have often been regarded as negligible, exceptional and infrequent, or irretrievable for other than the very recent period. However, far more is available than one may think; much of it lies hidden in non-obvious sources: oral testimony, mythology, life histories, genealogies, religious records, missionary and explorer accounts, archaeological excavations, language, legal codes, land tenure arrangements, oral and written literature, or cultural lore and fable. For women's histories, case studies often come after the general treatise, which frequently concentrates as much on exposing the lacunae and generating hypotheses as on synthesis. The historical literature on women in Africa, Asia, Latin America and the Caribbean, and the Middle East and North Africa has greatly increased in the years since these essays were first published, and that has led to their revision. Still, a great deal remains to be done. These general overviews are meant to acquaint scholars with the possibilities as much as to show what has been done.

THEORIES THAT EXPLAIN THE
SUBORDINATE STATUS OF WOMEN

Trained to look to the specifics of place and time more than to the creation of theory, historians have often left to anthropologists the task of theorizing about the origins of women's oppression or the factors that account for women's subordinate status. One basic division runs between biologically oriented and socioculturally oriented theories. The former finds significance in a relative universality of physical characteristics among humans and of a gender division of labor that assigns men to certain tasks and women to others, a division that sometimes characterizes the public sphere as a male domain and the private sphere as a female domain. This commonality is attributed to genetic or physical differences.

Environmentalists stress the equally apparent diversity of humans, physically and culturally, and claim that biology alone cannot cause this diversity. Moreover, they view "natural" features of society as fundamentally culturally and ideologically determined. Even childbirth and lactation, they argue, do not predestine women to stay at home; rather, societies can devise a division of labor that enables such women to be mobile.

Embedded in these positions are views about the appropriateness of men's and women's roles. Biologically oriented theories tend to assume that gender differences are best not tampered with. Sociocultural theories tend to see the pattern of women's subordination as subject to change; thus, the search for the causes of women's oppression becomes linked to the possibility of creating gender-equal societies. If the universality of women's subordinate status can be proved untrue, then the possibilities of creating gender-equal societies are strengthened; hence, some scholarship focuses on the search for matriarchies, or for gender-equal societies, past or present. While most scholars find evidence lacking, the discussions of matriarchy and gender-neutral societies have raised important questions about the relationship between the actual power of living women in a particular society and (a) kinship and residence patterns (e.g., matrilineality and matrilocality), (b) social structure and mode of production (e.g., patriarchy, pre-industrial), or (c) the ideological representations of women in art, ritual, or belief systems.

Another approach to the issue of the causes of women's oppression links women's power or lack of it to economic forces. Research in this area has generated questions about the link between gender inequality and levels of production or technology, class formation, women's and men's control of the products of their labor, etc. Furthermore, these theorists dispute the universality of the notions of public and private, arguing that these categories follow historically from the development of industrial(izing) societies. In the modern period discussion of women's oppression in postcolonial Third World countries must take into account the effects of colonialism and neo-colonialism on the construction of gender. In several places colonialism and neo-colonialism marginalized women in the economy, displaced them politically, cooperated with indigenous males to keep women socially subordinated, or increased the social subordination of women themselves.

Feminism challenges both European colonial and indigenous patriarchal ideologies regarding women. The relationship between Western and non-Western feminist thought has often, however, been adversarial. In part the tension between the two groups results from the explanation given for the oppression of women. Many non-Western women (even those who identify themselves as feminists) object to Western feminist theories that posit men as the primary source of oppression. Recently this debate has generated theories that focus on the interrelationship of multiple forms of oppression, such as race, class, imperialism, and gender.

THE INADEQUACIES OF THE CONCEPTS OF TRADITIONAL AND MODERN

The concepts of "traditional" and "modern" are often both ahistorical and value-laden. It may be legitimate to talk about ways people have done/do things "traditionally" (evolving at some unspecified time in the past) or in the "modern" way (coming into use relatively recently). However, for Africa, Asia, Latin America and the Caribbean, and the Middle East and North Africa, often the term "traditional" describes everything in the long eras before European intervention, and the term "modern" describes those phenomena following European intervention. This establishes a false dichotomy, with all things indigenous being "traditional" and all things Western being "modern." This usage often implies that the traditional is static and the modern, dynamic; it fails to portray and analyze each regional history within the context of its own internal dynamics, in which encounters with the West prove to be only one element among many. Such a view also obscures the fact that most societies were not isolated and had contact with other peoples before Western contact, that they are not homogeneous, and that several traditions often co-exist (to more or less peaceful degrees) within the same society or nation-state.

Sometimes this ahistoricity results from equating "modernization" with higher levels of technology; sometimes it is cultural arrogance and implicitly defines "modern/Western" as somehow better. Since colonialist ideology in Africa, Asia, and the Middle East often used indigenous "oppression" of women as a justification for intervention in these societies, colonizers promoted the belief that the arrival of Western civilization would improve women's lives. For example, in India in the early nineteenth century, one of the central arguments British officials employed to legitimate political control based on the use of military force was that British policies would "improve" the status of Indian women. Thus the colonizers made women central to the politics of colonialism.

The study of the lives of Third World women, in fact, challenges the legitimacy of the notion of a strict dichotomy between traditional and modern. Women's lives, especially, show that traditional cultures in these regions are not static, monolithic, or more misogynist than Western culture, and that there is no automatic linear progress made in the quality of women's lives by following a Western pattern of development. Regional studies provide evidence that the "traditional" ways of doing things, especially in the political and economic arenas, were often less inimical to women's collective interests than the "modernization" that colonialism purported to export.

The concept of tradition has also sometimes been used as a rallying point in anti-colonial liberation struggles. That is, by conceptualizing their struggle against European domination in "anti-Western culture" terms, various peoples have politicized the return to tradition as a liberating strategy. Because this "return to tradition" was often formulated during eras of high colonialism, when the promotion of Western culture was inseparable from the colonial presence, women were as central to the vision of tradition that emerged as they were to justifications for colonialism. Even after the colonial presence was gone, Western culture still symbolized continuing economic dominance. Gandhi claimed that women's superior ability at self-sacrifice made them better practitioners of *satyagraha* or non-violent resistance. In response to French cultural imperialism, wearing the veil became a political act of resistance in Algeria. Similarly, veiling became identified with opposition to Western influence and to the

Shah in Iran. In the 1970s, Mobutu Sese Seko of Zaire (now the Democratic Republic of the Congo) constructed his policy of *authenticité*, a major tenet of which was a return to the "traditional" value of women as mothers and housekeepers who obeyed male relatives. These are but a few examples that show women have often been on the losing end of a return to tradition—a "tradition" misused by ideologies of both colonialism and liberation. A view of culture as dynamic, as well as a better understanding of women's roles in the pre-European-contact periods, can help demythologize the concept of tradition.

RELIGION

Religion has been a source of power for women, or a source of subordination, or both.

Religious authorities have often functioned as politically powerful figures. In Inka society, women played important roles in the religious structure, even though male priests held religious and political power. As virgins, or *aqlla,* they were dedicated as "wives of the Sun" to prepare an alcoholic beverage for religious rituals and officiate at the same. Even in less-stratified societies of a much smaller scale, indeed perhaps more often in these societies, women acted as religious/political leaders. Charwe, a medium of the spirit Nehanda, led resistance to British colonialism in late-nineteenth-century southern Rhodesia. In the eighteenth century, the legendary Nanny drew upon her mediating relationship with ancestral spirits in leading her maroon community in Jamaica. Even where they did not hold religious office, women exercised power through religion: in peasant and nomadic regions of the Middle East, women continued, into the twentieth century, to control popular religious activities and thus to exert influence through their intercession with the supernatural.

Religious beliefs may point to the equality of women as sacred beings or the importance of female life force. Female clay figurines suggest the worship of female deities in Egypt around 3000 B.C.E., but we can infer little about the lives of women in general. Full-breasted female figurines, presumed to be fertility goddesses, are associated with the Indus Valley in South Asia around 2000 B.C.E. Aztec religion embodied many goddesses associated with fertility, healing, and agriculture. The presence of such goddesses did not signal a society of gender equality but rather one of gender complementarity, as in the Inka case. One of the largest temples in Ancient Sumer, at Ur, was headed by the priestess Enheduanna, who was also a renowned poet and writer.

On the other hand, religious beliefs may both reflect and reinforce the subordination of women. Women in many religious traditions are seen as polluting, particularly because of those bodily functions surrounding menstruation or childbirth. In West Africa, Akan fear of menstruating women limited even elite women's activities: the *asantehemaa,* the highest female office, could be held only by a post-menopausal woman from the appropriate lineage. Even though such beliefs may ultimately derive from women's power as procreators, women's status as polluting persons can restrict their activities and power. Moreover, traditions that stress the importance of male children to carry out ancestral rituals—for example, those in Confucianism—contribute to the negative valuation of female children and women. Other customs repressive and/or unhealthy to women—for example, *sati,* ritual suicide by widows—are sanctioned by religion. Finally, the traditions of Christianity, Confucianism, Hinduism, Islam, and Judaism all legitimate male authority, particularly patriarchal familial authority, over women: Christianity through biblical exhortation to wifely obedience, Confucianism in the three obediences, Hinduism in the Laws of Manu, Islam in the Qurʾan's injunction regarding wifely obedience, and Judaism in the Halakhah Laws.

However much these traditions carry profound gender inequalities in theology and in office, these same traditions spawn groupings that attract women (and other lower-status people). In India, the Gupta period, in which the Laws of Manu increased restrictions on Indian women, also witnessed the rise of Saktism, a cult derived from pre-Aryan traditions that envision the divine as feminine. In this set of beliefs, the female divinity appears in three major incarnations: Devi, the Mother goddess; Durga, the unmarried and potentially dangerous woman; and Kali, the goddess of destruction. Subsequently, in the Mughal period in South Asia, women in search of help with fertility or other psychological problems flocked to devotional Hinduism, becoming followers of *bhakti* saints, and to Muslim Sufi holy men. Women in the Middle East and in Muslim parts of Africa were also attracted to these mystical Sufi orders, which stressed direct union with Allah and believed there were no differences between men and women in their ability to reach God. Among syncretic Christian offshoots in Africa, women play much more central, albeit often expressive, roles.

SEXUALITY AND REPRODUCTION

Many theories about the origins of the oppression of women see control of female sexuality and the reproductive process (or female procreative power) as central. For this reason, it is useful to examine basic questions, if not patterns, in societies' construction of female sexuality. Just as gender is socially constructed, so too is sexuality— that is, which sexual practices (and with whom) were considered socially acceptable and which were considered deviant are specific to time and place, and often contested. Scholarship on homosexuality, for instance, is in its infancy in many of these histories, particularly that regarding lesbianism. Some scholars, though, posit the harem or *zenana* as a site of lesbian relationships.

Throughout history, societies have generated ideological systems that link female identity to female sexuality, and female sexuality to women's role in procreation. Thus one reason for controlling women's sexuality was to control their role in procreation. Women were aware of their important role in the procreative process, and sometimes used such sexual symbolism as a power play. African women on several occasions utilized sexual symbolism to protest threats to themselves as women. For example, in the Women's War of 1929, Nigerian women challenged the offending officials to impregnate each of them, drawing upon an indigenous technique to humiliate men: they were protesting men's right to interfere in women's economic power and thus women's obligations as wives and mothers. In 1922, Kenyan women, by exposing their buttocks at a public protest of colonial officials' actions, challenged their male colleagues to behave more "like men," that is, more bravely.

Religions project varied views of female sexuality. Islam acknowledges women's sexual pleasure, as it does men's, while advocating that it be channeled into marriage. In contrast, the Mahayana Buddhist views female sexuality as a threat to culture. In this religious group, women have been associated with bondage, suffering, and desire; female sexuality, then, is to be controlled by transcendence (or by motherhood).

Often the control of female sexuality and reproduction is linked to concerns about purity. The Aryan notion of purity was reflected throughout Hindu ritual and beliefs, but in particular it provided the impetus for early marriage and for *sati*. Colonial constraints upon Spanish women's behavior in the New World derived from the elite's desire to maintain "blood purity."

Expressed through virginity and chastity, in several cultural traditions a woman's purity had implications for her family. A Muslim woman's behavior affected her family's honor, for example, resulting in the ultimate penalty of death for adultery. Infibulation (briefly, the sewing together of the labia and one form of female genital surgery), found in both Muslim and non-Muslim areas, is commonly associated with virginity and the control of female sexuality. Although virginity was of little consequence in Inka society, adultery on the part of noblewomen was punishable by death. In seventeenth-century China, chastity was raised to a symbolic level not found in Japan or Korea. The 1646 Manchu rape law required women to resist rape to the point of death or serious injury; otherwise, they were considered to have participated in illicit intercourse.

The point here is not to list the multitude of ways in which women have been unfairly treated, but to understand the cultural construction of female sexuality. These examples, all drawn from religious traditions or the ideological systems of states, highlight the control of female sexuality. But the earlier African examples remind us that sexuality and sexual symbolism, like all cultural phenomena, are a terrain of struggle, to be manipulated by women as well as used against them. In their critique of Japanese society, the Bluestockings, a group of literary feminists in early twentieth-century Japan, saw sexual freedom as an integral aspect of women's rights.

Societies have sought to control men's sexual access to females through a combination of beliefs, laws, customs, and coercion. At times men enforced these sexual rules; at other times women policed themselves as individuals or curtailed the activities of other women—peers, younger women, daughters-in-law. Male control of sexual access to females has sometimes been a violent assault upon women, such as in enforced prostitution or rapes associated with wars. During the conquest of the Americas, for instance, Amerindian women were raped, branded, and viewed in general as the spoils of war. Also, enslaved women were often the sexual prey of their male owners, valued as both productive and reproductive laborers. Sexual tourism in the twentieth century, particularly in Asian and Pacific regions, exploits young girls primarily for the benefit of expatriate "tourists."

Concubinage, another institutionalized method of controlling female sexuality, existed in all the regions covered in this survey. Concubinage legitimated a man's sexual access to more than one woman outside of marriage. Although it clearly represented a double standard, concubinage as an institution offered certain protections or benefits to women. In the New World some Amerindian women gained substantial wealth and status as concubines; in addition, slave concubines might be manumitted at their owner's death and their children legitimized. Similarly, Islamic slave owners manumitted some concubines, encouraged by the belief that such action was rewarded by God. The protections offered by the institution of concubinage, albeit within a grossly unequal relationship, were lost with its abolition, and compensating institutions did not always replace concubinage. Hence, abolition in parts of Africa left poorer women, former concubines, without the legal rights of wives or concubines but still dependent financially. In contemporary Africa, women who in the past might have become concubines because of their economic or social vulnerability might today have children outside of formal marriage without the previous assurance that their children will be supported financially by the fathers.

Historically, prostitution has occurred under a variety of conditions that reflect different degrees of control of female sexuality. Prostitution may be seen as a strategy for a family's survival: impoverished Chinese families in the nineteenth century sold their daughters as prostitutes in the cities to earn money. Elsewhere in Asia, prostitutes functioned as part of larger institutions, or even imperial expansion. Hindu *devadasi,* or temple dancers, served as prostitutes tied to temples. In the nineteenth century the British, in an attempt to limit military expenditures, provided prostitutes rather than wives for non-commissioned British troops in India. During the period of imperial expansion in the 1930s, Japanese prostitutes were sent to service brothels in outposts of the empire, a process described in the film *Sandakan No. 8* (Brothel Number 9). Under these circumstances, prostitution did not mean increased autonomy for women, whether or not it provided subsistence.

In some places and times, however, prostitution has offered an alternative of increased autonomy. New colonial towns in Africa created spaces for women to escape from abusive or unwanted marriages. There, operating as entrepreneurs rather than under the supervision of pimps or other authorities, they supported themselves and their children by selling sexual and other domestic services to men, who frequently were migrant laborers. In addition, prostitutes were able to keep their children, an option that was not available to women in patrilineal marriages, where offspring belonged to the husband's patrilineage and were lost to a woman who divorced or absconded. Even under circumstances in which prostitutes had more control over their sexuality and their lives, it is important not to romanticize prostitution. It has been, and remains, an option for some women within a context of gender and class oppression.

The production of offspring (especially male offspring in strongly patrilineal societies) is often a measure of a woman's value. In some

African societies, this value is represented by bridewealth, the gifts that a groom must give to the bride's family in order to obtain rights to the offspring in a patrilineal society. The production of male offspring is essential for some religious rituals, for example, in Confucianism.

We have little historical information about control of reproduction. But even prior to the recent rise of reproductive technology, women found ways to limit birth. For example, in Congo in the late nineteenth century, slave women limited the number of children they had. In the complex conditions created by the internal African slave trade, slave women saw few advantages to producing children who belonged to their owners and who could not be expected to care for their mothers in old age. Advances in reproductive technology such as amniocentesis, which project the sex of an embryo or fetus, have sometimes been used to select male children and abort female children.

Recently, with the advent of population control programs adopted by nation-states and promoted by international agencies, control of reproduction has shifted away from individually initiated actions to highly bureaucratized operations. In that shift, the balance has slipped from birth control, which empowers women by giving them options, to population control, which regulates female reproduction in the interests of a nation-state or a donor country. Women may be encouraged or coerced to have babies for the nation, or the revolution, or conversely they may be manipulated or coerced into limiting childbirth. Stringent population policies were introduced in India, prompting protests by women's groups, and in China, where urban couples recently have been allowed to have only one child. In Puerto Rico one-third of the women of childbearing age were sterilized by the 1960s in one of the early attempts at widespread population control following policies initiated by the U.S. government. The white regime in South Africa promoted "birth control" among blacks as part of the larger plan of apartheid. In none of these population policies does birth control unambiguously empower women, since the elements of choice and safety have been compromised.

HOUSEHOLD RELATIONS

Household relationships are at the heart of most societies, since families act as the primary culture-bearing unit. In pre-industrial societies the family is also an important economic unit. Indeed, the way that families are organized is linked as much to the relations of production as to culture. Among other factors, a sedentary, nomadic, or hunting-and-gathering lifestyle, sex ratios, or the availability of land can affect family organization—and all of these factors also help determine the relations of production and culture. With few exceptions (Japan, for instance), the areas under discussion are still in the process of industrializing. Even while allowing for different levels of industrialization and cultural specificity, we can make some general observations.

In the Third World, historically and presently, domestic relationships have involved far more people than a nuclear family. The family most often functionally (not just emotionally) encompassed a wide range of relatives, including grandparents, parents, children, brothers and sisters, cousins, aunts and uncles, etc. Even when these people do not all inhabit the same household or compound, the sense of communal responsibility, obligation, and authority is wide-ranging and strongly felt and encouraged. The importance of the individual, as a general value, has been subordinated to that of the collective. Thus, domestic relationships and decision-making even between a husband and wife and their own children are often influenced by a wide variety of individuals and situations. Issues of polygyny, birth control, sexual conduct, education, allocation of economic resources, and so on are often group decisions, with elders frequently carrying more weight than younger members. The authority of a wide group of people who know about and sanction or approve behavior is accepted. Increasingly, however, factors such as class, personal mobility, and the proliferation of ideas about greater individual freedom are beginning to disrupt this pattern.

Historically, marriage was an important alliance that could not be viewed as a relationship between individuals, but between two kin groups, because the family was a primary unit for economic production and the concentration of wealth, for the allocation and legitimation of political power, and for conflict resolution. Consequently, marriages were often arranged for both women and men by other family members or by marriage brokers. Among the Aztecs, for instance, marriages were arranged by a go-between known as a *cihuatlanque*. Among the Spanish and Portuguese in Latin America, however (until 1776 when the Crown enacted new laws requiring parental consent for marriage), so long as a girl was twelve and a boy fourteen they could marry without such consent. Still, marriage was generally seen as an alliance between families by both the Spanish and the Portuguese, especially by those of the upper classes, where property was at stake and marriage between relatives was common. In the nineteenth-century Middle East, families exercised close control over marriage arrangements, and first-cousin marriage was commonly used as a method for ensuring political alliances and centralizing wealth. Arranged marriages seem to have held less importance for the poor, however, reflecting less wealth to protect and perhaps even the need to decrease the number of dependent kin. In Africa, also, arranged marriages were a prevalent means of ensuring the continuity of the transfer of resources. As men undertook wage labor their ability to pay their own bridewealth and hence arrange their own marriages increased, but rarely would this have been done over family objections to choice of a mate.

Gifts passed between families (and still do in many places) and between the bride and groom at the time of marriage. Dowry was brought by a bride to her marital home, and other transfers, such as bridewealth or brideservice, went from the groom (or his family) to the bride's family. The degree of access to and control over these gifts exercised by a bride varied greatly among the societies discussed here.

The institution of dowry served an important economic as well as social function. The dowry (or *dote*) was not a requirement for marriage among the Spanish and Portuguese in Latin America, but it served as a way of both compensating a husband for assuming the economic burden of a wife as well as providing a woman with some economic independence. Though it was administered by a husband, it remained the property of the wife and could not be alienated without her consent. If the husband mismanaged the dowry, a woman could petition in court to control it herself, and in the case of divorce, the dowry had to be repaid. In the case of the wife's death, however, the dowry was either divided among the children or returned to the wife's parents. In India, dowry encompassed both *stridhan*, which was usually jewelry and clothing belonging to the bride alone, and a broad array of household goods and other valuables that were gifts to the couple and to the groom's family, with whom they lived.

In various societies, wealth moved in the reverse direction, from the groom and his kin to the bride and hers. The system of bridewealth found in Africa was generally a gift from a man to the parents of his bride and signified their compensation for the loss of their daughter as well as his rights to the children of the marriage and, to varying extents, her labor. Among matrilineal peoples in Central Africa, a groom had to perform brideservice, (that is, labor in the bride's family's fields). Forms of bridewealth varied (including cloth, beads, cattle, and, after the introduction of wage labor during the colonial period, cash), and, in the case of divorce, it frequently had to be returned. In some places in Africa, women assumed control over a portion of their bridewealth. Some East Asian and Middle Eastern societies had both dowry and bridewealth. Under Islamic law, women retained rights to the personal ownership of their bridal gift, or *mahr*.

Polygyny, or the taking of more than one wife, was commonly practiced in a number of places. Sometimes, as noted above, it had an important political function in cementing alliances. In Islamic societies in the Middle East, Asia, and Africa, men could legally wed up to four wives. In non-Islamic areas of Africa and among some early Amerindian societies, such as the Inka in Latin America, polygyny also existed, but the number of wives was not limited. Judaism allowed polygyny by C.E. 70 in the Middle East. The economic obligations entailed by taking more than one wife could operate to curtail the degree to which polygyny was actually practiced; however, since women also produced wealth through trade, agricultural activities, and production of crafts, as well as by the exchange of bridewealth, it was often true that polygyny could be economically advantageous to men. Polygyny could sometimes be economically advantageous to women by allowing them to share household duties and obligations and by affording them more freedom to engage in trade and craft production.

Concubinage or the forging of sexual (and sometimes emotional) extramarital alliances was common in all four regions. Though concubines, as discussed above, were generally in a very vulnerable position, sometimes there were indigenous laws governing their treatment, and because these women often came from poor families, concubinage could represent a way of improving their economic position and even status. For example, Khaizuran, concubine of Caliph al-Mahdi during the Abbasid period in Iraq, saw two of her sons succeed their father as caliph, and she herself intervened in state affairs.

Since one of women's primary responsibilities was considered the production of heirs and the next generation, infertility could be a devastating circumstance and was the subject of many religious practices aimed at prevention or cure. Infertility was most often blamed on women until fairly recently. In Sumeria (3000–2000 B.C.E.) men could take another wife if their first did not bear children, historically a fairly common practice worldwide. Among the Aztecs a sterile woman could be rejected and divorced.

Some form of divorce or marital separation has existed for women nearly everywhere. (Among Zoroastrians, only men could divorce.) Although in general divorce was easier for men than women, there were exceptions to this rule. Extreme physical cruelty and neglect of economic duty were fairly common grounds by which women could petition for divorce. Adultery and a wife's inability to produce children, among a much wider range of other less consequential reasons, were common grounds on which men exercised their right to divorce women. In the early Spanish societies of Latin America, marriages could be annulled due to failure to produce children. Legal separation, known as *separación de cuerpos* (or separation of bodies) was also available on grounds of extreme physical cruelty, adultery, prostitution, or paganism, but such a separation forbade remarriage. From the sixteenth century onward, women were often the initiators of divorce in Spanish Latin America. In Southeast Asia women easily exercised their right to divorce, a situation some historians speculate was due to their economic autonomy. Prior to the twentieth century, however, divorce initiated by women was much harder in other parts of Asia, such as China and Japan. The ease with which divorce could be obtained was sometimes related to class. For instance, the divorce rate among the urban poor in nineteenth-century Egypt was higher than among the upper classes, for whom the economic components of marriage were more complicated. In Africa, because divorce often involved the return of bridewealth, women were sometimes discouraged from divorcing their husbands.

The treatment and rights of widows varied widely. During the Mauryan era in India (322–183 B.C.E.), widows could remarry, although they lost their rights to any property inherited from their deceased husbands. During the Gupta era (320–540), however, the Laws of Manu severely limited women's rights in marriage, including the banning of widow remarriage. Though its origins are unknown, the ritual suicide of widows among the Hindu known as *sati* is one of the most controversial treatments of widowhood. A complex practice, it appears to have economic as well as socioreligious foundations. Among the Aztecs widows not only retained the right to remarry but were encouraged to do so, especially if they were of childbearing age. In the colonial period in Spanish America, widows had the rights of single women who, after a certain age, were considered to have attained a legal majority. They could acquire control over their children or remarry. In parts of Africa, Asia, and the Middle East, widows were sometimes "inherited" by male kin of their deceased husbands. This practice, known as the levirate, could entail conjugal rights, but could also mean only the assumption of economic responsibility for a widow and her children. Women sometimes retained the right to refuse such a marriage. Among the Kikuyu of East Africa, for instance, women could opt instead to take a lover.

In many places women's activity in reform and nationalist movements, especially in the twentieth century, has been characterized by their struggle to liberalize laws governing marriage and family relationships. The Egyptian Feminist Union, led by Huda Sha'rawi, agitated for reform of laws governing divorce and polygyny in the 1920s and 1930s. Women (and men) of the May Fourth generation struggled in early twentieth-century China to make the reform of marriage and family law and practice central to their revolutionary effort. Even after the success of the Cuban revolution and the passage of a family code that explicitly gives women the same rights as men in economic and political arenas as well as in the family, women's organizations, with state support, continue to work to implement equality. In Africa women and men activists in liberation movements, such as the PAIGC in Guinea-Bissau in the 1960s and 1970s, clearly articulated the need to transform domestic relations as an important tenet of revolutionary ideology.

Women's roles, statuses, and power within the family have varied both through time within the same society and from one place to another. As reflections of material culture, they tell us more about societies than about women's place in them. For the regional areas under discussion, we can see the common threads, but we can also distinguish the wide variation.

WOMEN'S ECONOMIC ACTIVITY

In virtually all societies, the gender division of labor associates women with family maintenance. Overwhelmingly, gender segregation and domestic subsistence production have characterized the lives of women in the economic sphere, although before industrialization there was little distinction between the private and public economic spheres as most production took place in the family and in and around the home. In Nubian civilization in ancient Africa, for example, there is evidence that women were involved in the production of pottery for household use, while men specialized in producing wheel-turned pottery for trade. At times there were disincentives for women to be economic actors. In medieval Islamic society, elite urban men were cautioned not to marry women who engaged in economic activities in the public arena. But such observations should not be construed as an indication of lack of importance and variety in women's roles in agriculture, craft and textile production, the tending of livestock, trade, and other areas. In fact, many women engaged in economic activity that not only supplied subsistence but generated wealth, especially in agricultural and trade sectors of the economy.

In nearly all of sub-Saharan Africa, women historically played and continue to play important roles in agricultural production. In one of the few areas of sub-Saharan Africa where private property in land pre-dated European arrival, among the Amhara of Northeast Africa (present-day Ethiopia), women could control the entire agricultural production process. They owned, plowed, planted, and harvested their own fields. Amerindian women were important in agricultural production in Latin America before the arrival of the Spanish and Portuguese, who then sought to enlist men as agricultural laborers in cash crops. Although for the early centuries of the Atlantic slave trade the sex ratio was heavily imbalanced toward males, African women performed important agricultural labor, which was essential to the economies of colonial Latin America, the Caribbean, and what would become the United States. Women were cultivators in much of Asia, usually in family-centered production units. Even where women did not cultivate, they often performed other roles associated with agricultural production. For instance, in nineteenth-century Egypt, women did not plow land, but they worked at harvesting and in pest control activities.

Women undertook various kinds of manufacturing activities. In the Chewa-Malawi area of nineteenth-century East Africa, women were involved in producing salt and in other manufacture. In the eleventh-century Pagan Empire in Southeast Asia, women were important in the spinning of yarn and weaving of cloth. In eighteenth- and nineteenth-century Egypt, women were important in the textile crafts, though they were squeezed out by industrialization. In the nineteenth century, partially due to demand created by a European market, women became important to the growth of the silk industry in Lebanon and the carpet industry in Iran. Women were important weavers among the Inka, where they also worked in the mines. In the sixteenth and seventeenth centuries, women among the Shona of southern Africa worked in the gold mines.

Perhaps the most ubiquitous economic activity undertaken by women was that of trading. In Africa, Asia, Latin America and the Caribbean, and the Middle East and North Africa, women traded a number of items, including agricultural products, cooked food, cloth, beads, and handicrafts. Although women's trading activities were sometimes on a small scale, often referred to as "petty trading," that was not always the case. In Southeast Asia, women in twelfth- and thirteenth-century Burma were engaged in trade that included the large-scale buying and selling of rice and other commodities. They were also identified with the production and trade of a particular foodstuff, betel leaf, for which they made elaborate jewelled containers. Sometimes women engaged in long-distance trade that required their absence from home for extended periods of time. Among the nineteenth-century Kikuyu of East Africa, women engaged in long-distance trade and retained control over some of the wealth they accumulated. Even where women engaged in local, small-scale trade, they could be very important to the growth and development of long-distance trade and of port towns and urban centers. Such was the case with women traders along the west coast of Africa in the eighteenth and nineteenth centuries.

Residence in a harem and the practice of seclusion placed restraints on women's ability to engage directly in public-arena economic activity, thus forcing them to use intermediaries to conduct their business operations. This use of intermediaries, and the higher economic status that seclusion usually implied, meant women sometimes held considerable wealth and became significant economic actors. In the nineteenth century in parts of the Middle East (notably Cairo, Istanbul, Aleppo, and Nablus), upper-class women employed agents to conduct their business transactions in the public arena. They also invested capital as "silent partners" in other ventures and loaned money to men. Among the Hausa of northern Nigeria, Islamic women who were secluded used prepubescent girls to trade for them in public.

In some places, however, the strict gender segregation of Islamic societies in fact expanded women's economic alternatives, since only women could perform certain services for other women. In nineteenth-century Egypt women of lower economic status served as entertainers, cosmologists, and midwives to women of higher economic status who were in seclusion. Strict gender segregation opened up the professions (medicine, education, etc.) to women in the late twentieth century, especially in countries where economic resources are plentiful, such as Saudi Arabia.

The absence of male heirs, or the fact of widowhood, could also create economic opportunity for women. Under such circumstances women ran businesses and were important in trades. In sixteenth-century Mexico, Mencia Perez, a *mestiza*, married a rich merchant. When he died, she took over the business and became one of the wealthiest merchants in the province. In Syria, the *gedik*, a license that allowed one to practice a trade, was normally inherited by sons from their fathers. In the absence of a male heir, women could inherit the *gedik,* and although prevented from practicing the trade, they could sell, rent, or bequeath the license. In coastal West Africa creole women traders descended from African mothers and European fathers served as cultural intermediaries and often became very successful and wealthy businesswomen.

Yet women's tremendously varied and important roles in economic activity did not translate into economic, legal, or political equality with men. The more economic autonomy women had, however, the greater their freedoms. Whatever the origins of women's inequality, the complex processes through which it has been perpetuated will not fall in the face of economic parity alone.

POLITICAL POWER

In general histories of the Third World, political access is not normally discussed with gender as a factor of analysis, although frequently class, race, ethnicity, and other factors are considered. And being of a particular class, race, or ethnicity could influence women's power and status as much as gender. Still, the type and degree of women's political participation both as individuals and as a group have been underreported, and the present has frequently been mistaken for the past.

One of the most obvious ways women exercised direct power was by ruling. In the ancient African kingdom of Kush, women assumed power in their own right as well as sometimes co-ruling with their sons. There were women who ruled in early Austronesian societies from Polynesia to Madagascar, including the Philippines and Indonesia. In tenth-century Abyssinia in Northeast Africa, Gudit was a powerful queen of the Agao. Two African queens ruled in the sixteenth century, Queen Aminatu or Amina of Zaria and Queen Njinga of Matamba. The Mende of West Africa also had a tradition of women chiefs. Mwana Mwema and Fatuma ruled in Zanzibar in the late seventeenth and early eighteenth centuries, and Mwana Khadija ruled in Pate on the East African coast in the mid-eighteenth century. In India, several Hindu and Muslim women ruled small kingdoms during the late eighteenth century. In fifteenth- and sixteenth-century Burma and the Malay peninsula women also ruled.

What the existence of women rulers has to say about women's power qua women is a complex question. Most women who ruled were elite by birth, but then so were ruling men. However, Queen

Njinga certainly achieved rather than inherited her power, moving from the position of palace slave to that of a reigning monarch. Although the existence of women rulers indicates that women were not universally absent from the highest seats of power, having a woman ruler did not necessarily reflect the status of other women or empower them, any more than it does today.

Women also exercised direct power within arenas viewed as the female province; these varied based upon material culture. In Africa female networks seem to have arisen from the gender division of labor, and over many centuries women exercised considerable power and autonomy within society as a whole through all-female organizations. Women leaders of women such as the *iyalode* among the Yoruba and the *omu* among the Igbo are examples of such power. The *coya,* known as the "queen of women" among the Inka, is another example; she even had the power to rule in the absence of the male ruler. Women exercised considerable power within the royal harem in both Turkey and Iran.

Women exercised power as members of collectives of their own sex organized for particular purposes. Practices similar to the Nigerian institution of "sitting on a man" are found in various African societies. This phrase describes organized political activities of women who gathered as a group to protest policies or protect another woman by confronting a man and ridiculing him or making demands, sometimes even destroying his property as a punishment for some act against a woman or women as a whole. Women directed this practice against recalcitrant husbands and colonial officials alike. There is also evidence of the existence of this kind of activity in early twentieth-century China, where women forced husbands who had maltreated their wives to march through town wearing dunce caps.

Perhaps the most ubiquitous example of women's indirect and influential power is the existence of the queen mother, normally the progenitor of a male ruler although sometimes a woman appointed as his "mother." These women had power over women and men. Their power resulted not only from their access to the ruler, serving as his "ear," so to speak, but also because they often commanded formidable financial and personnel resources and/or had specific responsibilities over the governed. Queen mothers existed in ancient Kush, India, the Ottoman Empire, and West, East, and Northeast Africa, to name a few places. Some queen mothers, such as Shah Turkan of thirteenth-century Delhi, could be very instrumental in installing their sons on the throne, and consequently exercised considerable state power. Others, like Mihrisah, mother of the Ottoman ruler Selim II, who ruled in the early nineteenth century, exercised considerable power through largesse; she built a mosque and a medical school. Yaa Kyaa, mother of the West African Asante ruler Osei Yaw, also exercised considerable state power, even signing a peace treaty between the Asante and the British in the 1830s, and Yaa Asantewa led a large revolt against British rule. The *magajiya,* the title given to the queen mother in several of the Hausa states of the western Sudan in West Africa, even had the power to depose the ruler, or *sarki.* The queen mother, however, usually owed her power to her relationship to a male ruler and not to her relationship to other women. Even though she might be regarded as "queen of the women," she did not necessarily represent women's interests as a whole. Still, these women were often at the center of power, and many displayed formidable political acumen.

We also cannot discount the power and influence of women who were the wives, sisters, daughters, and consorts of powerful men. Precisely because of the intimate context in which such situations occurred, they are admittedly hard to document, but evidence exists. Women such as Inés Suárez, who accompanied Captain Pedro de Valdivia as his lover in his campaign to conquer Chile, played an important role as a spy and confidante and eventually took part in the conquest. Wives of emperors in the Byzantine empire wielded considerable political influence. Nineteenth-century Confucian reformers in China were influenced by increased contact with literate women at court and in elite families. The nineteenth-century Islamic reform movement led by Uthman dan Fodio in West Africa was certainly influenced in its ideas on greater education for women by the women in Fodio's own family, which produced five generations of women intellectuals who left bodies of written work in Fula, Arabic, and Hausa. In the West African kingdom of Dahomey, by the eighteenth century at least, no man could become king without the support of the powerful palace women. Royal women in nineteenth-century Iran also exercised considerable power and independence, even from inside the harem. There are many other examples which suggest to us that women's influential roles in politics were consequential.

Women's military participation as individuals and as organized corps of women fighters was also widespread. In many places women accompanied male troops, such as in Aksum and early Ethiopian kingdoms, in early Arabia, in Latin America, and elsewhere. But women were also actual combatants. The African Queen Amina of Zaria led troops into battle, as did the renowned Nguni warrior Nyamazana, of early nineteenth-century southern Africa, and Indian women in Delhi and Bhopal in the second half of the eighteenth century. In C.E. 40 two Trung sisters in Southeast Asia (in present-day Vietnam) led an army, including female officers. In eighteenth-century Jamaica, slave women played important roles as combatants in Maroon societies composed of runaway slaves. One woman, Nanny, is still revered as a fighter and ruler of one of the most famous Maroon communities, Nanny Town. Actual corps of trained women soldiers also existed, such as those in Java and in the West African kingdom of Dahomey, where they formed the king's bodyguard and were an elite unit of "shock troops." In eighteenth-century Egypt, women went into battle against Mamluks and the French. In the nineteenth century women fought in Japan, in the T'ai p'ing Rebellion in China, and in the Mexican Revolution. In early twentieth-century China, corps of women fought as the "Women's Suicide Brigade" and the "Women's National Army." Twentieth-century anti-colonial and liberation struggles are replete with examples of women as combatants, for example, in the 1950s "Mau Mau" rebellion in Kenya, the Frelimo liberation army in Mozambique, and the Cuban and Nicaraguan revolutions.

In addition to serving in military roles, women organized in other capacities with men and in women's groups against colonial policies that they viewed as inimical to their interests. In India at the turn of the twentieth century, women were active in the *swadeshi* movement, which sought to encourage the use of indigenously made products as opposed to European imports. In the 1930s Indian women participated in anti-colonial protest marches in Bombay and elsewhere. In 1929 the "Women's War" of the Igbo and Ibibio of eastern Nigeria was a massive uprising of women against the threat of female taxation by the colonial state. In 1945 the market women in Lagos, Nigeria were very instrumental in a general strike against economic and political policies of the British. Women in Egypt, Iran, and the Ottoman Empire worked with men in organizations promoting independence from European imperialism by participating in street demonstrations, public speaking, and writing. In the Algerian War of Independence against the French (1954–62), women were couriers of weapons, money, and messages, as well as actual combatants.

Women's participation in general strikes, major protest marches, economic boycotts, and armed rebellion was prevalent everywhere there was an anti-colonial struggle. As with any major societal upheaval resulting in challenges to existing authority, colonialism both created opportunities for and oppressed women. In the final analysis, however, the vast majority of women have opted to work for the independence of their societies and to pursue the issue of gender equal ity in the context of an independent and autonomous state.

Despite all of this, and despite the fact that improving women's status has often been a central point of anti-colonial ideology, women have usually not become the political and economic equals of men in newly evolving independent societies. In fact, the development of nationalist movements, at least in the nineteenth and twentieth cen- turies, has often operated to subordinate women. In nineteenth-cen- tury Japan the growth of nationalism and patriotism tended to subju- gate women, requiring that they be good wives and mothers as their first "patriotic" duty. Although initially instituting reforms that served to empower women, within a few years the Kuomintang national- ist movement in early twentieth-century China began to repress a developing feminist movement that had supported its rise to power. The 1922 Egyptian constitution denied women the right to vote and barred them from the opening of Parliament, despite the active role they had played in the nationalist movement. After the success of the Algerian Revolution, women's roles in the war were viewed as vali- dation of their "traditional" roles of wife and mother. After gaining independence, the Indonesian nationalist movement encouraged women to go back into the home to provide "social stability." In Nige- ria, although the nationalist movements of the mid-twentieth cen- tury had courted women and counted them as strong supporters in the independence struggle, women remained generally excluded from political power after independence and especially under military rule. In many disparate places and cultures, nationalism left women un- rewarded after independence was achieved.

There are exceptions, as some national liberation movements have challenged sexist ideologies regarding women. Frelimo in Mozambique criticized both the traditional initiation rites that included notions of female subordination as well as the colonial exploitation of women's labor. This kind of struggle was termed "fighting two colonialisms" by the PAIGC, a comparable liberation movement in Guinea-Bissau. In Cuba the government also sought to address the issue of women's equality in the post-independence period in a written family code that explicitly delineates women's equal status compared to that of men. The revolutionary Nicaraguan government of the 1980s also attempted to officially stipulate women as the equals of men. The positive difference in these countries, however, seems as related to women's continued organization as women (such as the Organization of Mozambican Women and the Federation of Cuban Women) as to state-supported revolutionary ideology.

CENTRALIZATION, BUREAUCRATIZATION, AND STATE FORMATION

Women's role in centralization, bureaucratization, and state forma-tion poses some challenging questions. In the processes of state for-mation and centralization, women often have tremendous importance and potential for autonomy and power as marriage partners who cen-tralize wealth, cement alliances, merge cultures, and produce heirs. In the Middle East the practice of first-cousin marriage helped estab-lish the family as a base of centralized wealth and political solidarity. In the pre-colonial West African kingdom of Dahomey, the king took wives from wealthy and powerful families to cement political alli-ances. Among both the Hindus and the Muslims in India, marriages reinforced political bonds with the nobility and among rival states. In Latin America the Spanish sought unions with elite Amerindian women to legitimize and consolidate their control over indigenous societies. However, it appears that when the state begins to bureau-cratize, making these relationships less important to state organiza-tion, women lose much of their potential for being central to state power. In the Middle East the growth of the state meant that the great family houses that had served as centers of societal organization and power lost much of that role. Similarly, in the West African king-dom of Dahomey, kinship ties became much less important in power relations as the state solidified and shifted to a merit system based more on service to the king than lineage connections.

Nationalist struggles in the nineteenth and twentieth centuries mobilized women nearly everywhere in the Third World. But once the state was established (or gained its independence from external conquerors), women often seemed to lose in the process. Particular and comparative research with gender as a central analytical factor can test this hypothesis and may open new windows on studies of state formation and the development of nationalism.

WOMEN'S CULTURE, NETWORKS, AND AUTONOMOUS SPACE

In male-dominant societies, women's activities, values, and interac-tions often form a "muted" subculture: their worldview is non-domi-nant and does not generally claim to represent that of the entire society of men and women. This subculture is reinforced by a strong gender division of labor that results in women and men spending most of their time in same-sex groupings and, occasionally, is augmented by ideological formulations of social rules (e.g., notions of pollution, or purdah).

At times, women demanded the separate space or take advantage of it as a refuge from oppressive features of their society. For example, the sisterhoods of silk workers in southern China, who pledged to resist marriage, provided an alternative to the patriarchal family. Buddhism allowed women to pursue the monastic life, albeit as less than equals to male monks. Still, Indian Buddhist nuns taught religion to other women and composed religious poetry. (Jainism accepted nuns as the equals of monks.) Women who joined Buddhist nunneries in China were criticized for ignoring female responsibilities of motherhood, although these nunneries, we might suspect, provided a space less controlled by male authority than the rest of Chinese society. Convents in colonial Latin America housed single women with various motives: some sought to escape marriage, others searched for religious fulfillment, and a few sought access to education. And not all who resided in a convent lived by vows of poverty and chastity.

Whatever its source or structural manifestation, this social space and the resulting female-controlled institutions offered women rich opportunities. Among the most important of these opportunities was the potential for female solidarity. Various African societies institutionalized female solidarity through activities such as "sitting on a man" (a Nigerian practice noted earlier). In Mende society in West Africa, the women's secret society known as Bundu (parallel to a men's secret society) provided a political base for female chiefs (it also perpetuated, as a central initiation ritual, the practice of clitoridectomy).

In addition to encouraging female solidarity, the separation of women and men had economic consequences at times. Islamic seclusion provided the impetus for the development of occupations serving the women of the harem or *zenana*, such as midwives, educators, entertainers, musicians, or cosmologists; for reasons of honor and modesty, these occupations were filled by women. The same rationale prompted the expansion of professions open to women: medicine, nursing, and teaching.

The physical separation of women contributed to a flowering of artistic, oral, and written culture from the female subculture. The world's first novel, *The Tale of Genji*, is only one example of the fine literary work of Japanese women writers in the eleventh century. Unlike men, who were restricted by gender norms to writing rather arid, but higher-status, poetry in Chinese characters, these women composed prose in *kana*, the language of indigenous expression of sentiment. Even where excluded from education and certain cultural outlets, women's networks produced a fine and rich tradition of oral expression, as in Bedouin communities in North Africa.

Women's networks and women's subculture, because they often derive from the marginalization of women from the centers of power, have been controversial in the scholarship. Even in extreme forms (perhaps more so there), the separating of women can provide a source of psychological support and connectedness and protection. In assessing the actions of women among themselves, the important issues of victimization and agency are played out and we must ask certain questions: On whose initiative are the women grouped? How do women respond to this grouping? How does the clustering of women, apart from men, empower and/or limit women? Is this a condition that encourages women's oppression of other women (since there are now distinctions of power drawn between women) as much as it encourages female solidarity?

WOMEN IN CROSS-CULTURAL CONTACT

Women are important intermediaries for cultural exchange. For several reasons, they are likely to end up marrying outside their community of birth. First, patrilineal societies outnumber matrilineal societies, and in patrilineal societies a woman marries into her husband's patrilineage and generally resides with her husband's kin (patrilocality).

Second, women have often been exchanged, as wives and as concubines, to cement alliances. In eighteenth-century Dahomey in West Africa, lineages were required to send their daughters to the king. During the same period in Java, the male ruler gave various women from his court to noblemen as wives. In sixteenth-century Japan, warrior families cemented alliances by the exchange of wives.

Third, in cases of European expansion into the Third World, the gender division of labor in Europe resulted in most explorers being male, which in turn created particular conditions for indigenous women to link with these men as sexual partners. Perhaps the best-known individual woman in this category was the slave Malinche (or Malintzin), who became the first Mexican mistress of Cortés. She served as translator in Maya, Nahuatl, and Spanish and apprised Cortés of the inland empire of Motecuhzoma. In the seventeenth century, the *signares* along the West African coast became wealthy traders and intermediaries through their relations with European men. Their mulatto children, familiar with two worlds, served as power brokers.

Similarly, initially in the seventeenth century, the Dutch administration encouraged the marriage of its junior officers to Indonesian women to provide a form of social order through mestizo culture on the frontiers of Dutch colonization. By the nineteenth century, the status of these mixed-race individuals had declined. The same gender division of labor, in which men were the agents of expansion, is also characteristic of societies outside of Europe. Most conquerors were male—for example, in the nineteenth-century Zulu expansion through southern and East-Central Africa, and among the Muslims who infiltrated Nubia from the sixteenth century on.

Women were thus well placed—as socializers of children, farmers, or traders—to transmit new ideas about social practices or mores, technology or techniques, religion, kinship, and so on to their new community. Female African slaves, valued for their horticultural labor and transported far from their natal villages, brought with them ways of planting or cultivating, thus encouraging agricultural innovation. Women, for the same reasons, were well placed to resist the cultural aspects of imperialism by perpetuating indigenous culture and customs. Amerindian women in Latin America, for example, continued indigenous religious practices in the face of Catholic proselytizing, as did African female slaves.

Women may become empowered by their intermediary position: it may give them pivotal control of information or material resources. On the other hand, as intermediaries they are sometimes marginal within their society of origin. They may lose the protections from their natal group accorded by custom without gaining those granted to indigenous women. As in-marrying strangers, they may suffer isolation. It is important to note, too, that the individuals and cultures resulting from these cross-racial liaisons were not valued everywhere: Anglo-Indians were shunned by both the English and the Indian communities during the Raj. The female intermediary risked being polluted by contact with outsiders and subsequently cast out or made a scapegoat when illness or other negative circumstances plagued a community. And some women who served as intermediaries—for example, Malintzin, or Eva in seventeenth-century southern Africa—have been labeled historically as traitors because they were seen as helping to facilitate conquest of their people by outsiders.

GENDER PLUS CONQUEST:
COLONIALISM AND IMPERIALISM

Contact resulting from conquest held vast implications for women as a group. Customs were transferred from one society to another. New practices that restricted women's physical mobility might be forced upon the indigenous groups or adopted by them in emulation. For example, although the *jihad* of Uthman dan Fodio improved conditions for Hausa women in numerous ways, such as providing greater access to Qur'anic education, it also led to the increased seclusion of elite women and a loss of their religious and political power.

Recent scholarship on women in European-dominated colonial societies presents evidence that there was no one colonial experience for all women, even within the same national boundaries. However, the position of most women declined under the aegis of colonialism both because of its sexist bias and because women were members of politically dominated and economically exploited territories. In general, women were dislocated economically and politically within a weakened indigenous order, and in those spheres at least, women were rarely compensated in the new order. Nevertheless, though women were often the victims of colonialism, they also took initiative both in resisting policies they viewed as harmful to them and in using new situations to their advantage. And sometimes the social fluidity created by the colonial experience allowed for the creation of alternative roles for women. As one scholar suggests, however, studies of gender need to be located as much in the changing relationships of production as in the political and social policies engendered by colonialism. Another scholar underscores this point in emphasizing that it was the integration of the Middle East into a global economic system which is the real canvas on which we must paint an analysis of women's changing economic roles.

Women were members of colonizing as well as colonized societies, and members of the former group eventually accompanied colonizers to conquered territories. For most of the regions under consideration here, these women were a small minority in colonial territories. In the initial phase of conquest, they were nearly absent; then a trickle came to join husbands; then more came, depending on the degree of expatriate settlement that the colonizers encouraged and the needs and size of the colonial bureaucracy.

In Latin America (and South Africa), however, the era of European conquest was marked by the rise of commercial capitalism rather than the industrial capitalism that would fuel the colonialist thrust of the nineteenth century, and it also pre-dated (by several hundred years) the colonization of other regions. After the initial phase of conquest, during which few women from the Iberian peninsula were in residence in Latin America, much larger numbers began to migrate there. The Amerindian population of Latin America was decimated due to European diseases and attempts at their enslavement (the Khoi Khoi of South Africa suffered a similar fate). Though the population of African slaves grew considerably from the sixteenth to the nineteenth centuries in Latin America, European immigration outstripped it. The region was effectively colonized centuries before widespread colonial penetration into other areas. Thus, by the nineteenth century, Latin American nations were gaining their independence, and the descendants of Europeans in Latin America were the predominant people in the population of the continent. In many regions Latin American culture became an amalgam of African, Amerindian, and European cultures, shaped on the anvil of a centuries-old slave mode of production and forced Amerindian labor. Therefore, the following discussion of women under European colonialism does not apply to Latin America after the early decades of the conquest.

Imperial and colonial expansion had economic, social, and cultural consequences for women. The greater development (or in some places the introduction) of wage labor that accompanied colonialism predominantly involved men, whom it drew away from work on the land, increasing women's subsistence agricultural labor. Among the Tonga of Zambia the absence of male laborers had a particularly deleterious effect on the agricultural labor of older women, who were no longer able to depend upon help from sons and sons-in-law. This situation was also common in West and West-Central Africa. Sometimes, however, women left alone on the land exercised greater power in the economic decision-making process. An example is late-nineteenth- and early twentieth-century western Kenya, where Luo women were able to experiment with new crops and agricultural techniques that improved their economic position.

In some places the existence of widespread wage labor among men eroded the importance of the family economy and women's role in it. In forcing male migration to wage labor in mining and other work among the Aztecs, Inkas, Mayas, and Arawaks, the Spanish eroded the significant role women performed in the pre-Columbian family economy. In Morocco during the French colonial era, women were only seasonal wage laborers but were still dislocated in the family economy.

The development of the cash-crop system created greater interest in establishing private property in areas where it had not previously existed. This change to private property often distorted land tenure arrangements and usufruct (usage) rights and seems to have operated overall against women's interests. In Morocco the French, pursuing a policy of consolidating landholdings, helped destroy a family-based economy in which women played an important agricultural role. The Swynnerton Plan, begun by the British in 1954 in Kenya, was a policy of consolidating and privatizing landholdings that severely disadvantaged women and set the stage for their loss of rights to land after independence. In West and West-Central Africa women also lost out in the privatization of land occasioned by the growth of wage labor and cash crops. In a few instances women were able to resist erosion in their economic viability; from the 1920s through the 1940s, women in the cotton-producing areas of Nyasaland (now Malawi) were able to utilize cash cropping to their advantage. There, remaining collectively organized, women delayed the privatization of land, participated in cotton production, and maintained their precolonial agricultural autonomy.

Competition from European imports often displaced women occupationally and pushed them to the margins of areas in the economy where they were formerly quite important. For instance, in the Middle East and North Africa, European cloth imports in the nineteenth century devastated local textile production in which women had been heavily involved. Among the Baule of the Ivory Coast, French monopolization of local cloth production, and its alienation to factories, displaced women's former predominance in producing cloth and related items, such as thread. Sometimes the colonial economy created jobs for women, and though they were often overworked and underpaid, this independent income still provided women with some autonomy. Often it was the situations fostered by the colonial economy, especially in the urban areas, that created room for women to establish their own occupations. These urban areas often had large populations of single adult men (or men separated from their families) and entrepreneurial women engaged in occupations that provided them with services normally provided by the family. Although sometimes these occupations were marginal (such as beer-brewing, selling cooked food, and doing laundry) or even dangerous and possibly degrading (such as prostitution) women seized whatever opportunity was available to stabilize themselves, and often their children, economically and to gain independence from men and other adult family members.

The colonial need to control the economy also marginalized women who had often exercised control over the production, pricing, and distribution of agricultural, textile, and household goods. In southwestern Nigeria, for instance, the British were constantly in disputes with Yoruba market women over the location of markets, their internal control, and the setting of prices for staple commodities—all areas women had formerly controlled and which the colonial state sought to regulate.

A small number of women in some places were able to benefit economically from an increase in market scale that accompanied European contact and colonial rule, such as Omu Okwei of Nigeria. This benefit came to few individuals and often at the expense of other women, since women's economic power had historically emanated from their operation in collectives.

Political independence in many countries did not eliminate economic dependence on former colonial powers and was often followed in the post–World War II period by the arrival of multinational corporations. Since colonialism situated women overall as an easily exploitable class of labor, this situation has had profound economic implications for women. On the one hand, a number of multinational industries, especially electronics and textiles, have shown a marked preference for female labor. This has meant women have been drawn into the formal wage-labor force and therefore have had independent income. On the other hand, it has also meant the severe exploitation of their labor at depressed wages in unskilled and low-skilled jobs with little stability or possibility of promotion, and under unhealthy conditions.

Yet colonialism was not merely an economic and political relationship; it was a social relationship as well. By the eighteenth and nineteenth centuries, European colonizers hailed from societies that had rejected prominent and public political roles for women and that empowered men to represent women's interests. Alternative colonialist definitions of femaleness reflected a European gender division of labor and sexist bias. Women's education was viewed as a vehicle for making them better wives and mothers, since women's role was to be domestic and dependent. The schools of colonial Latin America shared with those of colonial Africa, the Middle East, and India an emphasis on education for domestic roles. The provision of suitable wives for the male Christian elite and the importance of mothers as socializers of their children dominated the colonial agenda, as articulated by both the colonizers and the indigenous male elite. Colonialism sought to impose not only political dominance and economic control, but also Western culture.

Seeking to legitimate their presence, and based upon European views of women in society and their own notions of the value of human life, some colonizers and missionaries criticized polygyny and such indigenous women-oriented practices as clitoridectomy, *sati*, foot-binding, and seclusion. In the area of family law, especially relating to marriage and inheritance, Europeans did sometimes seek to provide women with increased individual rights. Among the indigenous Christianized elite in Nigeria, for instance, Christian marriage was initially popular with women for these very reasons; but because it also promoted women's economic dependence and reinforced a pre-existing sexual double standard without the historical protections provided by the extended family, women soon began to chafe under its restrictions. The arbitrariness with which European family law was often administered and its confinement primarily to urban centers combined with other factors to leave a number of states with more than one legal code—European, customary, Islamic, and so on—a situation still in the process of being reconciled in many places.

Gender—the roles, perceptions, ideologies, and rituals associated with sex—is constructed by society. All societies have broad experiences in common (everywhere people construct shelter, trade, procure food, resolve conflict, etc.), but they approach these tasks in vastly different ways. Similarly, with women, writ large, there is much that is the same in the construction of gender; writ small, there is much that is different.

Even accounting for the cultural and historical context, the commonalities in the construction of gender point to women as generally less privileged human beings than men. Women's sexuality has usually been more regulated than that of men. Women have been far more associated with household labor than are men. Women have been less likely to rise to the highest positions of political and/or religious power. Women as a group have exercised less control over wealth than men as a group. Even within the same space and time, gender has been constructed differently for certain women depending on class, race, ethnicity, religion, and other elements. Thus we must view constructions of gender related not only to sex, but to a number of other factors—mode of production, culture, religion, to name a few—that can sometimes operate to bond women and at other times operate to separate them. The fundamental construction of gender everywhere, however, has been to separate women from men—in role, status, privilege, access, and other ways.

Women in Latin America and the Caribbean

INTRODUCTION

Marysa Navarro and
Virginia Sánchez Korrol

Until recently, our knowledge of women in Latin America and the Caribbean was confined to a limited understanding of their role in the family and some information about the lives of a few individual women who had escaped anonymity by virtue of their familial relationships with historical male figures. The diversity of women's experiences in pre-colonial societies (under Spanish, Portuguese, English, French, or Dutch colonial rule) or in the twentieth century was largely ignored or misrepresented, especially when it was encapsulated in the lives of famous women.

In the last three decades, a growing number of monographs and articles have begun to retrieve the history of women in Latin America and the Caribbean. The new scholarship on women has not only deepened our understanding of women's roles in the family but also revealed a much richer social fabric that incorporates women who were slaves, nuns, domestic servants, prostitutes, and aristocratic landowners and, in the most recent past, *campesinas* (peasants), teachers, *mães de santos* (priestesses), writers, shantytown dwellers, *maquila* workers, and politicians. It has cast a new light on the emergence of *mestizo* and mulatto races throughout the continent; the establishment of racial barriers across gender, race, and class; and the creation of specific Latin American and Caribbean cultures.

Although much has been accomplished in the past thirty years, the record is far from complete. The history of Latin American and Caribbean women is presently a dynamic field of research, but it is still marred by too many gaps. We are just beginning to understand the role of women in pre-colonial societies; the social consequences of a colonial enterprise undertaken almost exclusively by men; and the impact of industrialization on working women in Argentina at the turn of century, the Dominican Republic in the 1980s, or on the U.S.–Mexican border in the 1980s and 1990s. Furthermore, not all areas or periods have received equal attention. We still lack substantial information on women in the Spanish, English, French, and Dutch Caribbean, especially during the colonial period, and on the lives of Indigenous women in Mexico, Peru, or Guatemala, both after the Conquest and in the more recent past. We also need to gain a better understanding of how women deal with transculturation and multiple national loyalties in the new migration movements.

As is the case in other areas, the difficulties we encounter in reconstructing the history of Latin American and Caribbean women are compounded by the nature of sources. The numerous and invaluable sixteenth-century Spanish accounts—written by explorers, missionaries, soldiers, and officials, for example—not only reflect deeply felt religious beliefs but also basic assumptions about human nature, how political society should be organized, and the role of men and women in it. Furthermore, in societies where most men and women were illiterate for centuries, and where female levels of illiteracy remain high, we rarely hear women's voices describing their own actions.

The new scholarship on Latin American and Caribbean women has not yet altered the periodization established since the beginning of colonization. The periodization adopted in this section therefore follows a traditional pattern, with a major division marked by the beginning of European colonization. We are aware that the use of the term "pre-Columbian" to describe the societies existing on our continent before the arrival of the Spanish may pose a problem. While contemporary anthropologists favor the use of "pre-Contact," the authors prefer to retain a name that emphasizes a precise historical and cultural moment. We also realize the difficulties presented by the word "Indian" both in English and in Spanish. In this text, we try to use it sparingly, understanding that it is a European misnomer, an invention, but the appropriate term in an account of the historical interaction between Europeans and the inhabitants of the Western Hemisphere.

Part I

WOMEN IN PRE-COLUMBIAN AND COLONIAL LATIN AMERICA AND THE CARIBBEAN

Marysa Navarro

PRE-COLUMBIAN SOCIETIES

At the close of the fifteenth century, the American continent was inhabited by a great variety of peoples who spoke many different languages, worshipped a multiplicity of gods and goddesses, and lived in distinct political and social organizations. The Caribbean islands, for example, were populated by Ciboneys, Taínos, Caribs, and Arawaks, who lived in small chiefdoms ruled by *caciques* (chiefs). By contrast, the central valley of Mexico, then called Anahuac, was densely populated by Nahuatl speakers, many of them subjects of the powerful monarch, Motecuhzoma Xocoyotzin. In South America, much of modern Brazil, Paraguay, and the Guyanas, regions of hot and humid rain forest, had a low population density. In this area, two semi-sedentary linguistic groups, the Tupinambas and the Guaraní, lived in villages of four hundred to eight hundred persons, divided into large families that shared four to eight houses. They practiced slash and burn agriculture and relocated to another place when the soil became unproductive. In contrast, the Andean region was the site of the Tawantinsuyu, the mighty empire created by the Quechua-speaking Inkas, where agriculture was a massive, collective enterprise directed by the state, involving the building of terraces and irrigation canals.

Despite the enormous cultural variations found throughout the continent, women everywhere were subordinated and excluded from public life to a greater or lesser degree. In Mexico and the Andean region, for example, the recent process of state formation had redefined women's roles along sharp gender lines diminishing their religious functions in the former, restructuring them in the latter, and in both cases reinforcing the reproductive duties of women.

Nonetheless, women everywhere performed important economic and social functions vital for the survival and welfare of their communities. In sedentary groups, both women and men practiced agriculture, whereas in semi-sedentary societies, field cultivation was primarily a female activity. Among the Tupinamba, for example, men's main activity was warfare. Captured enemies were consumed in cannibalistic rites that involved the whole community. Hunting and fishing were also the responsibility of males, while women were in charge of the production and processing of the staple food. Whenever the Tupinamba moved to a new site, women cultivated root crops from planting to harvesting after men had cleared the land of trees and burned the underbrush. In addition to food preparation—a complex process that required the grating, draining, and baking of bitter manioc root into unleavened flat bread—women's duties included the making of pottery and hammocks.

The division of labor along gender lines practiced by the Tupinambas was common to most pre-Columbian societies, from the Quechua speakers of the Andes to the Taínos of Borinquen (modern Puerto Rico). The Taínos occupied much of the Greater Antilles, except for western Cuba. They were agriculturalists, descendants of migrants who had left the coast of Venezuela and the Guyanas for the Lesser Antilles some twenty-five hundred years before. They cultivated cassava (their main food crop), squash, sweet potatoes, beans, peppers, and peanuts on earth mounds built on alluvial soil called *conucos*. They complemented their diet with fish and the meat of iguanas and dogs. Women cultivated the *conucos*, prepared the food (including the processing of cassava), made pottery, and possibly wove cotton and made baskets with sisal, while men prepared the fields, fished, hunted, carved canoes, and built houses. Their villages consisted of houses made of wood and thatch, built around a plaza. Each village was headed by a *cacique*. Villages varied in size but averaged from one to two thousand people. The villages were organized in district chiefdoms and the latter in regional chiefdoms. Taíno society was matrilineal and both men and women could inherit the position of *cacique*. In 1503, Xaraguá, the chiefdom of southwestern Hispaniola, was headed by a woman named Anacaona.

The Lesser Antilles were inhabited by the Caribs, relative newcomers to the islands. They, too, lived in small villages, although they did not have permanent chiefs. Carib men were great fishers, but they were above all warriors who raided islands inhabited by Taínos and Arawaks for additional wives and traveled great distances in large oceangoing dugout boats.

The Mexica-Aztecs (ca. 3000 B.C.E.–C.E. 1513)

In the late fifteenth century, Mesoamerica—the area that extends from the central valley of Mexico to the Isthmus of Panama—was the center of a complex civilization that included numerous ethnic groups, many of them paying tribute to Tenochtitlan. Built in the middle of Lake Texcoco, Tenochtitlan was the capital of a predatory, class-structured kingdom, where the most valued activity, warfare, was restricted to the male members of the nobility and was predicated on the labor of commoners, both men and women, and the reproductive labor of women.

On the eve of the Conquest, the Mexicas (known as Aztecs after they settled in the valley of Anahuac) were a relatively recent sedentary group. They were the last of the numerous waves of immigrants that shaped Mesoamerican civilization. Among their predecessors were the people who some 5,000 years ago began cultivating maize, one of the world's staple crops. They also created the mysterious female figurines with elegantly braided hair found in the tombs of Tlatilco, known as "pretty ladies." Other early immigrants were the enigmatic Olmec, a name that refers not to an ethnic group but to a culture that spanned from 1500 to 400 B.C.E. Although little is known of their origins or their social organization, the Olmec exerted a powerful influence in Mesoamerica because they created a counting system that included the zero (long before it was used by Europeans), one of the five known writing systems used in the area, and a calendar based on the solar and lunar year. Olmec influence was particularly strong and lasting on the Mayas, who developed their culture in the highlands of Guatemala and the Yucatan peninsula.

Other predecessors of the Aztecs were the people who built Teotihuacan, a large ceremonial center which flourished between c.e. 100 and 750 and may have housed between 100,000 and 250,000 people. We do not know the name of those who constructed this extraordinary city, with its imposing pyramids, large marketplace and wide thoroughfares, and temple to Quetzacoatl, the feathered serpent, a peaceful god who only demanded the symbolic sacrifice of butterflies and snakes. After this people's decline, the valley of Anahuac was dominated by the Toltec, a northern tribe which entered the area led by their leader, Mixcoatl. In c.e. 968, his son Topiltzin established the Toltec capital in Tula, a city that retained its religious and cultural preeminence until the twelfth century, when it was overrun by a Chichimec invasion. Tula was a major center of worship of Quetzacoatl and Tezcatlipoca ("Smoking Mirror"), a Toltec god who required human sacrifices. Women are credited with having played a leading political role in the city during this period, and matrilineal descent may have characterized Toltec society (Nash 1978: 72). The Toltec, known in Nahuatl as "the master builders," were also legendary warriors. Women appear to have engaged in combat as well, at least until the eleventh century. Tradition recalls the story of the "Warring Princess," who fought the enemies of her father and watched as the hearts of the men she had made prisoners were torn from their breasts.

The Mexica-Aztecs were the last to arrive in the valley. According to their records, they abandoned their mythical birthplace, Aztlan, in Northern Mexico, around c.e. 820 with Huitzilopochtli ("Hummingbird of the Left"), the tribal god who would guide their destiny. Led by four chiefs and a woman who carried a bundle that enclosed the spirit of Huitzilopochtli, they entered Anahuac in c.e. 1253. At that time, the valley was dominated by several lakes, the largest being Texcoco. On its shores, small city-states—among others Azcapotzalco, Culhuacan, and Texcoco—all claiming to be the heirs of the powerful Toltec, were engaged in constant warfare. The Aztecs settled on Chapultepec hill, began to learn warring skills, and became mercenaries of Azcapotzalco. The new arrivals also asked the chief of Culhuacan to give his daughter in marriage to a Mexica chief. However, Huitzilopochtli demanded her sacrifice, and, when her father came to the wedding, he saw a priest dressed in his daughter's skin. Culhuacan then launched a war on the Aztecs, who were roundly defeated and enslaved for twenty-five years. Finally, under the guidance of Huitzilopochtli, they settled on a swampy island on lake Texcoco, where they founded a city, Tenochtitlan, in c.e. 1325.

At that time, the Aztecs were a tribe of agriculturalists and hunters with a kinship system that included a minimum of status differentiation. The *calpulli*, their tribal-kinship unit, had governing duties through a male council of elders, the *calpullec*, who elected two male chiefs, one in charge of war and the other entrusted with civil or religious functions. They were known respectively as "the Father and Mother of the People" and the "Snake Woman," names that suggest that women may have played leading political roles in the past. Land was communally owned, and the *calpulli* redistributed it to member families according to their needs. After the Mexicas settled on Lake Texcoco, however, the egalitarian nature of tribal life was gradually eroded as the population increased, the need for more cultivable land became pressing, and the importance of warfare grew to the point of giving meaning to life.

Allying themselves with one powerful city after the other, shifting allegiances whenever they deemed it convenient, the Aztecs managed not only to survive but also to thrive. In 1376, they took a major step away from their egalitarian traditions and decided to establish a dynastic lineage that would give them legitimacy by sharing in the prestigious Toltec legacy. The *calpullec* asked Acamapichtli, the son of a Culhuacan princess, to marry Llancueitl, a young Aztec woman, and become the first Aztec king. Under the leadership of Izcoatl (1427–40) Tenochtitlan began an aggressive campaign against its former allies, the powerful Tepanecs from Azcapotzalco, and, after their defeat, acquired lands which were distributed to the members of the Aztec royal lineage and other warriors who had distinguished themselves in battle.

At the close of the fifteenth century, the Mexica capital had become the most powerful partner in a triple alliance composed of Tenochtitlan, Texcoco, and Tlacopan (Tacuba). When the Spaniards stumbled on Motecuhzoma's kingdom in 1519, its hegemony over tributary communities reached the coastal region of Veracruz, the Pacific Ocean, and the isthmus of Tehuantepec. Tenochtitlan, with its imposing central pyramid dedicated to Huitzilopochtli, its palaces, gardens, causeways, canals, and aqueducts, had a population between 250,000 and 400,000 and was one of the largest cities in the world. After visiting the great market, the Spanish chronicler Bernal Díaz del Castillo wrote: "Some of the soldiers among us who had been in many parts of the world, in Constantinople, and all over Italy, and in Rome, said that so large a market place and so full of people, and so well regulated and arranged, they had never beheld before" (Díaz del Castillo 1956: 218–19).

The defeat of the Tepanecs marked the transformation of the Aztecs into a society of "priest warriors." Political power became concentrated in a ruling class composed of priests and warrior-noble-men, the *pipiltin,* headed by an agnatic royal lineage with a ruler, the *tlatoani,* chosen by four lords of royal lineage from the siblings or male descendants of the king. Religious and political power, economic resources, prestige, and a luxurious life-style were largely restricted to the warrior-noblemen. The commoners existed to serve the nobility either as slaves, peasants, or merchants (*pochtecas*).

Women were crucial in this process of transformation. It was through women that the Aztecs were initially able to establish the necessary alliances needed to gain pre-eminence and legitimacy in the valley of Anahuac. Women belonging to the royal family remained an essential component of Aztec policy in the central valley because political alliances continued to be cemented with marriages. In the end, however, the institutionalization of dynastic agnatic rule and the right of royal males to practice polygyny, together with the over-whelming importance of warfare in Aztec society, weakened the role of noble women, because it re-emphasized their reproductive functions solely. A recent article by Louise M. Burkhart challenges this interpretation and suggests that "an ideology of male-female comple-mentarity was maintained through an investment of the home with symbolism of war" (Schroeder et al. 1997: 26). In the same volume, Susan Kellogg argues that complementarity and parallelism defined gender roles among the Aztecs. She sees the kinship system rooted "in a cognatic descent system"—that is, a system "in which genealog-ically based claims and rights to kin group membership, property, or positions of authority are rooted in the establishment of an individual's place in a line of descendants in which men and women are consid-ered to be genealogically and structurally equivalent" (125–26).

Since the time of Acamapichtli, the roles of Aztec women had been clearly defined. A noble woman (*cihualpilli*) transmitted the class and privileges she inherited at birth or acquired through marriage, and her role was to weave and bear children. A father advised his daughter to "learn very well and with care the task of being a woman, which is to spin and to weave; open your eyes to see how to weave delicately, to embroider and to paint cloth." He also reminded her of the differences that separated her from women of other ranks: "It is not proper for you to learn about herbs or to sell wood or peppers, salt or salpetre on the streets because you are generous and a descen-dant of noble family" (Ramos et al. 1987: 18).

At birth, the daughter of a *pilli* (singular of *pipiltin*) was shown spindles and shuttles and was told, "You must be like the heart in the body. You must not leave the home. . . . You must be like embers in the hearth." On the other hand, a son was shown a shield and four arrows and was told, "You are a quechol bird, your home, when you have seen the light of the world, is only a nest . . . you are predestined to delight the sun with the blood of your enemies and feed the Earth of Tlatccuhtli with their bodies. Your land, your birth, your father are in the land of the Sun, they are in the sky" (Anton 1973: 21).

Pregnancy and childbirth were crucial activities not only in the lives of Mexica women of all classes but also within broader local and familial contexts. A young bride's pregnancy was cause for celebration by kin and the birth of a child was a major event. Midwives—highly respected public figures—attended the laboring woman, whose travails were likened to those of the warrior on the battlefield, and named the child. Infant children, regardless of sex, were ritually welcomed into the world by a gathering of male and female family members who took turns holding and stroking the child to show their love and affection. Women breast-fed their children for several years. Boys and girls were trained differcntly from a very early age. As the Codex Mendoza (one of the Nahuatl pictorial manuscripts) indicates, by the age of five, little boys "were toting light loads of firewood and carrying light bundles to the *tiangues,* or market place. And they [mothers] taught the girls of this age how they had to hold the spindle and distaff in order to spin" (quoted in Smith 1996: 137).

The sexuality of pubescent girls belonging to the nobility was closely guarded before marriage. They lived apart, watched by old female servants, and were forbidden to walk in the streets of Tenochtitlan by themselves. They were supposed to hide their physical beauty and act at all times in a dignified manner. While boys went to school from age twelve to age twenty, receiving instruction in religion and the art of war, and training to become public officials, girls completed their education at sixteen, having learned to sweep temple courtyards, prepare food for the gods, and weave clothes used in religious ceremonies.

Their marriage, to youths of the same class but not necessarily of the same status, was arranged by a female go-between, a *cihuatlanque,* although a priest was consulted to determine the fate of the couple. The ceremony consisted of a feast; then the young couple was taken to the groom's parents' home, and her skirt and his cloak were knotted together.

Marriage was an important transition for both male and female youths. The young man would have his needs attended to by his wife rather than his mother, and the young woman exchanged the authority of her father for that of her husband. Brides moved into their husbands' families, where their duty was to produce children, especially sons, to replenish the ranks of the warrior class decimated by warfare. In her husband's house, a woman was under the supervision of her mother-in-law, and her status did not change until she had borne at least four children. Sterile women could be repudiated and divorced. On the other hand, desertion, physical abuse, or failure to support the family were grounds for a woman to ask for divorce. Widows, especially if they were of child-bearing age, were encouraged to remarry and frequently became the concubines of their deceased husbands' brothers.

Wives were supposed to remain faithful to their husbands, and female adultery was punished by death—the same penalty assigned to murder, rebellion, or wearing the clothes of the other sex. Not even the royal family was protected from this type of punishment. In order to strengthen Tenochtitlan's alliance with Texcoco, a young sister of Motecuhzoma, Chilchiuhnenetzin, was given in marriage to king Nezahualpilli. Unfortunately, her participation in secret orgies was discovered and despite the protection of her two thousand servants, she was garroted and burned, together with all her servants. On the other hand, men were allowed to have numerous concubines, and the Spanish chronicler Francisco López de Gómara recounts that Motecuhzoma had more than one hundred secondary wives. At a particular moment, some fifty of them were believed to have been pregnant.

Women's distinct nature and role was emphasized even after death. When a warrior died, he was buried on a pyre with slaves. A woman, on the other hand, was accompanied by her spinning and weaving instruments. These, when associated with a man, were seen as a symbol of subordination and humility. According to Ignacio Bernal, Tezozomoc, the ruler of Azcapotzalco, wishing to insult the king of Texcoco, Ixtlixochitl, sent him cotton to signify that "Ixtlixochitl [was] a weak woman who was only capable of spinning cotton" (Nash 1978: 356).

Power, wealth, status, housing, education, clothing, and even food separated the *pipiltin* from the *macehualtin*, the commoners. The commoners' lot was heavy, especially under Motecuhzoma. Their task was to pay the insatiable tributary demands of the nobility or of Tenochtitlan. *Macehualtin* married women carried heavy domestic burdens. Their duties included preparing maize for consumption, a heavy and long process that required shelling it, grinding it on a *metate* (grinding stone), washing it, and making and cooking tortillas. At times they also had to prepare food for the priests and for the soldiers who went to war. Additionally, they had to meet their weaving obligations for the family and work in the field with their husbands in order to produce the tribute owed to the *pipiltin* or to Tenochtitlan. Many also prepared food, beverages, and herbs to sell in the great market of Tenochtitlan.

As is the case with poorer sectors of the population in many parts of the world, among the *macehualtin* monogamy prevailed, and the marriage ritual was less important than for the *pipiltin*. Women were permitted to practice several trades and were therefore much freer in important respects than noble women. They could become, among other things, medicine women, midwives, street vendors, and go-betweens, although they were barred from certain activities open to lower-class men. Fray Bernardino de Sahagún—a Franciscan missionary who spent most of his life dedicated to the study of Aztec language and culture and author of the extraordinary *General History of the Things of New Spain*—indicates that men could perform thirty-five different trades, while only fifteen were available to women. However, one must consider the possibility that women's activities were far more numerous, but remained invisible even to Sahagún's sharp eyes or were deemed unimportant by his numerous informants.

Almost half of the Mexica calendar was dedicated to goddesses. The Aztecs had numerous goddesses identified with fertility, nourishment, and agriculture—reflections, perhaps, of a past when the status of women was higher; a time when deities suggested oppositions between light and dark, masculine and feminine, life and death; and a time without large-scale warfare, massive human sacrifices, and a demanding, male, bloodthirsty Huitzilopochtli. Dualism and complementarity still reigned in the Aztec pantheon. Coatlicue was known as "the Serpent Lady," the earth mother who gave light to everything, the mother of the gods, including Huitzilopochtli; but she was also Cipactli, the monster who devoured all that lived, including the stars and the souls of those who walked by fountains and caves. Her temple in Tenochtitlan was called "the House of Darkness." Chalchihuitlicue ("the Lady with the Jade Skirt") was the goddess of storms, springs, and streams. She was the sister/wife of Tlaloc, "Lord of All Sources of Water," an old Olmec god of fertility identified with rain, lightning, and mountain springs.

Despite the centrality of goddesses to Aztec religion, however, women played a secondary role in public religious ritual and men occupied the highest positions in the priesthood. Although they were not priestesses, women were responsible for maintaining the household shrines and performing rites, including sweeping, of vital importance in safeguarding the household from dangerous contamination. We may surmise that the importance of household rituals, and therefore of women's religious role, increased after the Conquest, when public rituals were no longer permitted.

At the close of the fifteenth century, Tenochtitlan was still expanding, exacting increasing tribute from subjugated populations. Its transformation into a powerful city-state, dedicated to warfare and supported by a growing number of commoners living in kinship units through which production was organized, had been rapid, and tensions in the valley of Anahuac were high. The process had included the adoption of a gender ideology that varied according to class but that excluded women from many benefits of the expansion.*

The Inkas (2500 B.C.E.–C.E. 1533)

The situation of women in the Tawantinsuyu, the major civilization in South America, differed in some respects from the conditions outlined for Aztec women, although both cultures' cosmological views stressed the complementary natures of masculine/feminine and male/female despite the radically distinct social roles prescribed for each sex. Like the Aztecs, the Inkas were heirs to very old cultural traditions, most of them developed by people who lived on the arid coast of modern Peru. Impressive ceremonial centers, pyramids, adobe palaces, irrigation canals, delicate jewelry, handsome vases, and exquisite textiles are witness to the achievements of cultures known today mostly as archeological sites or pottery styles: Chavín de Huantar, Paracas, Nazca, Mochica, or Chimú.

Around C.E. 600, the focus of Andean civilization shifted from the coast to the highlands with the emergence of Tiwanaku and the Wari empire. The former was a great ceremonial center which arose on the *altiplano* (high plateau) south of Lake Titicaca and extended its influence into northern Chile. The Wari empire was centered near modern Ayacucho and reached as far north as Cajamarca.

The great Andean conquerors, however, were undoubtedly the Inkas, who began their rapid expansion from the highlands under Pachakuti Inka (1438–71). His son, Tupak Yupanki (1471–93), extended the empire to the south and to the coast, and his successor, Wayna Qhapaq (1403–1527), pushed the empire's northern border into modern Ecuador and Colombia. When the Spaniards reached

*In addition to the works cited within this section, see Anton 1973; Clendinnen 1991; MacLachlan and Rodriguez 1980; Nash 1980.

the Tawantinsuyu, it was ruled by Wayna Qhapaq's son, Atawuall-pa, who had just defeated his brother Wascar in a bloody civil war. The Inka empire encompassed approximately nine million people living in some 380,000 square miles, an expanse that included most of modern Peru, southern Ecuador, western Bolivia, northern Argentina, and Chile. To its people, the empire was the Tawantinsuyu, "the land of the four quarters," and at its center was Cusco, "the navel of the world," "the sacred city" containing the Corincancha, the golden temple of the sun god Inti. Cusco was also sacred because according to Inka sources, it had been founded circa c.e. 1200 by the mythical Manqo Qhapaq; with Mama Oqllo, his wife (and his sister), he had founded the Inka dynasty. They established the parallel but complementary lines of descent for the inhabitants of the empire: "Women conceived of themselves as the descendants through their mothers of a line of women; men in parallel fashion, saw themselves as descending from their fathers in a line of men" (Silverblatt 1987: 5).

The Tawantinsuyu was composed of a multiplicity of subjugated ethnic groups, separated by different languages (although Quechua was the official imperial language), distinct institutions, and awesome geographic barriers, but united by a centralized state that sought maximum utilization of human, natural, and material resources. It was headed by the Sapa Inka, a descendant of Manqo Qhapaq and Mama Oqllo, an all-powerful figure, who was worshipped as the son of the Sun and ruled by divine right. He was married to the Coya, his sister, and although he was allowed to have many other wives, only one of her children could inherit the throne.

The Sapa Inka, the Coya, and their relatives—known as Inkas if they were male and *Pallas* if they were female—formed the ruling class of the Tawantinsuyu. As descendants of Manco Qhapaq, they were the True Inkas or Qhapaq Inkas, the only ones allowed to live permanently in Cusco. This class also included people known as Hawua Inkas or Outer Inkas, who were not born Inka but were granted the title by the Sapa Inka. They were usually *kurakas,* ethnic lords of conquered populations; despite their noble status, they lived outside Cusco. All other inhabitants of the empire were commoners. Political power was in the hands of the male members of the ruling class, especially the Sapa Inka.

Inka religion featured parallel cults. The premier religious figure, the Sapa Inka, was identified with the cult of the Sun; the Coya was identified with a parallel cult centered on the Moon, queen of the skies, mistress of the sea and winds, female fertility, and all other female divinities. The Coya, assisted by women, officiated in religious ceremonies honoring the goddess of women. Another important female divinity was the Pachamama (Earth Mother), worshipped in Andean communities since pre-Inka times. Just as the Moon was the complement of the Sun, the Pachamama was the complement of Illapa, the god of thunder and lightning, who dominated the heavens. According to the Spanish chronicler Bernabé Cobo,

> All adored the earth, which they called Pachamama, which means Earth Mother; and it was common for them to place a long stone, like an altar or a statue, in the middle of their fields, in honor of this goddess, in order, in that spot, to offer her prayers and invoke her, asking her to watch over and fertilize their fields; and when certain plots of land were found to be more fertile, so much greater was their respect for her. (quoted in Silverblatt 1987: 24)

Women had a special, sacred bond with the Pachamama, and, when planting time arrived, they were the ones in charge of putting seeds in the earth, after purifying themselves. Furthermore, because she embodied the regenerative forces of the earth, the Pachamama was also tied to female fertility through the midwives.

Although men occupied the highest positions in the Inka priesthood, women also played a pre-eminent and distinctive religious role as *aqllas* ("Wives of the Sun"). These were women, daughters of *kurakas* and commoners, who had been selected for their beauty by Inka officials and who were dedicated to the cult of the Sun and other deities. They were "chosen" before puberty and remained virgins for the rest of their lives. As Wives of the Sun, they officiated at religious rituals, figuring prominently at festivals, especially the Inti Raymi or Festival of the Sun. They also wove decorations for the temples and made the delicate alpaca clothes worn by the Sapa Inka and his family. They received their training in the so-called "nunneries" or *aqllawasi*, state-run institutions located in the provincial capitals where they lived, their sexuality rigidly guarded, with other beautiful girls. They learned "women's tasks": how to spin and weave wool and cotton and how to prepare *chicha*, an alcoholic beverage used in religious ceremonies. Not all the "chosen women" growing up in the *aqllawasi* eventually became Wives of the Sun. Some were taken as secondary wives by the Sapa Inka, and others were distributed by him, also as secondary wives, to whomever he wished, generally Inka officials, warriors, or—in order to cement political alliances—to *kurakas* of subjugated populations.

Silverblatt sees the institution of the *aqllas* as intrinsic to the ideological and political structure resulting from Inka conquest. The surrender of virgins who would become wives of the Inka or Wives of the Sun was "one of the major cultural transformations to emerge as the Incas built their Andean empire" (Silverblatt 1987: 85).

The Coya was unquestionably essential for the perpetuation of dynastic rule and the endless reproduction of the parallel and complementary order created by imperial expansion. She was known as "the Queen of Women," a title that suggests authority over the female world (Silverblatt 1987: 60). This authority was expressed in ceremonies, the right to receive gifts, the prerogative to throw lavish feasts, and the authority to arrange marriages for her female subjects. According to a Spanish account:

> The palace of the queen was located in this enormous construction, and it was almost as large as the Inca's; and since she held a preeminent office, she went about dressed with ornaments of *cumbi* [finely woven cloth] which represented the position she held in the palace. She had shrines, baths, and gardens both for herself and her ñustas, who were like ladies-in-waiting, of which there were more than two hundred. She was responsible for marrying them to lords who had achieved honorable offices under the Inca. It was truly marvelous when the great queen walked about; she was served, in every way, with the majesty shown toward the Inca. (quoted in Silverblatt 1987: 60)

Despite her centrality to the Inka state, the Coya's political duties were both exceptional and limited. When the Sapa Inka left Cusco for the battlefield, she could rule in his absence. However, neither she nor the *Pallas* formed part of the enormous administrative structure created by the Inkas, which was all in male hands. Noblewomen, like their Aztec counterparts, were educated to spin yarn, weave, and embroider; once married, their duty was to produce children in order to perpetuate the male lineage. Although pre-marital virginity was not required and noblemen were allowed to have numerous wives, marriage marked the beginning of a rigid control over the sexuality of noblewomen, and their infidelity was punished with death.

As in the Aztec case, the life of non-elite women was shaped by the labor requirements imposed by the state on the commoners as a whole and by the survival of pre-Inka institutions such as the *ayllu*, the basic social unit of the empire. The *ayllu* was a kinship group that owned land communally and whose members claimed descent from a common ancestor and married within the group. The labor requirements began with the incorporation of subjugated populations into the empire and were guided by the principles of reciprocity and redistribution, which were ritualized in an elaborate system of gifts and feasts. Conquest gave the Sapa Inka the right to take a portion of land owned by the *ayllu* for the state and the state religion, to redistribute the remaining land, and to request labor and *mit'a*, service labor, from the *ayllu* members. In exchange, the needs of the conquered populations were largely satisfied.

Women were exempted from certain *mit'as* carried out on a rotating basis, such as the maintenance of roads, building fortresses, temples, or cities, and serving in imperial armies. However, their labor was included in the demands imposed on the *ayllu* and performed by each household. They were responsible for weaving the assigned share of cloth. They also worked in the mines, and because all land was cultivated communally, they planted corn or potatoes after the men had broken the ground or had prepared the necessary terraces on the steep mountain slopes. In the northern frontier of the empire, all agricultural work was performed by women, and men's tasks, in striking contrast to practices elsewhere in the empire, were to weave and sew. Otherwise, throughout the empire, women had domestic duties that included spinning wool, weaving cloth, and making the garments worn by all the members of the household, as well as gathering wood for fuel, preparing food and *chicha*, and rearing children.

Pre-marital virginity among commoners was not expected in the Tawantinsuyu, but once a couple was married, both had to remain faithful. Adultery on the part of a man or a woman was punished by death. Marriage was compulsory, the household being the minimal unit into which the *ayllu* was divided in order to satisfy the labor requirements assigned by the state. The marriage ceremony was performed by an Inka official, and it was followed by a celebration, which varied in nature from area to area according to the traditions of the ethnic groups.

Compared to the Aztecs, the Inkas assigned women a prominent role in the public religious realm. Like many other pre-Columbian societies, however, the Inkas located women's central role in the household. Of course, the nature of women's duties and the circumstances in which they fulfilled them varied greatly by class. In all cases, however, the arrival of Europeans and the establishment of a new economic structure—which included private property, wage labor, the massive production of minerals, technological innovations, the importation of new plants and animals, forced migrations to the cities or mining areas, abusive labor requirements, and different social formations and values, accompanied initially by a dramatic demographic decline—directly challenged the viability of the pre-Columbian household and altered the roles that women performed in society throughout the continent.*

THE CONQUEST

Brazil

The first Portuguese expedition to Brazil took place in 1500. In the following years, much as they had done along the western coast of Africa in the previous century, Portuguese traders established posts on the coast between Pernambuco and São Paulo to obtain brazilwood and dyewood. Castaways, deserters, and occasional *degredados* (criminals exiled from Portugal), all male, were the first European inhabitants of the Brazilian coast. Many adapted so well to their new environment that they took on indigenous names, ways, and lovers. Diego Alvares (known as Caramurú) in Bahia, João Ramalho in Piratininga, Antônio Rodrigues in São Vicente, and their numerous offspring would prove invaluable when Portugal decided to colonize the area. Contrary to what would happen in Spanish America, the Portuguese Crown, concerned with its expanding maritime empire, initially showed limited interest in its American territories and consequently little concern with the sexual behavior of its subjects or the fate of *mamelucos,* the name given to the children of Portuguese men and Indian women.

When it decided to pay attention to Brazil, the Crown divided its territories into fifteen captaincies, which were granted to twelve *donatários* (grantees). In 1535, Duarte Coelho sailed to Brazil to take possession of his captaincy, Pernambuco. He was accompanied by his wife, Doña Brites de Albuquerque, but other women did not follow her example. Doña Brites was one of the first European women to perform administrative duties in the New World, taking care of Coelho's responsibilities during his frequent absences. Coelho also had the help of Vasco Lucena, a Portuguese who had lived many years in the area.

Relations with the Tupinambas soured because the Portuguese made labor demands which the former could not satisfy. Intent on producing agricultural products that could be sold profitably in Europe—cotton, tobacco, and sugar—the Portuguese needed a stable labor force and wanted the Tupinamba males, who were above all

*In addition to the works cited within this section, see Pescatello 1976; Silverblatt 1980.

warriors, to perform activities that were identified with the female realm. Enslaving the Tupinamba did not solve the problem. In 1559, the first epidemic, probably smallpox, hit the Brazilian coast and killed an untold number of Indians, enslaved and free. As cotton and sugarcane cultivation expanded, Amerindian labor proved unreliable, costly, and as epidemics spread, insufficient to fulfill the needs of commercial agriculture. The Portuguese, already involved in the slave trade, turned to a source of labor readily available to them: enslaved Africans. Indeed, the Portuguese had been trading in African slaves since 1441, when a shipload of slaves was brought to Portugal from Mauritania.

The prosperity of Pernambuco, despite Tupinamba resistance, was rivaled in the south by the success of the São Vicente captaincy, headed by Martim Affonso de Souza. He attracted sugarcane growers from the island of Madeira and by 1545 six sugar mills were actively processing cane. Notwithstanding the prosperity of São Vicente and Pernambuco, the *donatário* system proved a failure and was discontinued. In 1549, Tomé de Souza was appointed the first governor of Brazil. Accompanied by farmers, artisans, six Jesuits, and a few women, he arrived at the new capital, Bahia, to take over his duties and was received by Caramurú.

Although the Portuguese established towns along the coast of Brazil, it was the *engenho*, the sugar mill, that soon defined the character of the colony. Sugar planting and sugar mills required large expanses of land, a substantial labor force, and skilled workers. The last —coopers, blacksmiths, carters, sugar masters, and overseers—were generally male Europeans, at least in the early stage of colonization; in later centuries, holders of these positions included free male blacks and men of mixed race.

The importation of African slaves began in 1538 and proceeded rapidly. Although in the 1550s there were practically no Africans in northeastern Brazil, by the mid-1580s Pernambuco alone had some 2,000 slaves, once again mostly male, working on some sixty-six sugar plantations. The numbers of African slaves increased steadily, from 50,000 in the sixteenth century to 560,000 in the seventeenth century, to a high of 1,891,400 in the eighteenth century. By the end of the nineteenth century, an estimated total of 3,648,800 slaves had been imported to Brazil. In comparison, the total number of slaves imported to Spanish America has been estimated at 1,552,100. As for Amerindian slavery, it co-existed with African slavery throughout much of the colonial period.

In the second half of the sixteenth century, Portuguese men began to emigrate in greater numbers to Brazil as sugarcane production continued to expand. While the Crown sent a few female orphans of good family to the colony from time to time, the number of immigrant women remained very low, as it would throughout the entire colonial period.

In 1695, the colony was shaken by news of the discovery of gold in the southwest, in an area later known as Minas Gerais. Accompanied by their servants and slaves, large groups of colonists from Bahia, Rio de Janeiro, and Pernambuco rushed to the mining areas. As the gold boom began to decline, in the 1720s diamonds were discovered, also in Minas Gerais. Mining brought about an acute labor shortage in the sugarcane producing areas and increased the demand for African slaves.*

Spanish America

The establishment of Spanish colonial domination in the Indies (as the Western Hemisphere was called in the sixteenth century) was a gradual process that began in the Caribbean islands, jumped to the mainland, spread from different centers (Tenochitlan/Mexico, Panama, and Asuncion), and was largely completed by the second half of the sixteenth century. It was a process carried out by groups of men, organized as exploratory/military expeditions. The pattern first established in the Caribbean islands was repeated on the continent from Mexico to the Río de la Plata: Spanish men conquered new territories, and Spanish women followed as soon as the officials and the settlers began to arrive.

Christopher Columbus's first three expeditions, in 1492, 1493, and 1498, did not include women, although permission was granted for thirty women to travel to the Indies with his last expedition. Not until 1509 did a large group of women land in Hispaniola. They came with the new Viceroy of the islands, Diego Colón, and his wife, Doña María de Toledo. As settlers continued to arrive with tools, seeds, and livestock, the number of women began to increase, although they were consistently fewer than men. Between the years 1509 and 1539, women represented 5 or 6 percent of the total number of emigrants, and that figure only rose to 28 percent in the 1570s. Peter Boyd-Bowman states that between 1509 and 1519, 308 women sailed to the Indies, generally accompanying relatives. Between 1520 and 1539,

*In addition to the works cited within this section, see Pescatello 1976; Schwartz 1985; Klein 1986.

the number increased to 845, out of a total of 13,262 emigrants. The women traveled mostly to Mexico and Santo Domingo; of them, 252 were married and emigrated with their husbands, 85 were married and were going to join their husbands, 457 were unmarried, and 51 were widows or women whose marital status could not be determined (Boyd-Bowman 1973). However, even in this early period, the actual proportion of women in the Americas must have been higher than the numbers provided by emigration sources, because of the high mortality rate among men.

Relatively few Spanish women shared the experience of Inés Suárez, who participated actively in the conquest of what later became Chile. In 1537, accompanied by a young niece, she sailed to the New World to join her husband and landed in the Gulf of Paria. From Venezuela, she went to the Isthmus of Panama and then down the coast of Peru to Lima, founded by Francisco Pizarro in January 1535 as the new seat of Spanish imperial power after the collapse of the Tawantinsuyu. The number of Spanish women in the new viceroyalty at that time was very small. According to one report, there were only some 14 present in Lima in 1537 and four years later there may have been only 152. When Suárez arrived, she found the colony still torn by the bloody war between Almagro and Pizarro. The former's claim to Cusco exploded into a civil war, the first in a series of confrontations among Spaniards that would last more than fifteen years. The initial round had resulted in Almagro's defeat at the battle of Las Salinas and his prompt execution in 1533. Three years later, in 1541, a group of Almagristas assassinated Pizarro.

In Lima, Inés Suárez found out that her husband was in Cusco, and she proceeded to the highlands. In the former Inka capital, she learned that he had died during the great rebellion of 1536, when a formidable Inka army laid a year-long siege to Cusco. She settled in the city and lived from the revenues of a small *encomienda* that she had inherited from her husband. This royal grant gave an individual the right to collect tribute and labor from a certain number of Indians living in a specific area. In exchange, the *encomendero* (holder of an *encomienda*) was charged with protecting the Indians, ensuring that they became good Christians, and fostering their "hispanization." In most areas, however, the *encomienda* became in fact an institution that permitted the exploitation of the indigenous population. *Encomiendas* affected both men and women, generally forcing them to perform services away from their communities. The men worked in agriculture, construction, and mining, while the women went to the *encomendero's* home to be wet nurses, cooks, or maids. Although it was rare for Spanish women to be granted an *encomienda* in their own right, married women often managed estates in their husbands' absence and widows could inherit the grant. However, as Ida Altman reminds us, widows were "seldom permitted to remain single and retain an encomienda. As a result men often became encomenderos through marriage to widows who held grants" (Altman 1989: 223–24).

It was in Cusco that Suárez met Captain Pedro de Valdivia, campmaster at Las Salinas and a native of Extremadura like Pizarro and many other *conquistadores*. Although he was married to Marina Ortiz de Gaete, who had remained in Spain when he left for the Indies, Valdivia and Suárez became lovers. In 1539, Pizarro entrusted to Valdivia the task of expanding Spanish control over Chile. With some 150 Spaniards on horse and foot, 1,000 Indians, and some mares and swine, he set out for Chile. Suárez was granted permission to accompany him as his *criada* (servant) in charge of overseeing his Indian carriers. The Spaniards crossed the Acatama desert and had to engage in numerous skirmishes, during which Suárez took care of the sick and nursed the wounded. She also warned Valdivia of several plots against him, and, although she gained his trust, she also made enemies among the Spaniards. They finally arrived in the Mapocho valley where, on February 12, 1541, Valdivia founded a city which he named Santiago. The city was laid out according to royal instructions, a *cabildo* (town council) was created, and the Spaniards began to "pacify" the Picunches.

Six months later, while Valdivia was away on an expedition with most of his troops, Santiago was attacked and almost destroyed. It was saved, largely by Suárez, who, wearing armor, threw herself into the battle and, as the enemy was preparing the final assault, proposed beheading seven chiefs held as hostages in a stockade and hurling their heads at the attackers. She set the example herself, an action for which she was later rewarded with an *encomienda*.

Unfortunately, Suárez's life with Valdivia came under the scrutiny of the royal governor of Peru, Pedro de la Gasca. He ordered Valdivia to put an end to his relationship with Suárez and to bring his wife from Spain. Valdivia obeyed, and in early 1549 Suárez married Valdivia's captain, Rodrigo de Quiroga. She died in Santiago, in 1572, the revered wife of the governor of Chile. For his part, Valdivia did send for his wife, but he died in 1553, before she arrived, during a campaign against the Araucanians.

We have some details about Inés Suárez's life today largely because of her relationship with a prominent *conquistador* like Valdivia. Virtually no accounts by Spanish women of their adventures in the new world have survived, if they were ever composed, although further research on women may reveal sources heretofore overlooked. One exceptional account by a Spanish woman is a letter written by Doña Isabel de Guevara in 1535. She went to the Río de la Plata with twenty other women in a large expedition led by Governor Don Pedro de Mendoza. Three months after landing in Buenos Aires, one thousand men had perished for lack of food. Unable to survive, they decided to abandon Buenos Aires, sailed the Paraná River and settled in Asunción:

> The men became so weak that all the tasks fell on the poor women, washing the clothes as well as nursing them, preparing them the little food there was, keeping them clean, standing guard, patrolling the fires, loading the crossbows when the Indians came to do battle, even firing the cannon, and arousing the soldiers who were capable of fighting, shouting the alarm through the camp, acting as sergeants and putting the soldiers in order, because at that time, as we women can make do with little nourishment, we had not fallen into such weakness as men. (Hahner 1980: 18)

The initial absence of Spanish women, both on the islands and on the mainland, gave a specific dimension to the destruction and violence brought about by the Conquest, as the establishment of Spanish colonization in the Americas is called. Especially in places like Mexico and Peru, it produced a violence specifically directed against women, aided by the military nature of the process and the common practice throughout the region of exchanging women. Amerindian women were raped, killed, enslaved, branded, demanded or given as gifts or tokens of friendship, and were part of the spoils of war reaped by the conquerors.

But women were not only pawns, they were agents. On one hand, they satisfied the *conquistadores'* sexual appetites and took care of their everyday needs; on the other hand, women explained to the newcomers their own customs and traditions, at times protected *conquistadores* (making their task easier), and also used them to survive in a world that seemed to be falling apart.

The classic example, of course, is Malinche, Malinal or Malintzin, a woman the Spaniards called Doña Marina. Little is known about her today, although she was a crucial participant in Hernán Cortés's conquest of the Aztec kingdom. She was probably born in the Isthmus of Tehuantepec and, according to several accounts, was sold into slavery by her mother. She also lived for several years among the Tabascans, and by the time she came into contact with Cortés, she spoke several languages, including Chontal Maya and Nahuatl.

Malintzin met Cortés shortly after his expedition sailed from Cuba in February 1519. Within a few days of his landing on April 22, he had a skirmish with some Tabascans, and his victory over them was marked by a ceremony during which he was given numerous gifts, including twenty women and girls, whom he distributed among his men. Malintzin was awarded to Alonso Hernández Puertocarrero, but after he was sent to Spain with dispatches and booty for the Emperor Charles V, she became the first of Cortés's Aztec mistresses.

He was already aware of her unusual linguistic talents, which proved to be indispensable to him. Malintzin was able to give Cortés an exceptional understanding of his surroundings. Through her he learned that somewhere in the interior lived a powerful ruler whose name was Motecuhzoma. When the Spaniards entered Aztec territory, she helped Cortés to engage in negotiations with Motecuhzoma's emissaries. When the latter sent an embassy to confront the Spaniards, she translated their Nahuatl words into Maya for Jerónimo de Aguilar, who in turn translated the Maya into Spanish for Cortés and his men. Aguilar was a shipwrecked Spaniard who had lived in Cozumel for several years and had therefore mastered Maya. The need for triangular translation, however, was short-lived, because Malintzin soon learned Spanish and was able to communicate directly with Cortés. Bernal Díaz del Castillo called her the *lengua* (tongue) of Cortés. Their association was so close that he became known as "Captain Malintzin."

Although in his letters to the emperor Cortés barely mentioned Malintzin twice, her role in the conquest of Mexico was greatly valued by men like Bernal Díaz del Castillo, a foot-soldier in the expedition, and she is prominently depicted in sixteenth-century pictorial documents. She was able to provide Cortés with crucial information about the strengths and weaknesses of the Aztec kingdom as he prepared his march from the coast to Tenochtitlan. She was instrumental in establishing alliances with the enemies of the Mexicas, on several occasions thwarted attempts to massacre the Spaniards, and as Frances Karttunen notes, repeatedly assisted Cortés in creating discord among the Totonnacs, the Tlaxcalans, and the Cholulans, "playing people off against each other, misleading them to keep his potential enemies offbalance and acquiring allies through a mix of sweet talk and intimidation" (quoted in Schroeder et al.: 303). Sometime in 1522, she had a son by Cortés, Don Martín, who was brought up by one of Cortés's relatives and taken to Spain at the age of six. Years later, Malintzin's son was legitimized by Pope Clement VII and rose to be Comendador of the prestigious Orden de Santiago.

Cortés also used Malintzin's knowledge, intelligence, advice, and diplomatic skills in his 1524 expedition to Honduras. By that date, however, he had exchanged her for another Indian mistress and married Malintzin off to one of his men, Juan de Jaramillo. She had another child, a daughter, and died by the early 1530s.

When Malintzin became Cortés's mistress, he was already married to a Spaniard, Catalina Juárez, with whom he did not have children. She remained in Cuba and joined him in Mexico after the fall of Tenochtitlan. She arrived in 1522 with several other women, and died shortly thereafter. Cortés also left in Cuba his first Indian mistress, Leonor Pizarro, with whom he had an illegitimate daughter, the first of his four acknowledged *mestizo* children. In Mexico, he had several other mistresses besides Malintzin: Doña Ana, Doña Isabel, and Doña Isabel, all daughters of Motecuhzoma; Doña Elvira, niece of the Aztec king; and Doña Ana and Doña Francisca, both daughters of Cacama, king of Texcoco. When his wife joined him in Mexico, he was surrounded "by an infinite number of women," including some who were Spanish (Thomas 1993: 580). In 1530, after he returned to Spain a widower and was made Marqués del Valle de Oaxaca by the emperor, he married the young Doña Juana de Zúñiga (daughter of Carlos, Count of Aguilar, and niece of the Duque de Béjar), with whom he had five children.

Cortés's multiple successive relationships with indigenous women were not exceptional. In fact, the *conquistadores* who did not have one or several Amerindian concubines were the exception, although it is likely that few went as far as Alonso de Mesa, one of the "Men of Cajamarca" who accompanied Francisco Pizarro in the conquest of the Tawantinsuyu. He was eighteen and settled in Cusco, where he became a rich *encomendero*. He resisted marriage longer than most and lived with his six concubines, including a black slave woman, and six illegitimate children. He finally married an Amerindian noblewoman, Doña Catalina Huaco Ocllo, and he was the only Man of Cajamarca to do so. By the end of his life, he had at least four more children and legitimated only one. Francisco Pizarro, the *conquistador* of the Tawantinsuyu, who was illegitimate himself, had two Indian mistresses. The first was Doña Inés Yupanqui Huaylas, daughter of

Huayna Capac, with whom he had a son and a daughter who were legitimated. He eventually married Doña Inés to his retainer Francisco de Ampuero and had a second mistress, Doña Angelina or Añas Yupanqui, also of royal lineage, with whom he had two *mestizo* sons he did not legitimate. His most famous and long-lived offspring, writes James Lockhart, was his daughter Doña Francisca, who lived in Lima "and held a large encomienda as her father's successor. Sent to Spain at the same time as don Francisco [her illegitimate half-brother] she married her uncle Hernando [also a *conquistador*], to unite the Pizarro wealth and entails, and bore him seven children; she survived him and, before 1584, married the son of the Count of Puñoenrrostro" (Lockhart 1972: 154–55). The *conquistador* Hernando de Soto was married to Doña Isabel de Bobadilla in Valladolid, Spain, with whom he had no children. However, he left an illegitimate daughter in Nicaragua and had another one in Peru with Toqto Chimbu or Doña Leonor, one of Atawuallpa's wives.

The offspring of these unions were the first generations of *mestizos* and *mestizas*. Most of them were illegitimate because their mothers, noblewomen or commoners, were *barraganas* or *mancebas*: concubines. In Spain, Portugal, and the Indies, there were two kinds of illegitimacy. Children born to a man and a woman who were not married to anyone but could be married to each other were known as *naturales,* illegitimate. Children born to a man and a woman who could not marry were known as *espurios* or *bastardos* (spurious, bastards, illegitimate), conceived in sin and born of adulterous relationships, either because one of the partners was already married or because one of them had taken religious vows. Illegitimate children could be recognized or legitimated by their fathers. In the first stages of the Conquest, many *mestizos* were legitimated by their Spanish fathers, especially if they grew under their tutelage and if the mothers were of noble lineage. In the sixteenth century, they were accepted without much difficulty by the world of either parent. On the other hand, children born of African slaves were generally neither recognized nor legitimated by Spanish fathers.

Concubinage did not develop in the Indies. It was a very old institution in the Iberian world. Ida Altman points out that in sixteenth-century Extremadura, having children outside marriage was a well-established tradition for all groups: "Hidalgos might have one or two children by the same woman (usually though not invariably from the lower classes) before they married and established their legitimate family and household" (Altman 1989: 151). But it became so widespread in the early stages of the Conquest that the Spanish Crown from 1501 on repeatedly urged its subjects to marry their concubines. Governor Nicolás Ovando's instructions in 1503, which recommended that Christians marry Indians, were reiterated in 1514 and 1515. On the other hand, the Crown explicitly fostered the emigration of Spanish women to the Americas and went as far as granting only temporary emigration licenses to married men who left their wives in Spain.

The pro-marriage policy of the Crown did not lead to the formalization of mixed unions, at least among the most successful *conquistadores*—who were in a position, as a result of their successes in the Indies, to marry Spanish women of good (i.e., noble) lineage. After the fall of Motecuhzoma's kingdom, Cortés's lieutenant, Pedro de Alvarado, abandoned his mistress, Tecuelhuatzin, christened Doña María Luisa Xicotencatl. The daughter of the *cacique* of the Tlaxcalans, she had been given to Cortés by her father to cement the alliance. Cortés gave her to Alvarado, with whom she had two children, a son and a daughter. When he returned to Spain, rich and famous, Alvarado married a noblewoman by the name of Doña Francisca de la Cueva, who accompanied him to Guatemala and, like the Portuguese Doña Brites, took over his duties as captain-general whenever he was absent. They did not have children together but he arranged the marriage of his illegitimate son to the cousin of his legitimate wife.

The case of Garcilaso de la Vega's parents is another such example. Garcilaso de la Vega, also known as El Inca Garcilaso, was the *mestizo* son of Sebastián Garcilaso de la Vega, a captain in Pizarro's army, and Chimpu Oqllo (or Isabel Suárez to the Spaniards) granddaughter of the Sapa Inka Tupaq Yupanqhi and his sister/wife, Mama Oqllo. Before Garcilaso was born, his father had had a daughter with another Indian mistress and ten years later, the captain arranged the marriage of Isabel Suárez to Juan del Pedroche, a Spaniard of lesser social standing. In the meantime, the captain, in his forties, proceeded to wed Luisa Martel de los Ríos, barely fourteen but born of Spanish parents and of proper lineage in Panama.

The multiplication of the *mestizo* population undermined the initial Spanish strategy to create two separate worlds, *la República de los Indios y la República de los Españoles* (a Spanish world and an Indian world), mediated by an Amerindian nobility, the *caciques*. This strategy was supposed to permit the Crown to watch over the welfare of the Amerindians, who were declared legal minors, and to ensure their Christianization. To achieve this purpose, everywhere, the *cacique* nobility was granted special privileges. One of Queen Isabella's instructions to Governor Ovando stipulated that any Spaniard harming the Indian nobility would be severely punished. In Peru, the descendants of the Inka dynasty and Outer Inkas were declared the equivalent of *hidalgos* (landed gentry), and they were therefore entitled to economic and social privileges. In Mexico, in accordance with the Laws of Indies which required the creation of schools for *pipiltin* children, the college of Santa Cruz de Santiago de Tlatelolco was built for the education of boys, and Bishop Juan de Zumárraga brought several *beatas* (pious women who had taken simple vows) to undertake the education of noble girls. By 1534, the number of schools for elite Indian girls had grown to eight.

The extraordinary interchange of indigenous women among Spaniards had several political dimensions. In Mexico, it began as the military conquest itself unfolded, as part of the necessary strategy for a small band of soldiers who needed to gain allies among Motecuhzoma's friends and foes in order to bring about his defeat. During his march to Tenochtitlan, Cortés cemented his alliance with the Tlaxcalans with an exchange of presents. He received several hundred female slaves and eight daughters of noblemen or kings. As indicated earlier, he gave one of the daughters of the Tlaxcalan king to Alvarado and the other, Doña Elvira, to Juan Velázquez de León. Three other of his lieutenants—Gonzalo de Sandoval, Cristóbal de Olid, and Alonso de Avila—each received one, the rest being distributed among the soldiers.

In the immediate post-conquest period, Spanish men sought unions with elite women as a means of strengthening their ties with *caciques* or *kurakas,* widening their own legitimacy, tightening their control over the indigenous population, and easing the acceptance of Spanish domination. On the other hand, like most Spanish men in the peninsula and in many cases because of their newly acquired social status derived from the deeds they had performed in the Indies, they sought to perpetuate and strengthen their lineage through a marriage with a Spanish wife who would safeguard their newly acquired honor. This marriage was, in the words of Patricia Seed, "the ideological key to separating Spaniards from Indians and slaves" (Seed 1988: 97). In fact, even before a man could accumulate wealth with an *encomienda,* the Crown required him to be married and living with his wife. Additionally, if his wealth was to be inherited by his offspring, his wife and children had to be legitimate. However, this strategy was not available to all those willing or able to marry, because the number of Spanish women was limited. If the men did not go back to Spain, as most did not, then those who wished to marry had no other choice but to take either an Indian wife belonging to the nobility or a *mestiza* of good (i.e., noble) lineage.

For the Amerindian male nobility, the exchange of women also presented advantages. The exchange of women to reward accomplishments or cement alliances was a longstanding tradition. They continued to use it in order to retain their own class privileges in the new realm. During the conquest they sometimes took advantage of the tradition to shake off oppressive relationships. By giving their sisters or their daughters to the *conquistadores*, they allied themselves with the invaders and gained a new legitimacy, widening their powers of negotiation with the Spaniards and their indigenous communities. The strategy proved successful. Their renewed legitimacy transformed them into the mediators between the two groups and put them in charge of delivering the financial and labor requirements demanded from the commoners. Karen Spalding notes that by the middle of the seventeenth century, the *kurakas* of the central Andes formed an elite

> whose members were outwardly much like the Spaniards and the people of Spanish descent among whom they moved and lived. The kuraka of the repartimiento of Huarochirí, Alonso Quispe Ninavilca was the son of a mestiza and brother-in-law to a Spaniard. . . . Alonso's younger brother, Don Sebastián, was a young hothead who not only wore Spanish arms and knew how to use them but had childhood friends among the Spaniards, generally traders, resident in Huarochirí. (Spalding 1984: 226)

For their part, Indian noblewomen used their sexual relationships with the *conquistadores* to gain a foothold in the emerging social structure for themselves and their descendants, to retain their status and influence, to distance themselves from the *indios del común* (commoners who lacked privileges), and to obtain whatever gains were possible, including land grants and *encomiendas* or the opportunity to engage in mercantile activities. These women were quick to learn the new rules imposed by the conquerors and to take full advantage of them.

The life of Tecuichpotzin, also known as Doña Isabel Moctezuma to the Spaniards, is a case in point. Born in 1509 or 1510, she was the first child of Motecuhzoma. After he died and the Spaniards were expelled from Tenochtitlan during the famous *noche triste* of June 30, 1520, she was married to the new king, Cuitlahuac, her father's brother. Some sixty days later, like thousands of other Tenochcas, Cuitlahuac fell victim to the first smallpox epidemic. She was then married to the last Aztec ruler, her cousin twice-removed, Cuauhtemoc. She lived through the horror of Tenochtitlan's siege, when thousands died of smallpox, starvation, and dysentery while Cortés's forces attacked relentlessly. As the city fell on August 13, 1521, Cuauhtemoc and his wife tried to escape in a large canoe, but they were taken prisoner. Cuauhtemoc was brutally tortured by the Spaniards, who wanted him to reveal the whereabouts of the supposed treasure of Motecuhzoma. He then was forced to accompany Cortés on his 1524–26 expedition to Honduras and was finally tried, found guilty, and hanged for allegedly plotting a rebellion.

As one of Motecuhzoma's three heirs and the highest-status member of the depleted Mexica nobility, Doña Isabel was made a member of the new Spanish aristocracy when she received an *encomienda* in perpetuity from Cortés. Upon his return from Honduras, he granted her the rich *encomienda* of Tacuba, which included several thousand Indians; by the second half of the sixteenth century it would be the largest *encomienda* in the valley of Mexico. Then Cortés married her to Alonso de Grado, a member of his original expedition. They mere married less than two years when, in 1528, her husband died of unknown causes. Doña Isabel, then nineteen years old, became Cortés's mistress. Two years later, when she was five months pregnant, he again married her off, this time to Pedro Gallego de Andrade, an Extremaduran who had arrived in Mexico after the fall of Tenochtitlan. Her child by Cortés was a daughter, Leonor Cortés Moctezuma, who eventually married the wealthy founder of Zacatecas, Juan de Tolosa. Cortés took the child to the home of a cousin by marriage, who later became the administrator of his estates, and named him her tutor. In 1530, Doña Isabel gave birth to a boy who was named Juan Gallego de Andrade Moctezuma and baptized by the first Bishop of New Spain, Juan de Zumárraga. Two months later, Doña Isabel became a widow for the fourth time. In the spring of 1532, she was married, for a fifth and last time, to Juan Cano de Saavedra, a member of Pánfilo de Narváez's 1520 expedition to Mexico, with whom she lived for eighteen years. She had five more children and became an exemplary, pious Spanish lady, dedicated to her children and her charities. When she wrote her testament in 1550, she left the bulk of Tacuba to her eldest son, Juan Gallego de Andrade.

Ronald Spores has shown that in Oaxaca, Mexico, the Spanish allowed the Mixtec *caciques* and *cacicas* to retain their rights and privileges. The *cacicas* lived in luxurious houses, owned the best land, were exempted from tribute, were entitled to services by Indians, used the courts to protect their privileges, wore fine clothes and much jewelry, travelled in palanquins, "gave lavishly to the church, and, in return, they sat in places of honor at mass and were buried in the nave of the principal church of their cacicazgos" (Schroeder et al. 1997: 186–87).

In Mexico and the Andean region, indigenous noblewomen were able to take advantage of the chaotic conditions created by the conquest, but the fate of most non-elite, anonymous Indian women was much harsher. In Peru, the breakup of the *ayllu* weakened women's position. Large numbers were given to the Spaniards by their fathers or taken by force; separated from their kin, they were compelled to follow the *conquistadores*, providing them food and sexual satisfaction. In the early sixteenth century, most expeditions included a large number of Indian men who served as auxiliaries and Indian women who were servants/mistresses, cooks, and nurses. On the other hand, those who remained in their communities also felt the impact of contact with Europeans in new labor requirements, evangelization, the ravages of epidemic disease, and the destruction, to a greater or lesser extent, of the previously existing social fabric.

The establishment of Spanish domination was facilitated and reinforced by the imposition of Catholicism on the indigenous population. As successive expeditions brought new territories under royal control, groups of clerics arrived to undertake their missionary work and in so doing laid the foundation for the Catholic Church, the most powerful agent of social control in colonial society. Old religious symbols, beliefs, and practices disappeared gradually, though not without resistance; as the Christian liturgical cycle took hold, new festivals were celebrated, the names of the week were changed, and Amerindians were given names of Catholic saints, required to accept a different code of sexual behavior, and compelled to adopt such new institutions as monogamous marriage.*

COLONIAL SOCIETY

Throughout the continent, the turbulent years of the conquest ended with the arrival of royal officials who succeeded in bringing the unruly *conquistadores* under the jealous control of the Spanish Crown. Royal control was established even in Peru, where Gonzalo Pizarro, Francisco's brother, led a rebellion against the first viceroy, Blasco Núñez Vela, and the New Laws of 1542, which restricted the prerogatives of the *encomenderos*. In 1546, Pizarro defeated Núñez Vela and

*In addition to the works cited within this section, see Lockhart 1968; MacLachlan and Rodriguez 1980; Hoberman and Socolow 1996.

killed him in battle. Calm was restored after the Crown sent Don Pedro de la Gasca, who defeated Pizarro and had him executed in 1548. Although it had to retreat at times, the Crown persistently refused to allow the emergence of a powerful and feudal nobility. While a small number of *conquistadores* became rich, only a few were granted titles of nobility, among them Cortés and Pizarro, who were both given the title of *marquis* and were, unusually, allowed to bequeath their *encomiendas* to their legitimate heirs. The majority stayed in the Indies, entered the service of powerful Spaniards as their retainers and overseers, and lived with or married Indian women. Some acquired land grants and *encomiendas* which in some frontier areas lasted into the eighteenth century. The Crown, however, despite rebellions and protests, put restrictions on the *encomienda* and prevented its transformation into a fief. The ranks of the colonial nobility were enlarged in the eighteenth century, when the Crown was in need of funds. By contrast, the Portuguese Crown did not grant titles of nobility to wealthy planters.

In New Spain (Mexico), Peru, Cuba, or Chile, viceroys, governors, visitors, and *audiencias* (courts of law) brought with them clerics, bishops, inquisitors, lawyers, merchants, notaries, innkeepers, farmers, artisans, and small numbers of Spanish women. Complying with royal edicts that discouraged married men from emigrating without their wives or remaining in the Indies without them, they travelled in larger numbers than in the first decades. Between 1540 and 1559, the proportion of women jumped to 16.4 percent. Out of 9,044 travellers, 1,480 were women or girls: 675 were married, 76 were widows, and 805 were single (Boyd-Bowman 1973). A few camp followers went to chaotic Peru, but most came to settle and, like their male counterparts, to seek opportunities for social and economic advancement or recognition that were unavailable to them in Spain. As Ida Altman has shown, "the majority of the emigrants did not travel alone, especially after around 1540, but were accompanied by family, relatives, friends, servants, or slaves, or were themselves employed as servants, formed part of an entourage, or were recruited for some expedition" (Altman 1989: 178).

A new society began to emerge, influenced by Spanish institutions, economic demands, religious beliefs, values, mores, and conflicting interests, but also shaped by American reality. Perhaps the single most important cause for readjustment was the catastrophic demographic decline of the Amerindian population that fell prey to devastating epidemics of smallpox, measles, typhus, influenza, the bubonic plague, and other diseases, as well as famine and overwork.

In Mesoamerica the indigenous population fell from 25 million in 1519 to 2.65 million in 1568, and in Peru it dropped from 9 million in 1532 to 1.3 million in 1570. On the mainland the population continued to drop until the first decades of the seventeenth century and only began to recover in the second half of that century.

The dramatic population decrease and the restrictions placed on the *encomienda* system did not diminish the demands imposed by the colonizers on Amerindians. Male Indians were forced to pay tribute, and a new system, known as the *repartimiento,* was created. It compelled them to provide a certain amount of time every year to satisfy the labor needs of the European and indigenous elites working for token wages on their estates (*haciendas*), in textile workshops (*obrajes,*) in personal service, and in public works. When rich mineral deposits were discovered in Mexico and Peru in the 1540s, Indians were forcefully drafted to work in the mines, where they eventually replaced the African enslaved labor force. In Peru, Viceroy Francisco de Toledo used the *mit'a* as the basis for a brutal *repartimiento* system called *mita,* which supplied labor for the silver mines of Potosí and the mercury mines of Huancavélica, veritable death pits until the end of the colonial period. These compulsory labor systems were particularly disruptive of communities and households and placed additional burdens on the children and women left behind.

In the Caribbean islands the initial contact with Europeans was also devastating. The male population was compelled to perform tasks traditionally assigned to women; violent conflicts ensued. The population was practically exterminated by disease, violence, and the harsh labor demands of the Spaniards, who enslaved Amerindians to make them work in placer mining and agriculture. The Crown, loudly and passionately supported by some clerics, outlawed the practice, but it did not succeed in abolishing it. However, opposition to Indian slavery, combined with the drastic population decline, forced the Spaniards to look elsewhere for additional labor. As would be the case in Brazil somewhat later, labor demands were satisfied through the large-scale importation of African slaves.

The first shipment of seventeen enslaved Africans arrived in Hispaniola in 1505. According to Herbert Klein, by the end of the nineteenth century, "Latin America would become the destination for some 10 million to 15 million African slaves" (quoted in Hoberman and Socolow 1996: 167). They came to work on the sugarcane plantations that began to multiply after the 1530s. From there, sugar production expanded to the other islands as well as to the mainland, where African slaves constituted a sizeable minority. African slaves first appeared on the mainland as part of the *conquistadores'* expeditions. In the 1540s they were taken to work in the mines, but by the end of the century, they had been replaced by Indians. Nevertheless, even in such areas as the Viceroyalty of Peru, where mining was the most important economic activity, African slaves worked coastal plantations, including the establishments owned by the Jesuits. They were also part of elite households until the end of the colonial period.

Throughout the Indies, African slaves were synonymous with cultivation of sugar, coffee, cotton, and cacao. In the Caribbean they soon outnumbered whites, especially after the English, the Dutch, and the French took over several islands from the Spanish in the seventeenth century and established prosperous sugar plantations. By the middle of the following century, these plantations were worked by some 1.4 million slaves, born in both Africa and the Americas. On average, slaves were imported on a ratio of two males to one female, except in Barbados, where women slaves outnumbered men from the early eighteenth century. There, on sugar plantations women made up three-quarters of the field gangs, teams that prepared the soil, planted the cane, and cut it at harvest time. In other areas, however, they generally constituted at least half of the major gangs, groups that did the heaviest work. Most of the women on a plantation worked in the field gangs, while less than half of the men did so (Hoberman and Socolow 1996). Women performed the same heavy physical labor as men, were punished as the latter were, and received the same quantity of food and the same diet, but they were seldom allowed to perform any kind of skilled work inside the sugar mill.

While economic life was based in the countryside, urban centers were the seats of royal and ecclesiastical authority. New cities were created, at times, on sites where the vanquished had their capitals, but Lima, Santo Domingo, Montevideo, Asuncion, Santiago, and Buenos Aires were built in areas where no large concentration of population had existed. In contrast with the labyrinths of European cities, every Spanish American town was designed on the same model, following the grid plan around a central plaza, flanked by the cathedral, the governor's house, and other public buildings. The founders, *vecinos,* were given lots on which they could build their houses. Artisans and merchants set up shop in the central streets, and soon the cities were surrounded by *barrios* (neighborhoods) inhabited by *mestizos, mulatos,* freed blacks, and Indians who escaped communities weakened by disease, famine, and the exactions of the Spaniards. The countryside was inhabited by Indians, who lived in their towns, called reductions or congregations, created by the Crown to facilitate the collection of tribute. In the coastal areas where plantation agriculture expanded, the population was predominantly *mulato* and black.

While some *conquistadores* returned to Spain, most settled down in the cities, from which they could oversee their land grants, the *encomiendas* they had received for services rendered to the Crown, or their *repartimientos*. In Mexico, the greatest *encomendero* was Cortés, who in 1529 received an *encomienda* that included a large number of towns with at least some 23,000 "vassals." In the viceregal capitals, together with rich miners and, later on, landowners, the *conquistadores* built palatial homes worthy of their status and maintained large households with numerous servants, African slaves, and retainers.

Differences between urban and rural life became sharper. Although we know more about the former than the latter, recent research is revealing the many ways in which past practices and institutions persisted in the countryside, though adapted to the new context and transformed by Spanish beliefs and customs. Perhaps the best example is the development of the cult of the Virgin of Guadalupe in Mexico, after she reportedly appeared in 1531 to an Indian youth named Juan Diego in Tepeyec, a sacred site dedicated to the goddess Tonantzin. There are indications that Indian women everywhere were agents of resistance, containment, or the modification of Spanish or Portuguese beliefs and customs; women were active participants in the creation of the *"mestizo"* cultures that gradually extended throughout the continent. The same can be said for the African women who were brought to Brazil and the French- and English-speaking Caribbean islands. In a world in which the public realm had been dramatically transformed by colonial domination, the private sphere became a locus where old patterns of material culture could be reproduced by African and Indian women.

In her study of slave women in the Caribbean, Barbara Bush notes that in order to understand their contribution to slave society, it is necessary to distinguish their economic role within the plantation from their "private, domestic life," which was "part of the 'inner', more hidden slave community." This life—which included relationships with other slaves based on an unofficial slave code, childbearing, and child-rearing—was clearly influenced by African traditions (Bush, 1990: 6). Recent scholarship on the role of slave women in Caribbean society underscores their participation in all areas of life (Beckles 1989; Bush 1990; Morrissey, 1989). While more research needs to be done, there is little doubt that Indian women, like African women, were instrumental in the transmission of values, mores, and traditions that escaped the watchful eyes of plantation owners or royal and Church officials.

Women perpetuated tradition in the activities of daily life. In Peru, Indian women continued to cook with the same basic foodstuffs they had used in Inka times (maize, quinoa, potatoes, and llama meat) and even went on making *chicha,* although the beverage was no longer used in religious ceremonies. In New Spain, women still made torti-llas, although the Spaniards ate bread. Everywhere, weaving remained women's work, although women's and men's clothes, especially in the cities, gradually became different from the ones they wore before the Conquest. In Brazil, African slave women cooked with kola nuts and oil of the dende palm, imported from Africa with religious ob-jects (*cauris*) and items for personal use, such as cloth and soap from the African coast.

In addition to their more mundane activities, women were instru-mental in carrying on indigenous and African religious traditions. In the sixteenth century, according to the Inka chronicler Guamán Poma de Ayala, Peru's indigenous women openly rejected Catholicism: "They do not confess, they do not attend catechism classes teaching Chris-tian doctrine; nor do they go to mass. They do not even know who are their parish priests, *corregidores,* or *curacas;* they do not obey their mayors, or their *curacas.* . . . And resuming their ancient customs and idolatry, they do not want to serve God or the crown" (quoted in Sil-verblatt 1980: 177). Despite Spanish efforts to stamp out indigenous religious practices, missionaries and royal authorities were unable to prevent women from performing ceremonies connected with the *wak'as,* the *ayllu* ancestors' cults that predated the Tawantinsuyu. A 1660 investigation of heresy in Huarochirí, Peru, ended with 32 per-sons convicted, 28 of them women (Spalding 1984). African women emerged from the colonial era as priestesses of powerful religions that still flourish today in both the Caribbean and Brazil. In Bahia, they officiated at ceremonies in honor of the Yoruba god of thunder, Xango, and the goddess Yemanjá, queen of all waters and love. Throughout the Caribbean, the powerful *obeah* priests (secretive practitioners of magic who also dealt in herbs) were very frequently women. Their participation in clandestine religious practices often involved them in broader movements challenging the inequities of the prevailing order.

Both Indian women and African slave women took part in the movements of resistance against colonial domination and slavery. The great eighteenth-century Indian rebellion led by Tupac Amarú in Peru counted on the invaluable help of Micaela Bastidas, his wife and trusted military advisor. In Mexico, according to Stephanie Wood, women frequently filled "the ranks of rural demonstrations and riots" (Schroeder et al. 1997: 181). In his study of drinking, homicide, and rebellion in colonial Mexican villages, William Taylor has found that in numerous eighteenth-century rebellions, the authorities called in to restore order were likely to find "nasty mobs of hundreds of women, brandishing spears and kitchen knives or cradling rocks in their skirts. . . . In at least one-fourth of the cases women led the attacks and were visibly more aggressive, insulting, and rebellious in their behavior towards outside authorities" (Taylor 1979: 116). African women became runaway slaves, like their male counterparts. They joined numerous *quilombos* in Brazil and the Maroons in Jamaica and Suriname, contributing to the economic and physical survival of the community. In the Blue Mountains of eastern Jamaica, the present-day inhabitants of Moore Town claim to be descendants of Grandy Nanny, an Akan slave and *obeah* woman who fled to the mountains, from which she led a fierce guerrilla war against the British. The source of many legends still recounted today, the historical Nanny was a woman who had great authority, and her "influence among the Maroons was so great that the largest community of the Windward Maroons, Nanny Town, was named after her" (Bilby and Steady 1981: 460).

In Brazil, popular culture also rejoices in the memory of the legendary, flamboyant Xica da Silva, immortalized a few years ago in a movie of the same name by Carlos Diegues. Xica lived in the mid-eighteenth century in Arraial doTijuco, a town known today as Diamantina, in Minas Gerais. Though there is limited information about her life (most documents concerning her were burned), she was a slave among many until 1739—the year that a Portuguese named João Fernandes de Oliveira arrived in the colony. A wealthy entrepreneur who had obtained from the Crown a monopoly for the extraction of diamonds, de Oliveira proceeded to modernize the process of mineral extraction, became enormously rich, and fell madly in love with Francisca (Xica) da Silva, a slave he bought, freed, and elevated to one of the most powerful persons in Minas Gerais. For twelve years, she flaunted her freedom, his wealth, and her jewels, wore extravagant clothes, and gave dinner parties for the social elite, until Fernandes de Oliveira was recalled to Portugal, where he died in poverty; thereafter a curtain of silence was drawn on the story of Xica.

In addition to their involvement in slave revolts, Maroon communities, *quilombos,* and the religious aspects of community life, slave women (like slave men) resisted their exploitation in myriad ways. Daily resistance and non-compliance often took the form of malingering and insubordination, and occasionally led to sabotage. Plantation records provide evidence of these recurring offenses, as well as the harsh punishments meted out to female offenders (Bush 1990).

The flow of Amerindians to the cities continued to foster racial mixture and the creation of a culture that could not be a replica of the one imagined by the Spaniards. As did men, women moved to the cities for many different reasons, but in Peru, "one of the chief reasons for the migration of female Indians was sexual abuse by their corregidores or priests" (Wightman 1990: 51). In the cities, Indian women worked above all as servants in convents and Spanish households, rich or not. Even artisans could afford in the Indies what could never be available to them in Spain. "In Lima in 1546, the wife of one far from prosperous artisan was waited upon by a Negro woman slave, a freed Indian woman from Nicaragua, and a Peruvian Indian servant, aside from two slaves who aided her husband in his works" (Lockhart 1968: 159). Indian women also worked as cooks, nursemaids, wet nurses, and midwives or prepared food sold in the streets. In Peru, they "walked through the streets and squatted around the plazas, selling small prepared food items for residents and travelers. For the most part, they were vending *chicha* (corn beer), cheese, bread and fruit. However, in larger towns, especially Potosí, many of these women also sold soups and meals in the plaza and the market, especially to the Indian community" (Burkett 1978: 112). From the nearby countryside they brought produce, which they sold in the market or in the streets.

In the seventeenth century, the population of the Indies began to change substantially. As indicated earlier, the indigenous population reversed its downward trend and started growing. The numbers of Spanish also jumped. But the group that increased most, despite the concern of the Crown and the Catholic Church (as well as the activities of the Inquisition), was that sector composed of people resulting from the union of Spaniards with Indians and *mestizos/as*, and Spaniards with Africans and *mulatos/as*. To *mestizo*, a word which had long been synonymous with "illegitimate," was added *castas* (castes), a classification with numerous gradations of persons according to racial heritage and the color of their skin. The development of the *castas* was perceived as a threat and prompted the enactment of legislation that restricted their activities.*

*In addition to the works cited within this section, see Burkett 1977; Hahner 1980; Henderson and Henderson 1978; Silverblatt 1987; Spalding 1984.

Gender, Class, and Race

The colonial society that emerged from the Conquest is generally described by traditional historiography as a hierarchical structure theoretically divided along two axes, Spaniard and Indian, understood as two fundamental, racial denominations that entailed specific class divisions. Historians are careful to distinguish the rivalries among Spaniards because of their regional origins (between Castillans and Basques, between Old Castillans and Andalusians), or to take note of the distinctions between those Spaniards who had titles of nobility and those who did not, or those who became large landowners, miners, merchants, or simple bureaucrats. They also signal the differences that gradually developed among the Spaniards—that is, *criollos* (American-born Spaniards) and *peninsulares* (Spanish-born)—and point out that the division between Spaniards and Indians was far from rigid because racial mixing continued throughout the colonial period. These distinctions among Spaniards must indeed be taken into account, and others could be added: there were *mestizos* in the ranks of the Spaniards, there were whites who were poor, and there were important regional variations that changed throughout the colonial period. Furthermore, "Spaniard" and "Indian" are elusive, fluid words that are nevertheless generally used as if they were static, ahistorical, and implicitly well defined, although they changed through time; even in an age in which class distinctions and racial classifications tended to become more rigid, they could be manipulated by individuals for self-identification. Finally, traditional historiography tends to minimize the impact of Africans and, by systematically ignoring the role of all women, whatever their ethnic origin, it only provides a partial picture and fails to reveal the complex articulation of race, class, and gender hierarchies in colonial society.

When gender is taken into account, the following picture emerges, admittedly modified by exceptions. Although the *conquistadores* and their male descendants lost to the Crown some of the prerogatives they had sought to retain, and although the administration of the colonies remained in the hands of Spanish royal officials, because of their sex and race Spanish men (i.e., white men, born in either America or Spain) were nevertheless granted superior social and legal status, economic benefits, and a subservient labor force composed of men and women who were Indian, African, or belonged to a caste group. Spanish women, either *criollas* or *peninsulares*, were equal to Spanish men only in terms of race. In fact, they were legally subordinated to white men because they were viewed as the weaker sex, needing protection by the father if they were unmarried, or the husband after marriage. They could not hold public office or become lawyers, were banned from positions of authority, and were therefore subject to restrictions that applied to slaves or Indians. While their legal and economic status was defined by their father or their husband, because of their race, Spanish women were considered superior to Amerindians of both sexes, anyone of mixed race and, of course, slaves. Widows enjoyed considerably more freedom, being able, as long as they did not remarry, to manage their own business affairs and serve as guardian for their unmarried children.

Mestizos and *castas* were racially mixed groups that lived on the margins of the Spanish community, engaged in petty trades or manual labor. They were socially separated from the whites of both sexes because of their mixed racial ancestry and also because they worked. Physical work was considered a degrading activity for a Spaniard—as it was for a Portuguese—and was to be avoided whenever possible. In fact, throughout the Indies, work was the proper activity of Indians, castas, and slaves. Even in the Caribbean, for example, the entrenchment of slavery in Barbados meant that white indentured servants were no longer employed as field hands (Beckles 1989). *Mestizos* were excluded from certain public offices and could not be ordained unless they were of proper background and legitimate; free blacks suffered the same restrictions that were applied to the *mestizos* and, additionally, were forbidden to carry arms, buy liquor, or assemble. *Mestizas* were subordinated to *mestizos* because of their sex, but all in turn were considered superior to Amerindians.

In this latter group, women continued to be subordinated to men, as they had been since before the Conquest, and, although both men and women were legally subjects of the Crown and free vassals, they were also legally considered minors. Furthermore, because they had to pay tribute to the king or to the *encomenderos* and perform forced labor, they were in fact subordinated to Spaniards of both sexes and were regarded as fit only for servile tasks. On the other hand, Amerindians were also divided by class, although the Indian nobility stood substantially below the Spanish nobility. African slaves were at the bottom of the social scale because they were, legally, chattel. In many respects, women slaves fared worse than male slaves, once again because of the sexual dimension of their masters' power; however, precisely because of their sexuality, women could also and did at times manipulate their owners by means not available to enslaved men.

Spanish women, a minority within a minority, played a crucial role in the development of the colonial class and racial hierarchy.

They were its essential component, because through them the male elite could maintain its racial and class supremacy. They were the axis that permitted the articulation of all the other hierarchies. They were the necessary link for the proper transmission of material wealth, status, and honor from generation to generation, so as to give truth to the saying:

> "Antes que Dios fuera Dios
> y los peñascos, los peñascos,
> los Quirós eran Quirós
> y los Velasco los Velasco."

> Before God became God
> and the rocks became rocks,
> the Quirós family was the Quirós family
> and the Velasco family was the Velasco family.

Their assigned role required strict control of their sexuality because it was crucial not only for the perpetuation of Spanish hegemony but also for the maintenance of racial distinctions. The obsessive Iberian requirement to maintain *limpieza de sangre* (purity of blood) and "pride of lineage" for reasons of religious orthodoxy took on a new meaning in the Americas, where theoretically the danger of contamination from "Jewish blood" or "*morisco* blood" was greatly reduced because Jews and *moriscos* (Moors) were forbidden to emigrate to Spanish colonies. However, what was real was the problematic social origin of many *conquistadores*. In his study of the 168 men who captured the Sapa Inka at Cajamarca, for example, James Lockhart found 91 plebeians and 31 *hidalgos,* the rest being of unknown or uncertain origin (Lockhart 1972). Therefore, because of the questionable social origins of many Spaniards and the ever-growing numbers of *mestizos* and *castas,* "purity of blood" in the Indies came to mean above all "purity of race"—in other words, absence of Indian and, most especially, African ancestry.

In Brazil, the articulation of race, class, and gender was marked by the overwhelming presence of slavery. The existence of a large sector of the population, ethnically distinct and legally defined as the property of other human beings of a different race, created a fundamental cleavage between those who were owners and those who were owned. The slave-owning class, defined by the ownership of human beings and the fruits of their labor, was extensive. Slave labor was the predominant form of labor for most of colonial Brazil and affected all economic activities. Slaves were relatively cheap, abundant, and easy to replace, because of the constant supply from the Atlantic trade.

The slave-owning class was far from homogeneous, including merchants, lawyers, bureaucrats, artisans, miners, large numbers of *lavradores da cana* (sugarcane sharecroppers), religious orders, and, of course, sugar planters. Women in this class were subordinated to men, but since their status was defined by their fathers or their husbands, they were also slaveowners, and frequently held slaves on their own. At the close of the colonial period, in the Recôncavo, Bahia, women owned 20 percent of the slaves, though three-quarters of the women who owned slaves had fewer then five. However, the largest single slaveholder was a woman, Doña Maria Joaquina Pereira de Andrade, who had a total of 588 slaves in two parishes (Schwartz 1985).

In spite of Brazil's racial hierarchy, racial mixture continued unchecked because of the longstanding acceptance of miscegenation, the limited number of Portuguese women and the relative availability of slave women, the laxity of royal control over the colony, the small number of clerics, the predominance of an agrarian economy based on plantation agriculture, and the culture that system produced. In addition to the brutal field work that any slave could be forced to perform because of his or her status, women slaves were often burdened with the obligation to satisfy the sexual appetites of their masters. Ironically, this sexual exploitation could benefit women slaves if a master fell in love with his mistress and freed her after his death. More often, slaveholders freed their illegitimate children, on rare occasions even making them heirs. One interesting case is that of Aleixo Leme de Alvarenga, "who, while acknowledging paternity of children by slave girls, refused to allow bastards to be his heirs. But he made allowances for such children. Aleixo Leme left to his illegitimate daughter, Paula, her mother, who was still in bondage, and two more slaves. Should Paula die, then the mother would become the property of the other illegitimate children she had borne Aleixo" (Russell-Wood 1985: 227). Slave women were manumitted twice as often as male slaves, but the reason for this may have been that the labor of males was more valued than that of women. Persistent miscegenation in Brazil produced an ever-growing number of *mulatos/as* and persons of mixed descent as well as a substantial number of free blacks. A significant number of these non-whites could join the slave-holding class by acquiring slaves, but because of their origins and their color, they found their social mobility limited by restrictions intent on separating them from the whites.

By the seventeenth century, Bahia had a virtual monopoly on the European sugar market. The province's ethnically mixed and heterogeneous class of slaveowners was dominated by a relatively small group of *senhores de engenho*, the planters. Most of them were born in Brazil and were related by family ties. Their social origins in Portugal were undistinguished, and many were descendants of *mamelucos* (*mes tizos*), yet they constituted an untitled aristocracy of wealth and power. They lived as noblemen, with their wives and their children—legitimate and illegitimate—on large estates, amid the ostentatious display of luxurious goods imported from Europe, surrounded by numerous slaves and retainers, occupied in the running of the *engenho*, away from royal officials and clerics. Their wives were of similar background, but were subordinated to them, like their Spanish American counterparts. Women of Portuguese descent, too, were essential for the maintenance of *limpeza de sangue*, and the continuity of legitimacy, lineage, property, and honor of the male elite, which could only be achieved though the institution and sacrament of marriage.

Marriage, Legal Status, and Domestic Life

Marriage made possible the articulation of race, class, and gender and permitted the perpetuation of the system in an orderly fashion. According to the Catholic Church, marriage was a sacrament that tied the destinies of two individuals acting of their own free will, as long as the bride was no younger than twelve and the groom at least fourteen. However, the pair had to demonstrate that no impediments prevented their union, and if such impediments existed, they had to receive the necessary dispensation from the proper ecclesiastical authorities. Once permission had been obtained, the marriage banns were proclaimed on three consecutive Sundays, and the marriage could then be celebrated in a church or in a private home.

While the Church theoretically required that individuals marry of their own free will, that freedom did not imply necessarily that they had the right to marry whomever they chose. Both in Spanish America and Portuguese America, in fact, marriage among the elite had little to do with choice and was instead an alliance between families seeking to consolidate their patrimony and social position. Marriage followed the Iberian custom that granted preference to the eldest legitimate son yet allowed the division of property. The custom necessitated arranging lucrative marriages for daughters and sons, giving proper careers to the latter and sending the former to nunneries whenever necessary. Sons were clearly preferred to daughters, for as Cortés once wrote to the emperor, "If I did not have another [legitimate son] and God disposed of the one I have without leaving an heir, what would be the good of what I have acquired since when daughters inherit memory is lost" (Prescott 1936: 648). Ironically, one of Cortés's legitimate sons inherited his title—he had four legitimate children and five illegitimate—but by the third generation, the marquisate was inherited by a great-granddaughter and therefore "lost." In order to strengthen familial alliances and preserve the lineage and the family fortune, marriage between relatives was not uncommon. Upon the death of his wife, a widower could marry his sister-in-law, and an uncle could marry his former wife's niece. In Brazil, marriage between cousins was the rule rather than the exception for the elite.

In order to marry, it was desirable for a Spanish woman to have a *dote*, dowry, especially in the sixteenth and seventeenth centuries. Dowries were also necessary in Brazil. This was a donation offered by her family, stipulated in either a legal document or a *carta dotal*, a letter given to the groom. The dowry was not a requirement for marriage, but it was customary, especially among the elite. Its size varied greatly according to the wealth of the family, and there were numerous charitable religious institutions dedicated to providing dowries for orphans and other girls who lacked the means to be endowed. The dowry was a way to compensate a husband for the expenses that he would incur because of his wife, and it was also viewed as a way of providing a certain economic independence to women. In 1516, Doña Argueda de los Ríos y Lisperguer, the daughter of a prominent Chilean family, married Don Blas de Torres Altamirano, a member of the Lima *audiencia*. Her dowry consisted of 50,000 pesos, 30,000 to be paid before the wedding and the rest to be paid in three installments. The dowry was generally money, but it could also include land, furniture, animals, slaves, or rights to hereditary offices. Doña Lucia de Pastene's *carta dotal*—signed in Lima on February 5, 1635, for her marriage with Maese de Campo Don Bernardo de Amara Yturigayen —stipulated, among other things, a cash payment of 7,000 pesos; an estate with 1,200 head of cattle, 1,000 goats, 6,500 sheep, and 12 pair of oxen; 27 slaves; silverware; jewelry; and an *encomienda*. In seventeenth-century São Paulo, Messia Rodrigues, a widow, gave a dowry to one of her nine children that included 268,000 *reis* in cash and possessions for a total value of 450,000 *reis*, which included houses, eight dining-room chairs, clothes, one bed, eight mares, one colt, and forty calves.

In Spanish America, the dowry was administered by the husband, but it remained the property of the wife. He could not alienate any part of it without her consent, and, if he mishandled her affairs, she could go to court to request the right to administer her dowry. If the marriage was dissolved either by death or annulment, the value of the dowry and its income had to be repaid to the wife prior to any division of the husband's estate. If the wife died before the husband, the dowry was either divided among the children or sent back to her parents. If a widow remarried, she retained control of her dowry from her previous marriage, and her new husband could only administer her second dowry. At marriage, a woman also frequently received *arras*, a sum representing 10 percent of the groom's assets, which was added to her dowry. Some women took an active part in the management of their dowries.

Marriages could be dissolved, and the records of the ecclesiastical tribunal of the Bishopric of Lima, for example, show that from the sixteenth century onward, women were often the initiators of the proceedings, which were long and usually expensive. Cases brought to the tribunal could result in annulment, leaving the parties free to remarry. Alternatively, the pair might receive a legal separation, *separación de cuerpos*, which meant that the marriage bond was upheld, the partners remained spiritually bound, and, although they could live apart, they could not remarry as long as they lived. In such cases, if the woman was the aggrieved party, she recovered her dowry and her share of community property, and kept custody of the children. The most common grounds for annulment was the Church's acceptance that the parties were not married of their own free will, and because the main objective of a marriage was procreation, failure to produce children was also accepted. Grounds for legal separation included extreme physical or spiritual threat, physical cruelty, prostitution, the danger of heresy or paganism, and adultery. While a wife's adultery was always sufficient offense, a husband's affairs were only grounds for separation if he was found guilty of having adulterous relations inside the marital home or of maintaining a "notorious concubine."

Although the age of marriage for women varied according to region and also changed over time, Spanish girls were generally properly socialized from childhood for marriage with men of their class. In New Spain, some attended small schools called *escuelas de amigas*, spent some time in a teaching convent, or were taught at home by a tutor; but relatively few studied in *colegios* (secondary schools) like the Colegio de San Ignacio of Mexico City, endowed by the Basque community and commonly known as Las Vizcaínas. On the other hand, in Brazil, the children of the planter aristocracy were taught at home by a cleric or a relative. While the education of girls generally ended there, boys could go on to a Jesuit College; however, if they wanted to go to the university, they had to travel to Portugal, where they could study at Coimbra. On the whole, the education of elite women was largely limited to learning reading, writing, some arithmetic and some music, a few fundamentals of religious doctrine, how to manage a home properly, how to embroider, and how to accept the husbands chosen by their parents. Their lives were closely guarded, and they could not leave the home except in the company of *dueñas*, chaperones who prevented them from meeting undesirable young men.

While acceptance of paternal authority seems to have been the rule, if a young woman managed to fall in love with someone who did not meet with the approval of her parents, she could always elope and get married, and thus pave the way for the reconciliation that would ensue once the honor of the family had been re-established. Or like Juana Herrera and Gerónimo Valverde, the children of two well established rival merchant families of Mexico City, they could overcome parental opposition to their marriage by seeking church protection (Seed 1988).

Indeed, for much of the colonial period, minors could theoretically marry without their fathers' consent, as long as the girl was twelve and the boy fourteen, because the Church guaranteed freedom of marriage. However, as Patricia Seed points out in her study of conflicts over marriage choices in colonial Mexico, in the eighteenth century patriarchal control over marriage was tightened in Spanish America, just as it was loosened in Western Europe (Seed 1988). In 1776, the Crown enacted the Royal Pragmatic on Marriage, which restricted this freedom and also sought to prevent marriages among unequals by making offense to the family honor one of the grounds for opposition to a proposed marriage. The *Pragmática* made the permission of the father a formal requirement for marriage, and the penalty for infraction of the law was disinheritance. The law was explicitly not applicable to *mulatos*, free blacks, and other *castas*, who presumably had no family honor to protect.

Men and women reached adulthood at the age of twenty-five. Until then, they were under the *patria potestas* (paternal authority) of a father or guardian and required his permission to enter into contracts, court litigations, or marriage. By that age, women were expected to be married, especially in the sixteenth century, when girls eight and ten years old were married to much older men to cement profitable alliances. If a woman reached twenty-five (an age at which she was "past her prime") and was still single, she remained under the *patria potestas* of her father. However, if a father—of his own free will or by court order because he was incapacitated or had committed incest—released a daughter from his *potestas,* then she was *emancipada* (emancipated) and had total sovereignty over her legal acts. She could buy, rent, administer, bequeath, or inherit property; enter into partnerships; lend money; litigate; and appear as witness. This freedom was not available to many women, at least until the eighteenth century, largely because they were compelled to marry by their education, the very structure of society, and the dominant ideology, which viewed women as wives and mothers. Single women were anomalies because they lacked proper protection. If they did not live with relatives, they frequently sought shelter in convents or *beaterios,* religious associations of pious women who took vows of chastity, enclosure, and poverty.

Widows shared all the rights of emancipated single women and could acquire *patria potestas* over their children either by themselves or with another guardian. They were not expected to return to their fathers' homes, and if they did not remarry, go to live in a convent, or join a *beaterio,* they could achieve a great deal of independence without losing their respectability. Many did in fact pursue activities formerly performed by their husbands and took over farms, sugar mills, and other businesses. In New Spain, the Countess of Miravalle, married at eighteen and mother of eight children, found herself a widow at forty-two, confronting a bleak future because of the extensive debts that had been incurred by her husband. A shrewd and careful administrator, she managed to pay off her debts, provide a future for her children, and eventually become "one of eighteenth-century Mexico's most influential women" (Couturier 1978: 130). Because age differences between wives and husbands often amounted to several decades, a significant proportion of Spanish women were widows for some portion of their adult lives.

Married women were no longer under the *patria potestas* of their fathers or guardians, but under the authority and protection of their husbands. While the latter were legally required to provide, wives were equally required to obey. Wives lost the legal right to administer their properties, needed their husbands' permission to engage in legal transactions or any kind of public activity, and had to reside where their husbands determined; their children, because of the institution of *patria potestas,* were under the exclusive authority of the husband.

For all practical purposes, married women lacked sovereignty over legal acts and continued in (or returned to, if they had been emancipated or widowed) the status of minors, although they were assigned social responsibilities not identified with that status. Furthermore, in contrast to men, women could not be lawyers or judges, could not witness wills, and could not even normally be guardians of children. They were therefore legally of the same status as slaves, Indians, criminals, the mentally retarded, and the insane. According to Silvia Arrom, the difference between these groups and women was that these other disenfranchised groups were all regarded as deficient in some respect, but the restrictions placed "on women's activities were justified in terms of propriety and tradition" (Arrom 1985b: 59). On the other hand, these restrictions could be, and often were, legally circumvented simply by a husband's giving his wife a statement granting her permission to act of her own accord. Furthermore, among the nobility, women retained a substantial measure of control over their property if it was entailed, and although a husband might manage his wife's property, he could not dispose of it in any way without her consent. In her study of the Mexican nobility on the eve of Independence, Doris Ladd points out that the fifth Condesa del Valle de Orizaba managed her estates and "did not hesitate to correct her husband's business errors in public or to remind the authorities that she, and not he, was in charge" (Ladd 1976: 22).

The mission of Spanish elite married women was to be faithful and obedient wives, appearing pious and virtuous, and to bear legitimate children so that the lineage could be properly perpetuated. They also had to supervise the education of their daughters, transmit to them proper moral values and religious beliefs, and guard their virginity, counting for these tasks on the active collaboration of their spiritual advisors, their confessors, their husbands, and their sons. They were expected to remain at home and manage their large households, often no small task. Their influence often extended much beyond the household; while the final decision about a daughter's marriage rested with the father, the strategy for obtaining the best candidate was likely in the hands of the mother. In their homes, these well-to-do women organized the lives of relatives, dependents, servants, and slaves; embroidered; read pious works or devotional books; and left their seclusion only to go to church. Women needed to be restricted to the home because of the responsibility ascribed to them—the conservation of the family honor—and their alleged weakness, which made them less resistant to temptations and therefore a constant threat to the status of the family (Gutiérrez, 1985).

While it is important to take note of the legal status of women and the prescriptive literature defining proper behavior, elite women did in fact undertake many activities without opposition from their husbands. Some owned and managed property in the cities; others supervised agricultural estates. In Brazil, at the close of the colonial period, Doña Ana de São José Aragão owned two sugar mills with a total of 108 slaves in the Recôncavo, and in two townships, women held 16 percent of all the *engenhos* and 10 percent of the sugarcane plantations. In seventeenth-century Pernambuco and Alagoas, twenty-four women were sugarcane growers, and they comprised 17 percent of the *lavradores da cana* in the region. As Asuncíon Lavrin has pointed out, in Spanish America, seventeenth- and eighteenth-century notarial records provide ample evidence "that women were either active legal partners of their husbands or acted independently as legal persons. Thus they bought and sold property, founded charities, borrowed money, and took part in legal suits without any impediment from their husbands" (Lavrin 1978: 30). Similarly, while pressures to conform were undoubtedly strong and most elite women did obey the rules of proper behavior for their class, there were also exceptions, such as the case of Josefa Oñate y Azoca, who was disinherited for having married against the wishes of her family, or that of Melchora Hernández, who took her husband to court when he failed to give her the proper document confirming her dowry after two years of marriage (MacLachlan and Rodriguez 1980).

Although our information on the life of non-elite women in the colonial period is limited, both for Spanish and Portuguese America and especially for the Caribbean, there are indications that the prescriptions and restrictions (both religious and social) that affected the lives of elite women lost their rigidity in other social groups. In Spanish America, despite the power of the Church and its impact on everyday life, concubinage continued to be the rule for large sectors of colonial society for most of the colonial period, especially among the lower classes. The pattern was similar in Brazil. Elizabeth A. Kuznesof points out that concubinage and illegitimate births could be found in all social groups, though they were more frequent in the lower classes and the free black population (Kuznesof 1991).

Marriage as an institution remained far more identified with Spaniards than with *mestizas, castas,* or Indians. In her study on women and crime in eighteenth-century Buenos Aires, Susan Socolow remarks that "the high incidence of illegitimate births attests to the widespread acceptance of illicit unions of both casual and long-lasting nature" (Socolow 1985: 288). Furthermore, there is growing evidence that female-headed households were prevalent among racially mixed groups, throughout much of the colonial period. Marriage choice was also more possible among the lower classes, because the economic stakes were lower and left more room for sentiment. A pledge to marry, often sealed with an exchange of presents, bound a couple before the law. Many young, pregnant women complained of broken marriage promises and sought redress from a law that in fact viewed sexual relations under false premises as equivalent to a rape and stipulated compensation. White women appear to have preferred marrying white men and were pressured not to marry *mestizos* or *castas*. The Confraternity of Aránzazu that granted dowries to marriageable women did not make them available to those who were intending to marry *castas*. *Mestizas* married men of more diverse ethnic background, including *pardos* (free blacks) and *mulatos,* and Amerindian women tended to marry inside their group.

In Portuguese America, rates of formal marriage were low for mixed unions, free blacks, and slaves. Slaves faced restrictions that prevented them from marrying if they wished to do so. The number of female slaves compared with male slaves in a plantation was usually much lower, and a woman could generally only marry a man working on the same plantation. Slave masters did not encourage their slaves to marry, and those who permitted them to marry did not necessarily allow them to choose their partners. Recent research, however, has demonstrated that despite these impediments, many slaves formed long-lasting unions. Alida C. Metcalf has reconstructed slave family life in Santana de Parnaíba, a rural town in the Captaincy of São Paulo, Brazil, and found that in the late eighteenth century and early nineteenth century slave women had a high fertility rate and a large number lived in nuclear families (Metcalf 1992). However, her findings of high rates of female-headed households in other groups parallel those of other scholars (Kuznesof 1980; Ramos 1991).

There is fragmentary information indicating that non-elite women in Spanish America were involved in a multiplicity of remunerative activities, of very different scope depending on their economic conditions. Spanish women headed schools or taught in them. Artisan families were predominantly *mestizas* and *mulatas,* but they also included poor Spaniards who were recent immigrants. Many women took an active part in their husbands' businesses, running stores or working in artisans' shops, although they frequently did so behind the scenes. Others who were better off were sugar-mill owners, hog dealers, and owners of card factories and wine factories. In Mexico, Mencia Pérez was an illiterate *mestiza* from Tlaxcala who owned a small farm, but after marrying a Basque innkeeper in 1570, she and her husband moved to Huemantla, where they were able to acquire some real estate and a mill. Widowed in 1578, she remarried, to a prosperous carter and merchant; when he died, she took over the business and became one of the wealthiest persons in the province (MacLachlan and Rodriguez 1980).

More typical were the large numbers of women who, throughout the colonial period, prepared food, made candles, wove cloth, rolled cigars, or worked in factories or as domestic servants. In the cities of Spanish America, Indian women continued to dominate street selling and take part in the provision of food to most urban centers, while in Brazil these activities were in the hands of black women, both slave and freed. Those who remained in the countryside worked in the fields.

Life in Convents

If class, status, race, and physical work separated colonial women, so did religious life, because the decision to take vows, willingly or not, was only available to members of the Spanish elite. As mentioned earlier, in 1540 Bishop Zumárraga founded La Concepción as a religious school for Indian women, but the school soon stopped admitting them and instead opened its doors only to Spanish women. The same thing happened with the Colegio de la Caridad, initially created for the education of abandoned *mestiza* girls.

Convents, like monasteries, reproduced the hierarchical social structure in which they existed. Because by the second half of the sixteenth century Spaniards generally regarded Indians as inferior human beings, convents closed their doors to the vanquished and their descendants. Furthermore, before gaining entrance into a convent, a young woman had to provide proof of her *limpieza de sangre*, either because such specification had been made by the original founder or because it was the rule of the male religious order that had jurisdiction over the nunnery. Finally, although in both New Spain and Peru a few convents admitted a handful of postulants without them, most required dowries. In Mexico in the 1600s dowries were set at about 2,000 pesos and increased to 3,000 the following century. In seventeenth-century Peru, dowries ranged from 2,000 to 2,500 pesos, depending on the convent. In addition, parents were expected, among other things, to make a substantial donation when their daughter took the vows, provide for the numerous candles used in the ceremony, and sometimes also pay a heavy sum for her cell.

Not until 1724, when the convent of Corpus Christi was founded in Mexico, could Indian women enter monastic life. Corpus Christi was entrusted to a mendicant order (postulants did not require a dowry because the institution relied on the alms of benefactors), but postulants had to be legitimate, daughters of *caciques,* and of pure Indian ancestry. Furthermore, they and their families had to be free of having performed "vile offices" (occupations inappropriate for their class) or participated in idolatrous ceremonies. The young women also had to be at least fifteen, able to read Latin, and trained in sewing and embroidery, among still other requirements. In the century between its founding and the end of the colonial period, the convent admitted only 147 young women. Indian girls who did not belong to the nobility were largely illiterate, and if they learned how to read and write, they had probably been taught by the local priest.

Most convents in Spanish America were founded in the sixteenth and seventeenth centuries. By contrast, the first convent in Portuguese America, Santa Clara do Desterro, was not built until 1677, and despite repeated appeals the Crown did not authorize the construction of three more convents until fifty years later. The reason for the Crown's refusal to build convents was the scarcity of Portuguese women in Brazil. If women could not enter the convent, they would be compelled to marry. The policy, however, failed to deter all would-be postulants, and those who chose religious life travelled to Portugal: "In the absence of a colonial convent the daughters of prominent settlers persistently risked the dangers of the open sea and the threat of piracy to profess in the nunneries of the Atlantic islands or in Portugal itself" (Soeiro 1978: 176). Even after the Convent of the Poor Clares was founded, women continued to go overseas, because it admitted only fifty nuns. Perhaps as a direct result of these religiously motivated departures, in 1732 the Crown forbade women to leave Brazil without royal permission. Like the convents in Spanish America, Brazilian female orders required dowries and were closed to those who could not attest to *limpeza de sangue.* While some women of dubious ancestry or behavior could live in the convent if they had the means, they could not become nuns.

The explicit purpose of the first convents in Spanish America was to provide shelter for single women. Every major colonial city had at least one or two, though Lima had thirteen and by the seventeenth century Mexico City had twenty-nine religious institutions for women, founded by the nobility, rich miners and merchants, and in the eighteenth century by wealthy *hacendados* (landowners). Many convents ran girls' schools, hospitals, and orphanages. Although many were small institutions where meditation, austerity, prayer, and monastic discipline mere rigidly followed, others presented a very different picture. La Encarnación and Santa Catalina, two of the largest convents in Lima, occupied more than two city blocks. They were enormous structures that each included well-kept gardens, chapel, the common offices where maids and black slaves did their chores, dormitories, the *seglarado* that housed the young girls educated in the convent, the novitiate where postulants lived for a year before taking their vows, an infirmary, a jail, the quarters of laywomen who retired to live their last years in the convent, and the *celdas* (cells), small houses, some two stories high, where the nuns lived. In 1700, La Concepción, one of Lima's great convents, had 1,041 women, of which 271 were nuns and 17 novices; 162 were either ladies living in retirement, schoolchildren, or babies; 290 were servants and maids; and 271 were slaves (Martín 1983). In these convents, postulants brought their slaves and servants and could live a comfortable life among friends of their own class. The nuns of the Convent of Poor Clares, in eighteenth-century Bahia, came from prominent families, wore fine jewelry, and had numerous personal servants—and scandalous morals.

Iberian women entered conventual life for a variety of reasons. Some took the vows because they had not gotten married or because they were pressured by their families. Others took the vows because they searched for spiritual and religious fulfillment, and still others went into convents because they sought escape from temporal society or the pressure to marry. An exceptional few saw in religious life the chance to obtain a knowledge otherwise denied them. This was the reason that compelled Sor Juana Inés de la Cruz to take the vows.

Juana Inés de Asbaje y Ramírez de Santillana was an illegitimate child, born in 1648 at the *hacienda* of San Miguel de Napantla. She was a genius who learned to read at the age of three. "I remember," she wrote, "that in those days, although I had the healthy appetite of most children of that age, I would not eat cheese because I heard that it made one dull-witted, and the desire to learn was stronger in me that the desire to eat, so powerful in children" (Hahner 1980: 23). At the age of six or seven she learned that there was a university in Mexico City where men could study. She begged her mother to let her put on men's clothing and attend the university, but was unable to convince her:

> I began to study Latin, in which I had barely twenty lessons; and so
> intense was my application that although women (especially in the
> flower of their youth) cherish the natural adornment of their hair, I

would cut off four or six fingers' length of mine, making a rule that
if I had not mastered a certain subject by the time it grew back, I
would cut it off again . . . for it did not seem right to me that a head
so empty of knowledge, which is the most desirable adornment of
all, should be crowned with hair." (quoted in Hahner 1980: 23)

At thirteen, this extraordinary child became maid-in-waiting to the
Marquesa de Mancera, the wife of the viceroy. Under her protection,
Sor Juana continued to indulge in her passion for learning, and her
erudition was so extraordinary that the viceroy arranged a public debate with the most learned men in the viceroyalty, some forty profes-
sors of the University of Mexico. She was required to expound her
knowledge in several fields, among others theology, philosophy, history, mathematics, and poetry.

At sixteen, she suddenly decided to enter the Jeronymite Order,
where she spent the following forty years of her life, satisfying her
insatiable intellectual curiosity and writing poems, essays, and plays.
Called the Ninth Muse by her contemporaries, she is still considered
one of the great lyric poets of the Spanish language. Surrounded by
books—her collection of mathematical works was exceptional—she
pursued her studies in her cell despite the disapproval of her superiors. She maintained contact with the best scientific minds in the
viceroyalty and was frequently visited by the famous scholar Don
Carlos de Siguenza y Góngora, who taught mathematics and astro-
nomy at the University of Mexico. She confronted her superiors' opposition and brilliantly defended herself and the right of women to
acquire knowledge in a letter she wrote to the Bishop of Puebla entitled *Respuesta a Sor Filotea de la Cruz;* in the words of Margaret Sayers
Peden, her translator into English, this was "the first statement in our
western hemisphere to argue a woman's right to study and teach and
learn" (De la Cruz 1997: v). But the pressures exerted on her and the
criticisms of her superiors finally triumphed. In a move that has puzzled
and fascinated students of her life, Sor Juana gave up all her worldly
possessions and scholarly pursuits, undertaking a life of penance. She
died in 1695, while nursing her sister nuns during a plague.

The Eighteenth Century

In the eighteenth century, both Portuguese and Spanish America underwent a series of commercial, administrative, and political reforms
enacted by monarchs influenced by the ideas of the Enlightenment.
In Brazil, the reforms were undertaken by the Marquis of Pombal,
prime minister of Dom José I. Seeking to centralize control of the

Crown over the colony, Pombal curtailed the privileges of the municipalities and increased the powers of the viceroy. He also banished the Jesuits from Brazil and Portugal, secularized education, promoted schools, and named viceroys committed to reforming agriculture and encouraging industry. In Spanish America, three Bourbon monarchs enacted a series of measures tending to make colonial administration more efficient, increase Crown revenues, and bolster American defenses against rival European powers. By the end of the eighteenth century, colonial trade was revived, agriculture and mining had substantially expanded, new administrative units had been created, and the *intendent,* a new official who answered directly to the Crown, replaced local *corregidores.*

Although the Bourbon reforms were largely administrative and fiscal, because they were rooted in the Enlightenment they also included changes that affected women, at least those who were white and belonged to the elite. Following other European Enlightenment writers who advocated the education of women, in Spain Father Benito Jerónimo Feijóo published his 1739 *Essay on Women, or Physiological and Historical Defence of the Fair Sex.* In it, Feijóo "suggested that the female's brain was too soft for her to comprehend as much as a male" (Pescatello 1976: 161). Nevertheless, he acknowledged the place in history of exceptional women, such as Queen Isabella and Sor Juana Inés de la Cruz and also argued that with proper education women could be valuable members of society.

Enlightened reformers demanded the creation of new values in the population, and, because of women's crucial roles in instilling values in their children, "motherhood took on a civic function, increasingly exalted in the writings of the time. And since mothers could fulfill their responsibilities only if they were themselves enlightened, reformers vigorously advocated the education of the Fair Sex" (Arrom 1985b: 15).

In the colonies, the Enlightenment brought about the creation of "economic societies" and several journals in Lima, Quito, Buenos Aires, Mexico, and Bogota, where the new interest in elite women and their maternal role was widely discussed—by men. Articles about women filled the pages of these journals with many themes: health care, character, luxury and extravagance, and domestic problems. The nature of the material was instructive, rather than entertaining. Women, however, would have to be literate before they could be receptive to the ideas pronounced on their behalf. Therefore, the need for feminine education was a subject that recurred time and again (Mendelson 1978).

In the second half of the eighteenth century, teaching orders for girls began to establish branches in Buenos Aires and Bogota. Although the new schools sought above all to educate women for their roles as wives and mothers, young girls were now exposed to an "enlightened" curriculum that included Latin, arithmetic, and other sciences, alongside the traditional subjects of reading, embroidery, religion, sewing, and music. In Mexico City, three new boarding schools were created, one of them—*La Enseñanza Nueva*—for Indian girls. Furthermore, in the 1780s, when migrants deluged the capital escaping from a famine in the countryside, the city council sought to occupy young vagrants by making them study, and existing institutions were encouraged to enroll non-paying students. By 1802, some 3,100 girls studied in "70 convents, parish, municipal, and private schools" (Arrom 1985: 18). Although the numbers being educated had increased substantially, most girls remained unaffected by the new institutions.

In New Spain, the promotion of education for elite women was accompanied by measures that sought to incorporate lower-class women into the labor force. Royal decrees abolished guild rules preventing women from entering crafts and ordered public schools to include vocational training in their curricula.

Yet the effects of the Bourbon reforms and the new views on women had little time to take hold. As the nineteenth century began, events in Europe would force the colonies to set aside the question of women's education and take up the cause of independence.

Part II

WOMEN IN NINETEENTH- AND TWENTIETH-CENTURY LATIN AMERICA AND THE CARIBBEAN

Virginia Sánchez Korrol

WOMEN AND THE STRUGGLES FOR NATIONAL INDEPENDENCE

As the nineteenth century began, the Ibero-American empire stood poised on the brink of formidable transformations that would bring independence from colonial rule, carrying promises of equality for all. However, the social, political, and legal status of women would remain virtually unchanged despite their valiant efforts and highly visible presence in the struggles for independence. In addition, other economic and ethnic hierarchies also persisted into the national period.

Many factors contributed to the wars for Latin American independence in the first third of the nineteenth century. Spanish restrictions on colonial political and economic aspirations, the influence of French and English liberal philosophies, and the examples set by successful American and European revolutions combined to ignite long desired changes in the social order. The immediate cause of the Spanish American revolutions was the occupation of Spain by Napoleon's forces in 1808. However, colonial discontent stemmed from the period of the enlightened Bourbon Reforms when the Crown bolstered American defenses against rival European powers, increased colonial revenues, and instituted administrative and political reforms.

The French occupation of Spain in 1808 sparked the onset of insurrection by providing the opportunity for colonial leaders to take matters into their own hands. Following the example set by peninsular Spaniards in resisting the French invasion, American *criollos* (American-born Spaniards) established governing *juntas* to fill the administrative void left by the capture of the Crown. Viewed by those more loyal to the crown as rebellious and seditious behavior on the part of the colonists, these activities soon led to open conflict between colonial patriots and ruling *peninsulares.*

The restoration of a conservative monarchy in 1814 re-energized Spanish American frustrations and rekindled the struggles which culminated in independence. In South America battles were fought on several fronts. The first, led by Simón Bolívar, occurred in the northern part of the continent or the Viceroyalty of New Granada, whereas the second front, under the leadership of José de San Martín, was confined predominantly to the countries of the southern cone, the Viceroyalty of Rio de la Plata. In Mexico the insurrection began in 1810. Under the leadership of Miguel Hidalgo and José María Morelos, this movement combined pro-independence sentiments with a social reform program on behalf of the indigenous and *mestizo* (individuals of Native and European parentage) population.

The Participation of Women in the Independence Struggle

Women did not remain passive spectators throughout this period. Women from all class and racial groups joined the movements for independence, took sides on political issues, and participated on many levels. On a personal level, women could not help but be involved as the wives, mothers, daughters, and sisters of those who fought. Some chose to lend their support as combatants, spies, couriers, or informants. Others served as hosts and organizers of political meetings, as quartermasters and camp followers. They donated monies, food, and supplies, and they suffered the loss of loved ones, property, and wealth.

Many died for their actions. Some women remained loyal to the crown and others did not become involved in the conflicts. Yet all were affected by the wars as social and economic communal foundations were disrupted because of the rebellions and subsequent restructuring of the newly independent states.

There was, after all, sufficient motivation for women's involvement, and they responded to the crisis in many ways. Government policies on taxation affected women's property or inheritances as well as men's, and many women openly protested against increased taxation and other burdensome regulations.

At another level, women were openly courted, often through gender-specific propaganda, to assist the war efforts on one side or the other. Throughout Latin America, particularly within cosmopolitan or urban sectors, the notion of women's social usefulness was gradually replacing more traditional ideas of female seclusion. Institutions such as convents or retirement homes, which had provided cloistered havens away from secular affairs for elite Spanish or *criolla* women, were on the wane or leaning toward increasing their social service orientation.

In small numbers, women were spearheading nascent efforts in education by sponsoring *colegios* (secondary schools) for girls and forming organizations. The Patriotas Marianas, among the earliest secular female groups in Mexico to support the royalist cause, was but one of the many examples of women's political activities (Arrom 1985b).

Not surprisingly, nationalism and other political sympathies elicited multiple forms of resourcefulness. These included more direct participation in the conflicts, for the wars also provided an unexpected opportunity for personal rebellion against legal and social constraints. The latter relegated women to prescribed roles, often in the domestic sphere, in virtually all social classes.

Whatever their reasons for involvement, the fact remains that women were actively present throughout the period of conflict. In Mexico, Josefa Ortiz de Domínguez, also known as La Corregidora, and Leona Vicario were among the many who supported the cause of independence. The former sounded the cry for independence and alerted the rebels of imminent danger, while the latter left a comfortable home "first to give material aid and then to join the embattled insurgents in rural Mexico" (Macías 1983: 6).

In Venezuela and Colombia, the arena of some of the bloodiest battles, women were not expected to fight, but some—like Evangelista Tamayo, who fought under Simón Bolívar in the battle of Boyacá—

joined the armies. Others, like Teresa Corneja and Manuela Tinoco, fought in numerous skirmishes disguised as men. Although the actions of women like Tinoco and Corneja or Domínguez and Vicario were probably the exceptions, many women fought to defend their homes and cities. On at least one occasion Bolívar acknowledged their valiant efforts, but at the same time, he romanticized them in the stereotypical manner of that period:

> . . . even the fair sex, the delights of humankind, our amazons have fought against the tyrants of San Carlos with a valor divine, although without success. The monsters and tigers of Spain have shown the full extent of the cowardice of their nation. They have used their infamous arms against the innocent feminine breasts of our beauties; they have shed their blood. They have killed many of them and they loaded them with chains, because they conceived the sublime plan of liberating their beloved country! (quoted in Cherpak 1978: 222)

As nurses in field hospitals, women provided vital services. The military hospital in Caracas, for example, relied on the volunteer efforts of "the most beautiful and pleasant ladies in the world," according to Trinidad Morán. "Each one of us believed to have in these ladies a mother or a sister interested in our health and I am not mistaken in saying that many escaped and owe their salvation to such merciful offices" (quoted in Cherpak 1978: 224).

On the home front, creole women, particularly from among the upper and middle classes, were more likely to organize and host *tertulias* or *veladas*. These were often intellectual, social-cultural gatherings, which provided the meeting ground for political discussions. In Caracas, Josefa Palacios and her husband, José Félix Rivas, were instrumental in bringing together Venezuelan liberals and intellectuals to vent political grievances and articulate viable solutions. In Quito, Ecuador, Manuela Canizares launched the 10th of August insurrection in one of her *tertulias*. The Puerto Rican María de las Mercedes Barbudo, agent for the island's separatist movement in San Juan, opened her home for that group's meetings until her exile in 1823. Seducers or propagandists, on the other hand, were, in the eyes of the nationalists, women who attempted to sway royalist opinion to their cause. Regarding this group, one army officer remarked, "Nothing can be more prejudicial to the troops than the women who dedicate themselves to seducing . . . individuals and to deceiving them by telling them fabulous lies" (quoted in Gross and Bingham 1985: 147).

In general, common opinion held women as innocents, incapable of deception and inappropriate behavior, and this attitude aided their wartime efforts. As spies and couriers, they took advantage of the unsettled state of affairs to come and go without arousing suspicion. Some confined their activity to espionage and gathered information on royalist troop movement or the state of military affairs in Spain. They supplied the rebel forces with a network for communication. In this regard few achieved the fame or notoriety of the young Colombian Policarpa Salavarrieta, known as La Pola. Nurtured in a family of separatist sympathizers, La Pola employed her skills as a seamstress to gain entry into creole homes. Once engaged, she could justifiably spend long periods of time working on her assignments. This gave her the opportunity to determine which families supported the royalist cause or shared divided loyalties, to uncover valuable information on troop movements or maneuvers, and to pass such information on to the rebels. In 1817, La Pola was captured and sentenced to die in the plaza of Bogotá. Surrounded by curious onlookers, she admonished the crowd at her execution: "Indolent people! How different would be our fate today if you knew the price of liberty! But it is not too late. Although I am a woman and young, I have more than enough courage to suffer this death and a thousand more. Do not forget my example!" (quoted in Henderson and Henderson 1978: 119)

As the wars progressed, attitudes toward women involved in revolutionary activity changed radically. Women's actions had provided alternatives to the stereotypical notion of themselves as the harmless, gentle, and weaker sex. Their organizational and leadership abilities had to be acknowledged, and as their visibility and effectiveness increased, women insurgents received harsher punishments. Like La Pola, other rebellious women were also executed as traitors; they were sent to prisons or convents or were exiled for their subversive roles. Other women exchanged the ravages of war for the unknown and emigrated to those areas, like Cuba and Puerto Rico, more firmly under royalist control. The lot for exiles was dismal, since women often found themselves as heads of households without benefit of the material and emotional resources available to them in their native lands. But others, particularly *castas* (racially mixed women), who did not enjoy such options as emigration, followed the common soldier into battle, providing food, clothing, and other necessities. As wives, mistresses, or companions of soldiers they extended invaluable domestic and personal services, guiding the armies along familiar ground, ministering to the wounded, and burying the dead. Many bore their children on the battlefront.

The *Rabonas* of Peru, for example, sometimes viewed as precursors to contemporary women soldiers, or the *soldaderas* of the 1910

Mexican Revolution, maintained a semblance of normalcy throughout a period of extreme stress and chaos. They were described as "women who provide for all the soldiers' needs, who wash and mend their clothes, receive no pay and have as their only salary the right to steal with impunity" (quoted in Gross and Bingham 1985: 45). These women were not usually married in the eyes of the church and state, but lived with their *compañero* soldiers, ate with them, and experienced the same dangers.

Unlike its Spanish colonial counterparts, Brazil escaped with a bloodless revolution and entered its imperial epoch when Napoleon invaded Portuguese shores in 1807. Protected by the British royal navy, the entire Portuguese court fled to safety in Brazil. There Dom João VI severed ties with Lisbon's commercial monopoly by opening Brazilian ports. Distressed by what he perceived as a backward, undeveloped society lacking libraries, printing presses, academic faculties, and commerce, the Portuguese monarch created new institutions in exile, including a national library, museums, and a botanical garden. Professionalism was fostered in the plastic arts and foreign immigration encouraged. Fourteen years later, when the restored monarchy in Portugal attempted to curtail Brazilian autonomy, the heir apparent, Dom Pedro I, defied Lisbon and remained in Rio. He convened a constituent assembly to proclaim the country's independence and in the process launched the period of empire in Brazilian history.

Even in Brazil, where the road to independence was largely devoid of the bitter hostilities to be found in surrounding republics, women participated in liberation efforts. One fanciful incident is described by Graham, regarding a young, ardent nationalist, Maria de Jesus, who donned men's clothing to join a regiment.

> She is illiterate, but clever. Her understanding is quick, and her perceptions are keen. I think, with education she might have been a remarkable person. She is not particularly masculine in her appearance, and her manners are gentle and cheerful. She has not contracted anything coarse or vulgar in her camp life, and I believe that no [scandal] has ever been substantiated against her modesty. One thing is certain, that her sex never was known until her father appealed to her commanding officer to seek her. (Graham 1969: 294)

While Latin Americans waged long, arduous battles to gain their independence, their counterparts in the Caribbean islands of Haiti, Cuba, the Dominican Republic, and Puerto Rico followed a different path. Inspired by the French Revolution, the slave rebellion led by

Toussaint L'Ouverture in 1804 concluded with the proclamation of Haitian independence. Santo Domingo, the eastern half of the island shared with Haiti, declared its independence from Spain in 1822 only to suffer a Haitian invasion and occupation that would last until 1844. In the aftermath and devastation of the Haitian Revolution, Cuba supplanted many of the activities of the former French possession and developed into a major sugar producer and slave entrepôt. Immigration from Florida, Louisiana, and Santo Domingo contributed to expansion and diversification of trade and to the introduction of large-scale sugar production. As a result, Cuban elites generally favored the economic changes that had led to increased prosperity and, fearing slave rebellions similar to those fought in Haiti, remained loyal to Spain.

In contrast to the very visible *criollo* leadership forged in Cuba, Puerto Rican national consciousness was in its early stages when the Wars of Independence erupted. Although limited armed confrontations took place in the Spanish Caribbean compared to the rest of Latin America, similar sentiments and grievances were already being articulated regarding the position of *criollos* in colonial Cuban and Puerto Rican society. As the islands were key to the colonial defense network, they served as points of disembarkation for Spanish troops deployed throughout the continent. Although Latin American, particularly Venezuelan, rebels sought to secure Antillean independence, it was virtually impossible to do so given the heavy Spanish military presence in the islands. By 1824, Cuba and Puerto Rico were all that remained of the Spanish Empire in the New World. Throughout the remainder of the century, Spain would try to recoup her losses by intensifying the colonialization and economic production of both island colonies.

We know little about the direct involvement of women in these early stages of Caribbean pro-independence political activity, but by mid-century their presence was indisputable. Throughout the decade of the sixties, small bands of women collaborated with separatists who persisted in their efforts and struggles to attain Antillean independence. These revolutionary movements peaked simultaneously in 1868, with the proclamations of the *Grito de Yara* in Cuba and the *Grito de Lares* in Puerto Rico. Independence and the abolition of slavery were the primary objectives of the insurgents, but the Pact of Zanjón, which brought hostilities to an end, accomplished neither. By the 1890s the movement for Antillean independence was rekindled, and exiles formed the Cuban and Puerto Rican Revolutionary Party to obtain, as the patriot José Martí declared, "with the united effort of all men of good will, the absolute independence of the island of Cuba, and to foment and aid that of Puerto Rico" (quoted in Keen and Wasserman 1984: 407). In spite of the gender reference made in the statement, women were integral to the insurrections and political conflicts of both countries, but they achieved limited modifications in their own legal or social status as a result. Elite women like Lola Rodríguez de Tió, credited with writing the revolutionary anthem, and Mariana Bracetti, who sewed the banner of Lares, were instrumental in the Puerto Rican cause. Less prominent sympathizers joined secret societies that orchestrated the revolts. More often than not, the members of these societies were related by blood or marriage and were intent on protecting class interests. As was the case throughout the rest of Latin America, political affiliations were serious business and usually lifelong commitments.

In Cuba, elite and non-elite families were brought directly into the conflict when hundreds were imprisoned, exiled, or executed for the deeds of their loved ones. Following the examples set by people like Mariana Grajales, the mother of insurgent Antonio Maceo, and María Cabrales, his wife, women provided shelter, safety, and provisions for the rebel armies. In her sixties when the war shattered her past life, Mariana was able to put the experiences of a comfortable lifetime behind her. She watched over the families of the soldiers and nursed the wounded. Her daughters and daughters-in-law joined the women of the fighting men to work beside her in providing refuge.

The poet-patriot of the Cuban Revolution, José Martí, described Mariana Grajales in the newspaper *Patria* as a faithful revolutionary who, as her husband lay dying, urged her compatriots to continue the battle. She was lauded for nursing the wounded on the battlefield —Spaniard and Cuban alike. On bleeding feet, she is said to have followed the stretcher carrying her wounded son, Antonio Maceo, but admonished his followers against despair. In Martí's words, she was truly the mother of the Cuban nation.

More than half a century separated the experiences of Cuban women from those of Gran Colombia in the struggles for political determination, yet Martí's praise of Mariana Grajales echoes Bolívar's admiration of Venezuelan women rebels. Both illustrate the stereotypical tropes of women's sacrifice and devotion to family.

Women's Status Following Independence

The image of women as subordinate yet supportive individuals, providers of shelter, warmth, and nourishment, was a traditional one in keeping with Ibero-American heritage. For the most part, the activities of the women who emerged in participatory roles throughout the period remained within prescribed boundaries. In the aftermath of independence, women were fully expected to return to their traditional, subordinate, and proper sphere as wives and mothers. However, women had demonstrated admirable intelligence and a remarkable capacity for political and social participation in revolutionary activities, particularly with regard to organization and insurrection. Their support and pursuit of political stands on behalf of the new republics afforded adequate preparation for full and equal participation in political affairs. Yet, despite the fact that some limited transformations in women's roles were already in evidence in the period before independence, their social and legal status remained virtually unchanged in the newly formed republics, regardless of their class or color. Contradictions abounded in countries where constitutions promoted equality under the law, qualified male suffrage, and abolition of slavery, but denied women emancipation and the franchise. In effect, women could not hold public office, vote, advocate, be a witness in a court of law, or adopt or become a guardian over minors. With few exceptions—most notably widows—women formed part of a disenfranchised group that included minors, slaves, invalids, criminals, and the retarded.

With the exception of Cuba and Puerto Rico, which remained directly under the corpus of Spanish law, civil codes were enacted throughout Latin America that, more often than not, upheld the legal status of women based on Hispanic law. Under such laws paternal authority predominated in society and in the home. Neither single sons nor single daughters became independent during the father's lifetime. Although personal and juridical independence could occur at twenty-three to twenty-five years of age, single women often remained at home under the protection of male relatives. Widows and single emancipated women on their own could exercise a substantial degree of control over their legal matters, but married women were less privileged as they retained fewer rights. Although they could inherit and bequeath wealth, hold property, retain custody of children in most separations, and keep their maiden surnames, in legal matters married women were almost completely subordinate to their spouses. It is known that some exceptional women like Soledad Román de Nuñez, who married the divorced president of Colombia in 1877, defied convention. Others successfully sued for the dissolution of their marriages, but in general, divorce was rare (Delpar 1989; Arrom 1985b). Matrimony continued to be the institution that accorded husbands administrative control over their wives' properties, even though some exceptional women succeeded in negotiating favorable marriage contracts that gave them varying degrees of control. For the most part, however, women could not enter into legal contracts, work, or utilize their wages without their husbands' approval. Moreover, the *patria potestas* that had given fathers legal, personal, and economic authority over their children throughout the Colonial period remained very much in effect throughout the nineteenth and much of the twentieth centuries.

Nevertheless, despite de jure subordination, some women exercised considerable control over personal wealth and family politics. It is also plausible that women from the lower classes—for instance, those who were more likely to earn monies from work outside of the home—retained control over family income. This was certainly the case in female-headed households.

Historians contend that the transformations of the early decades of the nineteenth century had minimal effects on women's roles. With few exceptions, attitudes regarding gender remained intact in spite of women's demonstrated ability for full participation and integration into all levels of society. Periods of violence, political unrest, economic instability, and pronounced foreign influence characterized many of the new republics in the first four decades of the nineteenth century. Frequent shifts in government between liberal and conservative orientations necessitated a preoccupation with establishing economic stability and sound political systems rather than social reforms.

To be sure, class, status, race, and work continued to separate women much as they had done in the past. For most women, life was centered in the countryside, where Indians, blacks, *mestizos,* and mulattos formed the bulk of an agrarian labor force as they had done in centuries past for wealthy landowners and their families. The gap between elite women and all others was wide, but the upper classes nonetheless set rigid standards of behavior over less-prestigious social groups. Ideally, women were expected to live and die within the context of patriarchal societies strictly ordered on gender roles sanctioned by centuries of legal and cultural institutions. In more practical terms, while they were subordinate to men in each class, women continued to wield influence in pivotal social roles. Upper- and middle-class women could be found as heads of households, owners of mines and *haciendas,* active entrepreneurs, and benefactors of religious and charitable institutions. Among the lower classes, women participated in the economic life of their households and communities as agricultural producers, shopkeepers, laundresses, domestics, market vendors, and artisans. If land was available for subsistence farming, patriarchal households predominated among Indians and *mestizos*. However, when the numbers of people within the household surpassed the availability of land, family configurations shifted. Lynn Stoner (1987a) suggests the emergence of a market economy, commercialization of land and labor, and a reduction in accessible land often resulted in an increase in female-headed or extended households. In fact, the existence of parallel-structured, female-headed households at all levels of society is evidenced by census and baptismal documentation (Lavrin 1987; Arrom 1985a and 1985b).

Although men were considered the undisputed heads of their households, at another level, women found strength and sources of empowerment in home and family. They supervised their children's training and education, and some administered well-staffed estates with servants, cooks, and extended-family members. Protected by church and state, women fulfilled their roles as wives and mothers through the ritual of wedlock. Marriage in turn ensured legitimacy, and, while the state protected the institution of matrimony through legislation, the church sanctioned its moral codes. Along with indigenous women, blacks, and *castas,* white females outside elite circles were less restricted in terms of marriage. Many among the lower and lower-middle classes lived in consensual unions rather than legally recognized matrimony. Regardless of the type of bonding and the configuration of the home, the family and women's place within it continued to be regarded as an important social pillar.

Ancestry predominated as a key factor in social mobility throughout Spanish and Portuguese America and in the islands of the Caribbean. Family organization especially flourished following independence. By the mid-nineteenth century, a few elite family networks came to dominate regional and national affairs. In some cases, ties continued between old colonial families and "new" ones founded by eighteenth-century immigrants who married into creole families. But the breakdown of administrative and financial structures in the first decades of the nineteenth century also paved the way for new familial ascendancy. Families represented stability and reliable members could be counted upon in commercial and economic transactions. Through the careful manipulation of marriages, and kinship and its relationship to the state, families achieved and expanded their power into the public arena. Indeed, connections between powerful families dating from the late colonial period and the political parties of the national period are well documented (Balmori et al. 1984). Interconnected family networks extended their hegemony beyond the provincial and regional levels through the political party structure. Moreover, it was precisely through the construction of notable or dynastic families, founded on kinship and marital alliances, that nineteenth-century economic activities translated into power, prestige, and wealth. The placement of family members in key government positions assured protection and patronage for the interests of the group. In the cities, small groups of well-to-do old families, also united to one another for generations through marriage, dominated the political and economic structure. In all, these networks operated on a common understanding that enabled them "to expand their power and pre-eminence until they dominated Latin American society at all levels" (Balmori et al. 1984: 43). By the first decades of the twentieth century, the influence of some elite family networks begins to give way to interest-based political and bureaucratic structures. Significantly, contemporary non-elite families utilize marriage, ritual kinship, business association, and political influence as did the earlier elites, "thus confirming the strength of cultural traditions supporting the institution of the family regardless of class" (quoted in Lavrin 1986b: 6).

Caribbean Societies

In and of itself, slavery was not the sole defining feature of the slave experience; however, slave society predominated in Brazil and the islands of the Caribbean for a good part of the nineteenth century. To be sure, the expansion of sugar and coffee plantation or *hacienda* societies following the decline of Haitian sugar production was formidable. Cuba, as but one example, witnessed a growth in the numbers of plantations from 1,000 in 1827 to 2,430 in 1862 (Pérez, Jr. 1992: xv). The dominant social, cultural, and economic institution, plantations were the major centers of agricultural and industrial production. Scarano points out the importance of such centers as population nuclei "in which power was rigidly exercised by a ruling minority over a large group of subservient workers, whose labor in every phase of the production process was organized according to strict rules of efficiency" (Scarano 1984: 3).

In these societies race, color, and ethnicity were facts of life, the "indelible badge of status and condition" (Knight 1978: 130). Much of the population in plantation areas, and to a lesser extent in urban areas, was enslaved. Generally speaking, the broadest social base represented the vast majority of enslaved individuals. Originally, most slaves were African-born, but the end of the slave trade in 1807 had contributed to an increase in the number born in the Americas. Despite the British decree outlawing the slave trade, Africans continued to be imported to Brazil, Cuba, and Puerto Rico as slaves for several decades. In the British colonies such as the Guianas, the end of the trade resulted in a dramatic and sustained increase in the importation of indentured laborers, the vast majority of whom came from British-ruled India. Individuals of mixed ancestry were found within the group of American-born slaves. A middle group consisted of free people of color—blacks and *mulatos*—who enjoyed few of the privileges of the ruling class. The smallest group—the white population—controlled the political and economic apparatus and exercised enormous social influence.

In Caribbean societies many black women worked the land, and some researchers believe that prior to emancipation (1833 in the British colonies and 1848 in the French) they toiled longer in the fields than did male slaves (Higman 1979). In such societies as British Guiana, where indentured laborers took over the work of cane cultivation from African slaves, Indian women also worked in the fields. However, sex ratios of imported workers were heavily skewed in favor of men. In contrast to field hands, domestic slaves were frequently born into hereditary service. Thus, the children of house slaves often associated with their young masters during their juvenile years, and inherited the responsibilities of their parents upon the latter's demise. Mulatto female slaves were often found as house servants, where many were said to have enjoyed advantages denied to field slaves. They were accorded more leisure, for example, were less subject to physical coercion, and had greater opportunities for manumission. Their presence in the house, however, left them more vulnerable to the sexual advances of the master and his male descendants.

Mulatto offspring were also a fact of life and the travel literature of the period seldom fails to point out the intermingling of the races. In a visit to a Cuban plantation in 1875, one traveler observed:

> We passed through a trap-door on the upper floor and found ourselves in a wide gallery running round the court. On this gallery opened large and tolerably well ventilated rooms, used as nurseries, sick-wards, lying-in rooms, saddle's rooms and stores. Dozens of naked children of every age, from the fly-devoured baby in its cradle to the black-eyed, round-bellied urchin of three or four years old, swarmed along the gallery. Their number and various shades of colour, from jet black to nearly white proved that the negro women were certainly not barren, and that the white man did not disdain to make a concubine as well as a slave of the African. (quoted in Pérez, Jr. 1992: 87–88)

After abolition, a small independent peasantry arose that farmed less productive land; but the status of former slaves as free men and women made little difference in the social or economic order. In most of the Caribbean islands, whites continued to form a small but powerful minority. Following emancipation, women were the first to retire from agricultural work, but differential migratory patterns—at first rural to urban, then in the twentieth century from colony to metropole—often left women as the sole support of their children. Females in Caribbean households frequently combined multiple survival strategies such as owning their own farms, marketing their produce, and working as agricultural laborers on a part-time basis (Henshall 1981).

The actual contributions of both female slaves and free women of color to the social and economic development of Caribbean plantation society are still to be detailed. However, research in this area is rapidly increasing. The many roles of Afro-Brazilian women slaves, for example, indicate that their contributions were far-reaching and multifaceted. In addition to their participation in agricultural production and domestic work, they served not only as mothers for their own children but also as surrogate mothers and wet nurses for the children of their white masters. They were central figures in the Afro-creole matriarchal family and exerted broad influence as priestesses *(mãe de santos)* in transplanted religions such as *candomblé*. Priestesses kept and transmitted ritualistic customs and traditions. Fugitive slave communities called *quilombos* profited from the leadership roles of Afro-Brazilian slave women. And it was also women as tellers of tales who passed down the richness of their African heritage, maintaining connections with their ancestral past (Davis 1995).

In the Hispanic Caribbean colonies, creoles accounted for a sizable portion of the total population, the remainder composed of free *mestizos,* blacks and slaves. This situation had motivated the creation of a legally enforced system of labor in Cuba and Puerto Rico. Regimented through a passbook system, in effect from 1849 to 1873, the work and mobility of peasant men and women over the age of sixteen was regulated. Workers were required to carry their passbooks at all times. If unable to produce the document, workers were classified as vagrants and thrown into jail. Free women of lower socioeconomic status had therefore been accustomed to agricultural and other types of work and to struggle for survival on meager wages. Women picked and thrashed the berries in the coffee fields, and in the tobacco industry women stripped, classified, and bundled tobacco leaves. They toiled on sugar plantations and in subsistence farming. In the towns working class women took in laundry, and girls were hired out as domestics at an early age. Commonly referred to as *criadas,* they worked day and night subject to the whims and demands of the employing family. Others worked as street vendors, as seamstresses, and in food services. As the century came to a close, however, urban women of the middle, and to a lesser extent the upper classes, were already found in the teaching and nursing professions.

EDUCATION

By the mid-nineteenth century enlightened leaders in many Latin American countries, cognizant of the strides necessary for the progress of young nations, proposed reforms intended to raise social and economic standards and formulated the first opportunities to bring about changes in women's status. These included expansion and revisions in secular education. In general, education for women was perceived as one way to eradicate backwardness and promote national progress. In countries like Cuba, Puerto Rico, and Brazil, movements for the abolition of slavery in the last third of the nineteenth century parallelled attempts to integrate women into expanded educational structures. Emancipation for slaves, it was generally believed, would spark awareness of the lack of consideration, equality, and opportunity where women were concerned. However, other Caribbean nations in which slavery had already been abolished experienced limited educational growth, through lack of either financial or social support. In some countries, financial support for educating boys and girls was generally problematic regardless of gender. Where strict separation of the sexes in public affairs was customary, nations were not prepared to establish coeducational, secular school systems. The need to educate women was perceived by some people as frivolous, but others feared the move as the initial steps toward future demands for equality.

In contrast to the Hispanic Caribbean, the British West Indies developed different traditions regarding education. Because of an intensive plantation economy that exported sugar to a global market, slavery accounted for a majority population of African descent. The West African heritage had included greater freedom for women, who were expected to control village trade and manage individual households in polygamous marriages. Slavery in the Americas frequently meant the breakup of family structures, underscoring what current research indicates as functioning and viable matrilocal households (Bilby and Steady 1981; Mathurin 1975). West Indian Maroon societies, for example, established by runaway slaves throughout the Caribbean, were also matrilocal in organization. In both Maroon and slave communities women, although customarily subordinate to men, represented a valuable and stable element. This was particularly true with the abolition of the slave trade to the British colonies in 1807. Women cultivated the land, controlled the Sunday markets, and provided the basic necessities of the family. In shaping their societies, women forged their African heritage with the culture of resistance, survival, and solidarity that evolved in many West Indian slave communities. Traditions that had aided the survival of the family in the past now functioned as the foundation for the free agrarian societies that characterized many of the islands throughout the nineteenth and twentieth centuries. Because of the historically more independent roles played by women and the degree of influence exerted by the metropoles, island colonies like Barbados and Jamaica readily supported education for both sexes, in contrast to their Spanish American counterparts. As a result, educated women were valued and rapidly became employed in such professions as teaching and nursing, which would eventually be considered typical feminine work (Gross and Bingham 1985).

Initially, education throughout Latin America, including the Hispanic Caribbean, was intended to strengthen women's primary role within the context of the family, as reproducers of the citizenry and transmitters of culture. Women teachers emerged from these early educational systems and returned to reform them. Once educated, a cadre of experienced, often middle-class, women turned their attention to their own emancipation, demanding their rightful place in the development of their countries.

In Mexico, considered a fair barometer for change in Latin America before independence, developments in education advanced significantly after the Bourbon Reforms (Arrom 1985b). As early as 1807, the *Diario de Mexico* supported the rights of women to an education in the belief that, once enlightened, they would contribute to the state's progressive aspirations. For example, the writer Fernando Lizardi focused his novel, *La Quijotita* (1817), on the theme of educational reforms for women. Between 1831 and 1843, legislation was proposed regarding the establishment of schools for girls in Puebla, Mexico's second largest city. Arguments about the education of women were utilitarian in nature. One priest, director of the Colegio de Enseñanzas de Nuestra Señora de los Gozos, remarked: "It does not escape you how much influence mothers have in the education of their children and once mothers are educated, in great part will public customs improve, since their example will at least serve to moderate the violent passions of their children" (Vaughan 1986: 28). By 1842, legislation in Mexico City approved mandatory education for both sexes, ages 7 to 15 (Arrom 1985b). The earliest schools for girls in Mexico City appeared in 1869, followed in the next five years by similar establishments in other provincial cities. By the 1880s, legislators supported compulsory education and the adoption of a single, well-defined school curriculum.

If the curriculum established for Puebla serves as a prototype for other cities and provinces, it can be assumed that religion played a significant role in the secular schools. Children were taught reading and writing from catechisms. At public examinations, catechism was recited for government officials. Before class, children prayed *salves* to the Virgin; they added the rosary on Saturdays. Many of these activities took place in classrooms adorned with religious icons and holy images. By 1842, President Santa Anna decreed the Virgin of Guadalupe Holy Protectoress of all the schools in Mexico (Vaughan 1986).

Late nineteenth- and early twentieth-century liberal reformers included influential individuals such as President Benito Juárez, educator José María Vigil, and legislator Justo Sierra. This group generally approved secular education for women, not only as a means of female advancement but also to lessen conservative-supported, Catholic Church control over females and, consequently, the family. Well-prepared teachers were expected to graduate from the normal schools purified of "superstition and thoroughly imbued with the values of science, work, time, patriotism and citizenship" (Vaughan 1986: 30). Educated women were expected to become supportive wives, efficient homemakers, and enlightened parents of strong, active, and decisive children. Widows and other single heads of household also needed the skills acquired through education in order to make a living for themselves and their families. It was, after all, the family that wove together the fabric of Mexican society. Sierra believed, for example, that Mexican schools were "forming men and women for the home; this is our supreme goal. In doing it, we believe firmly that we are performing a service beyond comparison with any in the benefit of the Republic. . . . The educated woman will be truly one for the home; she will be the companion and the collaborator of man in the formation of the family" (Vaughan 1979: 66–67).

Within this context the notion of earning advanced degrees not geared toward the performance of maternal duties met with considerable resistance; only in 1888 were women permitted to study for the professions. Matilda Montoya, the first woman to attend classes with male students at the National School of Medicine, inspired Columba Rivera to matriculate and graduate as Mexico's second female physician. As Anna Macías points out, by 1904 there were at least three practicing female physicians in Mexico City, with twice that many enrolled in the medical school (Macías 1983). In addition, vocational schools assumed the responsibility for preparing countless young women for employment in clerical, telephone, telegraph, and other industries.

Education for women became a symbol of progress and culture in many of the new Spanish-American republics, in Brazil, and in the Caribbean. In Argentina, the earliest institutions to promote educational opportunities for girls came about with the establishment of the Society of Beneficence of Buenos Aires (1823–1948). This organization was charged with operating a public elementary school system. Administered by a group of government-appointed elite women, the Society provided the model for other charitable institutions and a place for the talents of academically prepared women but had minimal impact on mass education. In time, the Society shifted its focus to social welfare projects and offered a wide range of services for women and children.

By mid-century, such leading intellectuals and reformers as Juan Bautista Alberdi and Domingo Faustino Sarmiento advanced progressive ideas regarding the place of women and public education in Argentine society. Exiled during the Rosas regime, Sarmiento and others viewed firsthand the advanced educational processes under way in Europe and the United States. Sarmiento, who had the opportunity to put many of his ideas into practice during his presidency (1868–74), was convinced that government-supported free public schools were essential for national progress. He founded a secular coeducational school system in Parana which trained the nation's first generation of normal-school teachers. Normal schools, established by the state along the lines of North American pedagogical philosophies and methods, emphasized questioning, reasoning, self-discipline, physical fitness, and manual labor. Since female students in particular would generate great influence over Argentine youth, their program of study combined domestic economy with courses in scientific child-rearing, furniture purchasing, budgeting, and household management.

In Argentina education went beyond the primary levels to include vocational training that prepared women for diverse types of employment. By 1870, commercial progress resulted in a demand for workers in numerous sectors. Industrial, trade, agricultural, and commercial institutions emerged to prepare young people to meet the challenge. Commercial schools for women added classes in typing, telegraphy, accounting, stenography, and other subjects to their curriculum. By 1907 aspirations to study on the secondary level were met with the opening of the National Girls' High School #1 in Buenos Aires. The curriculum encompassed course work in chemistry, natural history, anatomy, psychology, and geography. Domestic science, needlework, music, and physical education completed the women's program. Interestingly enough, it was middle-class youth and those of immigrant stock who readily availed themselves of such opportunities. Centers of learning such as those described would produce the educated elite responsible for the initial transformations in women's roles in the first decades of the twentieth century. However, as Cynthia Little cautions, despite the degree of academic proficiency or comprehensive preparation for a career, "the restrictive nature of the Argentine Civil Code as it related to women hindered them from competing as equals in business. For example, a married woman had to receive her husband's permission before engaging in any profession, and she could not sign a contract" (Little 1978: 241).

Among the northern republics of South America, Colombia's earliest public schools appeared in 1821, following precedents set in the late eighteenth century when instructional centers for boys and girls were established sporadically in some of the provinces. At that point plans to expand educational opportunities, especially for girls, had been hindered by lack of resources. By 1832 however, intent on improving the condition of women, the Colegio de la Merced opened its doors offering, in addition to a traditional curriculum, courses in Spanish, French, drawing, and music. Efforts were renewed in 1870 to unify public instruction throughout the nation and to establish normal schools for teacher training in each state. The inauguration in 1872 of the first normal school class of eighty students in Bogota signalled an important but lengthy process in increasing the educational opportunities for women.

Education in Brazil was largely the prerogative of those entitled to its benefits by birth, color, or gender. As Hahner illustrates, the Brazilian census of 1872 counted a total population of 10,112,061. However, only some 1,012,097 free men, 550,981 free women, 958 enslaved men, and 445 enslaved women were able to read and write. In 1873, nearly 5,077 primary schools, public and private, were established in the empire. These schools had a total of 114,014 male and 46,246 female pupils. As in Argentina, the children of wealthier families were often educated at home; in Brazil, however, home tutorials were preferred because the public schools were frequently poorly run (Hahner 1980).

As early as 1827 girls had been admitted to primary schools in Brazil and instructed in domestic science. Normal schools for teacher training appeared almost a decade later, and these offered a rare opportunity for female education. The lack of coeducational facilities, particularly in higher education, inhibited women's academic advancement. Those persistent few who clamored for learning left the country to pursue their own aspirations. Before women like Rita Lobato Velho Lopes could study in Brazil, María Augusta Generosa Estrella and Josefa Agueda Felisbella Mercedes de Oliveira came to the United States to train as physicians. By the end of the century, the health field, which included nursing and midwifery, gained social approval as a career for women and, along with education, provided the few outlets available to women who formed the newly educated elite. It bears repeating, however, that many (if not most) Brazilian women already worked in agriculture, as domestic servants, as laundresses, and in other service sectors.

Significantly, although Cuba and Puerto Rico remained Spanish colonies, the islands experienced intellectual currents that reflected the rest of Latin America. Liberal reforms in education, emancipation, and the rights of working-class women merited consideration along with the abolition of slavery (Puerto Rico in 1873; Cuba in 1886) and the passbook—the aforementioned legal document that restricted workers' mobility. Building on the legacy of pioneers like Celestina Cordero, a Puerto Rican educator of the 1820s, women founded organizations advocating the expansion of education for women (Acosta-Belén 1986). Liberal reformers implored women to free themselves from injustice and contribute productively to society. Alejandro Tapia y Rivera, for example, wrote numerous plays that illustrated the important role of women in Puerto Rican society, and historian Salvador Brau went so far as to defend the education of peasant women and laborers (Jiménez de Wagenheim 1998). By the last third of the century, an educator, Eugenio María de Hostos, was instrumental not only in establishing the island's public school system but in extending his educational philosophies to Chile, Cuba, the Dominican Republic, and other countries in the hemisphere.

Throughout Latin America and the Hispanic Caribbean, similar patterns emerge regarding women's education. Resistance to educating women rested on the belief that they would overstep their proper place in the home and society, ultimately challenging male authority. Whereas some individuals maintained that women would merely abuse the privilege of literacy, others feared educated women might be thought—or think themselves—too worldly for marriage. Moreover, education had been traditionally reserved for the upper classes. The notion of educating the masses, which included indigenous non-Spanish-speaking people as well as the lower classes, heightened class prejudices.

More often than not, the curriculum designed for girls differed from the one prepared for boys. It was intended to prepare young women for roles as enlightened housewives rather than as active, equal partners in society. The only accessible road beyond the primary school for women was the normal school. This resulted in the feminization of the school systems, most evident at the primary levels. It is not surprising, therefore, that significant movements to initiate changes in women's social and legal status, particularly from the 1880s to the 1930s, would disproportionately come from teachers. In addition, this period was one in which women became primary players in rural to urban migrations, increasingly integrating into an industrialized work force. The period also witnessed the formation of numerous workers' organizations. Imbued with socialist or anarchist ideology, these groups would ultimately challenge the status quo, demanding social justice and economic reforms.

SOCIETIES IN TRANSITION: 1880–1930s

Conditioned by geography and resources, the pace and nature of social, political, and economic change in the decades bridging the centuries varied widely across Latin America and the Hispanic Caribbean. Shifts in women's roles and status accompanied broader societal transformations generally influenced by forces affecting society at large. Cuba and Puerto Rico entered into an international market, characterized by an intensification of a more modern and technologically improved sugar-production system, but development was largely curtailed by the Spanish-Cuban-American War and the islands' passage into U.S. hands in 1898. Regionalism increased in Brazil throughout the last third of the nineteenth century, but the advent of the railroad, steamships, and communications stimulated development in southern urban centers. Brazilian wealth and power continued to rest firmly on a traditional plantation economy. Despite some economic shifts occasioned by the abolition of slavery in 1888, this picture did not undergo great changes with the establishment of the

Republic in 1889. In Mexico and Central and South America, politics and economics responded to European industrialization by accommodating foreign investment and technology, which in turn created the necessary infrastructure for expansion but bound nations into dependent neo-colonial relationships with industrial powers in Europe and the United States. Economically, many Latin American countries continued to rely on the export of raw materials, for either agricultural or mineral production; however, industrialization and modernization in countries like Argentina, Chile, Mexico, and Brazil became a significant factor before the onset of the twentieth century. Urban societies and the economic growth of urban areas promoted population movements from country to city, contributing to the growth of a new proletariat. In addition, the period witnessed massive European immigration, especially to Brazil, Argentina, and Chile, which satisfied a growing demand for labor but also introduced new social and political ideologies, including anarchism.

In the cities, urbanization and industrialization coincided with the search for equal rights. By the turn of the century, increasing numbers of women were employed as seamstresses, artisans, and food processors. In Colombia, for example, 70 percent of those classified as artisans in 1870 were women (Delpar 1989). Throughout the continent they entered domestic service, and although those in that sector disproportionately suffered abuse and exploitation, for many it became the middle passage between rural and urban life. Teaching, nursing, and clerical employment offered the first opportunities for middle-class women to work outside the home, while factories and cottage industries incorporated women of the lower classes as a cheap source of labor.

Agricultural Economies

The continuing demand by Europe and the US for raw materials, sugar, coffee, wheat, henequen, copper, nitrates, and other commodities intensified land and labor expansion throughout Latin America. As land remained concentrated in large plantations or *haciendas,* under the control of a landed elite, a landless peasantry formed that was forced to trade or sell its labor for survival. *Haciendas* were self-sufficient, large farms based on semi-feudal labor relations, and plantations were large land holdings based initially on enslaved or indentured labor and, following abolition, on salaried workers. Both exported commercial agricultural products to a world market and imported manufactured goods, machinery, and equipment from Europe and the United States. The landed elite family, now involved in an international capitalist system, became more cosmopolitan and frequently moved between the estate, city homes, and residences abroad. The daily task of managing the estates was left to hired overseers.

As in the past, women of the lower classes in rural, non-industrialized areas continued to perform important social and economic functions as producers and reproducers of the labor force. Peasant families were bound to the *hacienda* through coercion, often debt peonage, but they had access to the land for subsistence farming. Women's work in the fields was augmented by their responsibility to process food, cook, sew, weave, and raise livestock. Insufficient wages, food scarcity, and unsanitary living conditions frequently resulted in illnesses also treated by women adept in healing. In addition to sustaining their own families, they provided for the welfare of the *hacendado*'s family.

In indigenous communities where fertile land was valued for commercial export production, it became fair game for appropriation. Many displaced Native Americans became laborers on the *haciendas*, with some exceptions. In areas like southern Mexico, Central America, and the Andean region, where agricultural production was controlled by the peasantry, or where Native exploitation was less direct, these communities became vulnerable but were not destroyed (Greishaber 1979). Various systems emerged, depending on the region and its resources, to draft Indians as contract laborers for the *haciendas.* Such arrangements led to significant community relocation and, at least in Guatemala and Peru, to a re-indianization of the coastal areas.

One response on behalf of the indigenous communities to resist the changes exerted on their internal social organization was a conscious effort toward non-assimilation, isolation, strict adherence to their native traditions, and protection for land and way of life. Current research indicates that women played key roles in these efforts, as agents of resounding cultural and economic impact. Indian women transmitted the customs and work ethics of their ancestors, maintaining communities impervious to the dominant cultural and religious order. They operated village and small urban markets supplying woolen goods, farm produce, and household crafts to townspeople. Testimonials like those of Rigoberta Menchú (1984) and Domitila Barrios de Chungara (1978) represent a contemporary discourse extolling a steady, unbroken chain of traditional behavior passed from one generation to the next in indigenous societies. These portraits of indigenous women as nurturers and transmitters of tradition rely, to a certain extent, on stereotyped images of women's virtues. However, in these cases, women's roles are vital not only for the survival of the group, but for the ancestral community as well.

WOMEN AS FEMINISTS AND WORKERS

In response to the challenges posed by societies at different stages of transition, aggressive leaders sought to broaden their electoral bases by adopting legislative and educational reforms relevant to both support a growing economy and alleviate social conditions for the less privileged sectors of the population. Within this climate small groups of women, often educated and middle class, led an important struggle to transform the status of women. Although they did not represent a majority of the female population, which had been conditioned for generations to support a traditional male-dominant patriarchal way of life, their movement offered a viable ideology for coping and explaining transitions in women's roles at a critical historical juncture. In many countries it coincided with another movement led by working-class activists stressing protection, equality, and rights for women and children.

The idea of gender equality, referred to as "liberation" or "emancipation" in the literature of the period, was considered by a core group of progressive women as the logical evolution of the relationship between the sexes. However, significant numbers of women, as well as men, opposed such views, fearing that equality spelled the initial breakdown of home and family. Many women supported traditional gender roles that oriented the female toward the home, while men, accustomed to societies that stressed male values and roles, were understandably reluctant to compromise their legally sanctioned power. The majority of women who sought advancement and increased rights for their sex sought to mediate between two extremes: they advocated neither for "sameness" with men nor for a status quo that perpetuated female legal, professional, and economic inferiority. In this mixed climate, advancement for women—by attempting to restructure the civil codes, increase education, improve wages and work conditions, and eventually gain political enfranchisement—meant confronting formidable opposition. Achievement of these goals proved to be a lengthy and uneven process throughout the hemisphere.

The concerns of women activists covered a wide range of issues. They sought equality before the law: to make their own decisions, eliminate the double standard, expand their educational horizons, and aid in the progress of their countries. Simply stated, these women wanted self-sufficiency for themselves while also working for improvements in the circumstances of others less fortunate. Moreover, imbued with a sense of moral guardianship toward society, women stressed the deplorable conditions affecting working women, children, and the poor and articulated the need for protective legislation in this regard. Although the term "feminism" was rarely used, by the last third of the nineteenth century an ideology of activism oriented around issues of concern to women became evident. This continued into the early decades of the twentieth century, culminating in a second feminist wave in modern times, which influenced the reforms of the civil codes and secured the vote for women.

For some, feminist consciousness evolved as a result of education. Asunción Lavrin (1986) suggests that changes in women's status in Argentina accrued primarily from the impetus of middle-class, educated women. And both June Hahner (1980) and Anna Macías (1983) highlight the extraordinary work of teachers in Brazil and Mexico, respectively, in fomenting feminist ideology through their writings and organizational activity. For others, travel abroad or awareness of the impressive gains made by women in progressive European countries or the United States inspired a shift in consciousness and commitment to work for social change.

Cecilia Grierson, for example, Argentina's first female doctor and author of several medical treatises, travelled extensively throughout Europe, where she studied the latest techniques in the treatment of the blind and hearing impaired. In her native country, Grierson organized one of the earliest academies for the study and teaching of retarded children. The Brazilian feminist Bertha Lutz was also educated in Europe, and the Chilean Amanda Labarca, who organized reading circles between 1915 and 1918 on the writings of earlier feminists, received her academic foundations in the US. The inter-American and intra–Latin American conferences that helped provide opportunities for contact and dialogue with similarly minded women were also vital for the development of this educated elite.

Feminism and its goals were defined in many ways. Writing in *La ondina de plata,* published in Buenos Aires in the 1870s, María Eugenia Echenique debated the benefits deriving from the emancipation of women to the individual and society. To Echenique, emancipation meant "absolute freedom to work and to carve their own destinies, although remaining as men's companions" (Lavrin 1986a: 4). Uruguayan feminist María Abella y Ramírez defined feminism as "nothing else than a new doctrine of freedom for the woman who proclaims herself as an enemy of all slavery. . . . When feminism triumphs, we will not be dominated by men; we will enjoy freedom and so will be as happy as they are, because being free is one of the greatest things in the world" (quoted in Lavrin 1986a: 6). In Colombia's *La mujer,* founder and editor Soledad Acosta de Samper stressed the role of women in history along with the feminist movements of the hemisphere in the 1870s. The Argentinian Adelia de Carlo spoke of freedom in the 1920s, when she defined feminism as liberation from the state of servitude and proposed human dignity for all women. By the decade of the thirties, Isabel Andréu de Aguilar, among the first graduates of the University of Puerto Rico, described feminism as a doctrine that "establishes equality between the sexes as a fundamental principle, equality in duties and rights in order to build a more perfect society within its ideology of liberty" (quoted in Valle-Ferrer 1986: 77).

Latin American feminists were concerned about their gender image from the inception of the movement and dedicated enormous energy to clarifying their position. In formulating feminist ideology, gender roles, so much a part of Latin heritage, were not discarded. One of the underlying premises in some types of feminist discourse was that the philosophy enhanced the traditional role of women as wives and mothers. In her 1901 study on the subject, Elvira López emphasized the fact that feminism in Argentina, Chile, and Uruguay was not the struggle of women against men. Rather, it was a battle to gain economic and educational opportunities equivalent to men's. A similar outlook was proposed by the Argentinian socialist feminist Dr. Alicia Moreau de Justo: "For me, feminism is not apart from social reality. The woman liberates herself along with the man and not against him. That liberation is a particular form of the struggle against capitalism and social injustice" (quoted in Corbiere 1982: 73). Clearly such principled positions also had political ramifications. Justifying women's advancement in terms that stressed the common interest of the sexes appeared to be less threatening.

The education of women was one of the feminists' most important causes and was routinely defended on the grounds that education would enable women to better fulfill their honorable and socially indispensable roles as mothers. The editors of *La mujer mexicana* (1904–08) stressed education along with equality as the ultimate strength of the home and society. In the first decades of the twentieth century, Cuban feminists advocated changes in women's status by praising motherhood and upholding the sanctity of the home. The Brazilian

Bertha Lutz, generally more radical in her approach to feminism, also viewed the emancipation of women as beneficial to society. Initiating the suffrage movement in 1918, Lutz qualified the establishment of a League of Brazilian Women in the following manner:

> I am not proposing an association of "suffragettes" who would break windows along the street but, rather, of Brazilians who understand that a woman ought not to live parasitically based on her sex, taking advantage of man's animal instincts, but, rather, be useful, educate herself and her children, and become capable of performing those political responsibilities which the future cannot fail to allot her. Thus, women shall cease to occupy a social position as humiliating for them as it is harmful to men. They shall cease being one of the heavy links that chain our country to the past, and instead, become valuable instruments in the progress of Brazil. (quoted in Hahner 1979: 203–04)

The initial steps taken to dramatize emancipation and other women's issues lay specifically in the publication of journals, essays, and books; the mobilization of women into associations; and organizational participation in regional, national, and international forums. As early as the mid-nineteenth century, Brazilian feminist newspapers and journals such as *O jornal das senhoras* prioritized the "social betterment and the moral emancipation of women" (quoted in Hahner 1978: 257). Edited by former school teacher Joana Paula Manso de Noronha, the journal operated on the premise that women were intelligent and capable, and merited equality. The journal portrayed women as integral and contributing partners in the home, dispelling stereotypical images of the female as a doll-like, spoiled, one-dimensional producer of children. If men were truly concerned about their sons' futures, the editors reasoned, mothers would be respected as the first educators. Subsequent editions connected women with the Virgin Mary and stressed her veneration based on their perceived emotional and spiritual superiority. Other publications accepted the elevated position of women in society in principle but chose to concentrate on improving their lot in the practical world.

The 1870s witnessed a surge in the publication of feminist materials in Brazil. Another former teacher, Francisca Senhorinha de Motta Diniz, published *O sexo feminino,* dedicated to "the education, instruction and emancipation of women" (quoted in Hahner 1978: 262). This was followed by *O domingo, Jornal das damas,* and *Myosotis. Echo das damas* appeared under the guidance of Amelia Carolina de Silva Couto. These journals reiterated the importance of education

for individual as well as public gains, but while earlier endeavors concentrated on ameliorating male opinions of women, the latter focused
on bringing about change to benefit women directly. Feminists like
Francisca Diniz stressed the economic and moral benefits accruing to
a country whose women became active participants in its national
life.

In Argentina, the feminist struggle for women's civil rights, education, improvement in the conditions of the working class, and suffrage
assumed international proportions, and solidarity was established with
corresponding women's groups in other countries—Brazil, Paraguay,
Uruguay, and Chile—with the celebration of the Congress of 1910.
The First International Feminist Congress in Buenos Aires, coordi-
nated by Drs. Cecilia Grierson and Petrona Eyle, debated civil rights
issues, progressive and special education, divorce, female health concerns, and the application of domestic economy to the home. The
congress aimed to establish unity among all women of the world and
orient women of diverse social positions to a common understanding. Some participants were more concerned with portraying a positive feminist ideology that would ultimately benefit the family, society,
and the nation. Others hoped to modify prejudice among the classes
in an effort to better the social conditions of all women (Landaburú
et al. 1982: 62–67).

Determined to promote feminism as well intentioned and intelligent, an influential force that transcended the individual, the congress drew support from leading feminists and professional women
of the period. These included Dr. Julieta Lanteri de Renshaw, founder
of the National Feminist Party and proponent of women's suffrage;
Fenia Chertkoff, one of the first to promote the defense of children's
rights and denounce the social, sexual exploitation of women; and
Dr. Alicia Moreau de Justo, socialist founder of the Committee for
Women's Suffrage and the National Feminist Union. The congress established wide feminine networks by drawing on a multinational audience which included such notables as French scientist Marie Curie
and Italian educator Maria Montessori. The importance of this first
attempt to unite women the world over is evidenced by the wide
range of official languages utilized in the proceedings: Spanish, English, Russian, French, Italian, and German.

By the 1920s, such Argentine groups as Julieta Lanteri Renshaw's
Nationalist Feminist Party and Elvira Rawson de Dellepiane's Wom-
en's Rights Association lobbied for political and civil emancipation.
The urgent need for the Argentine government to present a progressive and enlightened image to the outside world culminated in the

reforms of the Civil Code in 1926. Women gained limited rights to their own earnings, to inherit in any amount, and to engage in contractual agreements. These reforms and other legislation regulating the working conditions of women and children were due in no small measure to persistent feminist activity.

The Mexican feminist movement, on the other hand, had a character all its own, according to Anna Macías (1983), primarily due to the critical role of the governors of Yucatan. Before the outbreak of the Mexican Revolution in 1910, small groups of educated women began to demand educational opportunities for all women, decent wages, and reform of the Civil Code with a view toward eliminating the double standard and inequality. Under the leadership of socialist governors Salvador Alvarado (1915–18) and Felipe Carrillo Puerto (1922–24), the progressive state of Yucatan, well endowed with the profits of the henequen industry, emerged as the center for the advancement of women. As early as 1870, poet and school teacher Rita Cetina Gutiérrez had set precedents for feminist action by founding the journal *La siempreviva*. The journal's editors established a secondary school that eventually became the government Instituto Literario de Niñas, an institution now credited with the preparation of generations of teachers.

Along with Cetina Gutiérrez, Consuelo Zavala y Castillo, and Dominga Canto y Pastrana, Governor Alvarado was instrumental in calling the first two feminist congresses in Mexican history, in January and November 1916. Their agendas included the role of women in the political sphere, the primary school, and the work force, but issues of divorce, birth control, and the vote were also discussed. Attended predominantly by teachers, the congresses approved resolutions favoring progressive education, increased vocational and educational opportunities, political participation for women, and reforms in the Civil Code. Carrillo Puerto, who succeeded Alvarado as governor, continued many of his predecessor's programs and accelerated others, including proposing the right for women to vote in municipal elections and run for public office.

Although electoral participation was halfheartedly embraced in Mexico throughout this period, it was overwhelmingly endorsed almost a decade later by the feminists who attended the First Feminist Congress of the Pan American League in Mexico City in 1923. Participants, many of whom also represented the various women's organizations of the period, were sent from twenty Mexican states. In addition, participants from the National League of Women Voters, the Women's International League for Peace and Freedom, the Parent Teachers Association, the YMCA, the Los Angeles Council of Catholic Women, and the American Birth Control League ensured international support.

Feminism throughout Latin America and the Hispanic Caribbean directly benefitted middle-class women and drew support from an urban, professional, or white-collar sector. There was, however, a conscious effort on the part of some feminists to address the needs of all women, regardless of class. In achieving this goal, feminists tended to expand their agendas to include the poor and the working-class population that was increasing at an alarming rate throughout the continent. Despite the fact that poor and working class women were not integrated into feminist circles, the concerns of both groups frequently meshed.

Throughout the continent working conditions were brutal. With the rare exception of educated professionals, women were expected to work long hours for low wages in factories and sweatshops, and provisions for childcare, health, sanitary conditions, or safety were unheard-of. As mechanization increased, jobs became highly skilled and working conditions declined even further. The early decades of the twentieth century also witnessed an increase in internal migration of people in search of better-paying industrial employment. In Colombia, for example, the Civil War of 1899 aided migration, industrialization, and the emergence of a salaried labor force. Women were incorporated into this labor force in domestic service and textiles in record numbers (Leon de Leal 1977).

In Mexico, the era of the *Porfiriato* (1876–1910), with its emphasis on progress through industrialization, paved the way for middle-class women to enter the professions, but it also brought countless women into textile factories, railroads, and other commercial-industrial enterprises. These industries were notorious for exploiting their workers. Moreover, industrialization also meant internal migrations and urbanization. According to Macías, the numbers of women who came to the cities and became domestic servants or prostitutes rose dramatically. In 1895, the Mexican population reached 12.7 million. Of these over 275,000 were domestic servants. By 1907 Mexico City had twice as many prostitutes as Paris, even though the former contained one-fifth the population. Moreover, 30 percent of Mexican mothers were single parents, while 80 percent of the adult population lived in consensual unions. Women not legally wed were considered to be more vulnerable to the vicissitudes of life. This "immoral" situation concerned elite women, who often saw themselves as the guardians of the nation's moral and social fabric. In the journal *La mujer mexicana,* published in Mexico from 1904 to 1908, Professor Esther Huidobro de Azúa lamented, "Unless educated women come to their aid, many such women would swell the already large ranks of prostitutes" (quoted in Macías 1983: 14).

Increasing numbers of women and children in the work force parallelled the growth of factories in most urban areas. This translated into urgent preoccupation over the administration of women's earnings and property, exploitation, unemployment, and decent wage scales, particularly for female heads of households. In many countries socialist or anarchist workers' groups had already begun to advocate equality before the law and protective legislation to ensure justice for women in the work force. Thus, working-class women responded to feminism as part of a broader concept of social justice and personal freedom. Rather than stressing perceived contradictions, working women appeared to interpret compatibility between feminist ideology and workers' goals. To be sure, the vast majority of sources present the situation from the viewpoint of the educated elite. We cannot be sure to what extent working women perceived agreement between feminist ideology and workers' goals.

The experience of working women in Puerto Rico illustrates some of the major dynamics of incorporating female labor into industrial work. Puerto Rico underwent a rapid shift from an economy organized around *hacienda* agriculture to a capitalist system following the United States takeover in 1898. In 1899 a striking 91 percent of employed women worked as domestic servants, seamstresses, cooks, or laundresses on the haciendas. Between 1899 and 1910 the number of employed women increased by 61.2 percent, largely in response to the new organization of the work force, while the corresponding increase in male employment was only 17.7 percent (Rivera 1986). By the 1930s women laborers were clustered in three sectors: the tobacco industry, needlework, and domestic service. Over the course of the first three decades of the twentieth century, diverse ideologies about female labor force participation had a decided influence on women's work-force experience in Puerto Rico.

Opinions about women's salaried employment ran the gamut from assertions that women's rightful place was in the home, to the recognition that their work was necessary, to endorsements of increased female employment as advancement for the individual and the nation. Interestingly, Catholic clergymen and male anarchists both supported the ideology of domesticity, although for different reasons. The

Church sought to maintain the economic and political status quo, including the natural division of labor and hierarchical authority within society and the family. The rhetoric of home and hearth was used by some anarchists to condemn female paid employment, which threatened male wages, and indeed employment stability, by providing a cheaper pool of labor.

In Puerto Rico, the labor press focused attention on pragmatic details, such as how to prevent women from exercising a downward influence on male wages. One solution was to unionize women. The Federación Libre de Trabajadores urged more women to unionize and struggle for their rights.

Organized groups of women workers had formed before the turn of the century. By 1901, in the newspaper *Pán del pobre* (Workers' Bread) Puerto Rican Josefa Maldonado appealed to other workers to fight for equal pay. As early as the 1910s, unions such as La unión de damas de Puerta de Tierra (Women's Union of Puerta de Tierra), La unión de escogedoras de café (Coffee Pickers' Union), and La unión de obreras domésticas de Ponce (Domestic Workers' Union) strove for recognition and collective bargaining. Many of these groups unfurled the banner for women's rights, and, since most were affiliated with the Puerto Rican Socialist Party, political gains for women were also defended (Silvestrini 1986). In 1907, Gregoria Molina, president of a ladies' union chapter, urged women to form unions as a weapon for the workers' struggle. She reported that women were no longer timid beings tied to their homes but rather the vanguard of the workers' army in the war against oppression.

Between 1911 and 1916, the Puerto Rican socialist and union organizer Luisa Capetillo agitated for emancipation for women and improvement of working-class conditions in the pages of her publication, *Ensayos literarios, Mi opinión sobre las libertades, derechos de la mujer como compañera, madre y ser independiente.* Capetillo denounced the double standard as well as those state and religious institutions responsible for over-burdening the working class. Capetillo incorporated class analysis into her feminist perspectives and went further than most in her discourse on social motherhood by criticizing class-based attitudes and middle-class women's abuse of the poor.

For the most part, middle-class women throughout Latin America as well as the Hispanic Caribbean reflected moderate thinking focusing on moralistic and legal methods to improve the conditions of the poor. They seldom invited working-class women into their ranks, arguing that until the latter became respectable, decent, or proper women the needs of the working-class or the poor could only be responded to through philanthropic, charitable works. The predominant attitude among the middle class was that women were expected to remain at home, even though their own professional and political activities took them away from the familial hearth. Work was unfeminine and women were not meant to work for wages.

The Cuban socialist Ofelia Domínguez Navarro shared Capetillo's sentiments. Under her direction the Alianza nacional feminista (National Feminist Alliance) attempted to include women of all classes. However, like their counterparts throughout the hemisphere, the Cuban feminist movement was also predominantly middle class. The average feminist was a wife, a mother, and a professional. Seventy percent of the feminist leadership was married to wealthy men, employed three to seven servants, and had 2.6 children as opposed to 4.5 in the average Cuban family. Thus, their emphasis, in addition to advancing the rights of women, was understandably the preservation of home and family according to their standards (Stoner 1987b).

Workers' unions and organizations were critical instruments for more accurately articulating the needs, issues, and concerns of working-class women. As early as 1880, strikes led by organized women workers in the tobacco and textile industries were already taking place in Mexico. In general, Mexican unions demanded higher salaries and improved working conditions in the factories. By 1905 the goal of numerous workers' groups, such as the Hijas de Anahuac (Daughters of Anahuac), which organized women in the textile industry, included minimum wages and an eight-hour day. Such groups ultimately fought against the government of Porfirio Díaz in 1910 and in the revolution that ensued. Their concerns were ultimately recognized and addressed in various measures by the post-revolutionary government.

Even in the newspapers of the workers' organizations, contradictions sometimes appeared regarding working women. Such newspapers as *El socialista, La internacional,* and *La comuna* denounced the oppression of women and defended their right to work, but they, too, were known to publish articles that connected women's oppression to their female nature (Towner 1979). In Chile, working-class women addressed key issues of wage earnings and exploitation in their organizations long before university graduates discussed the tenets of women's liberation in 1915 (Lavrin 1986a). Such journals as *La alborada* and *La palanca* aligned themselves with working-class interests and feminist ideals. By the decade of the thirties the Argentine Socialist Party's women's journal, *Nuestra causa,* along with others like the Chilean *El mercurio* and *La mujer nueva,* reiterated the sentiments of the earlier publications when they once again stressed the conditions of working-class women and the need for protective legislation.

Whether the impetus came from feminist groups or workers' organizations, agreement existed on the need to improve the status of women.

Political Action and Electoral Participation

Following the First World War, feminists broadened their agenda to include the vote in the belief that social change would only be achieved if women were politically empowered. "Winning the vote," as Lynn Stoner surmised, "depended upon three conditions: a crisis in democratic rule; the organization of feminist groups; and the involvement of feminists in national struggles for political order" (Stoner 1987a: 108). Past experience in the feminist movement with socialist, anarchist, and workers' organizations had paved the way for mobilizing women around common interests and raised levels of awareness about the effectiveness of group pressure. Moreover, the participation of women across class and color lines in the Mexican (1910) and Bolivian (1952) revolutions, among other similar causes, reinforced women's recognition of the dismal reality that they were still subordinate in spite of the limited advancements they had achieved.

The right to vote was seen as an important step in combating women's continued legal and social disadvantages. However, opposition to female suffrage remained formidable. In countries like Mexico that had experienced violent confrontations between church and state, it was feared that women would be unduly influenced by the Catholic Church in their political decisions. In some nations, the very idea that women were capable of reaching decisions on national affairs was difficult to accept. Still others judged women to be politically astute and quite capable of independent political action but harbored concerns that enfranchised women would support conservative policies, as they had done in Spain's second republic (Macías 1983; Lavrin 1986a). Opponents of female suffrage often argued that politics was a masculine activity in which women, because of their very nature, should not be allowed to participate.

Among the earliest Caribbean countries to grant the vote to women, Cuba (1934) and Puerto Rico (1932) generated suffrage movements similar to those of other Latin American nations, even though both islands were heavily controlled by U.S. economic and political interests. Puerto Rico was ruled directly as an American colony during this period, while Cuba endured the earliest in a series of United States–supported independent but weak and corrupt governments. By 1930 President Gerardo Machado exercised oppressive control over Cuba, but mounting opposition to his regime included university students, intellectuals, Communists, labor unions, and feminists. Until then, the Cuban feminist movement had been divided between moderates and radicals, split over the issues of illegitimacy and unwed motherhood. However, the Cuban Committee for the Defense of Women's Suffrage, directed by Pilar Jorge de Tella and Ofelia Domínguez Navarro, united all feminists in 1928, regardless of political orientation. The catalyst for unity developed when President Machado, in an attempt to buttress an eroding electoral base, promised but then rejected the idea of universal suffrage. His ouster from office in 1933, uniformly supported by feminist groups, cleared the way for granting suffrage in the next administration (Stoner 1987b).

Women secured the vote in Puerto Rico in 1932. In spite of the fact that feminism as a movement had become diffuse, 113 women, among the first to hold public office in Latin American and the Caribbean, were elected to the municipal councils in following elections. The first woman to be elected to the island's House of Representatives was María Luisa Arcelay-Rosa. The owner of a needlework factory in Mayagüez, Arcelay-Rosa was among the earliest proponents of a day-care system, improved working conditions, and progressive managerial techniques. By 1936, María Martínez de Pérez Almiroty was elected to the Senate, initiating a consistent electoral female representation which continues to the present. On the municipal level, the election of the internationally known Felisa Rincón de Guatier as mayor of San Juan from 1948 to 1968 was but one example of the many women elected to that post in municipalities throughout the island. In a period of thirty years, thirty-nine Puerto Rican towns or *municipios* out of a total of seventy-seven elected women mayors.

Also granted the vote in 1932, Brazilian women built on the achievements of nineteenth- and early twentieth-century feminist pioneers, but unlike their predecessors, who struggled for substantive changes for all women, they merely demanded some of the rights reserved for men of their own class. Some made use of the vote, but the majority of Brazilian women did not. Excluded from leadership positions, often because of prejudices regarding the role of women in public life, many remained behind the scenes of a male-dominated society.

Argentinian women were granted the vote in 1947, one year after General Juan D. Perón was elected to office. Between 1911 and 1946, fifteen separate bills favoring women's suffrage had been defeated by a conservative-dominated Senate. Perón supported yet another bill, but this one was overwhelmingly approved.

Peronismo was a populist movement with an ideology that emphasized the dignity of workers, including women, who through their work and home life contributed to Argentine development. Although other women worked in the informal sector, by mid-century women's participation in the formal labor force had dropped to 20 percent of salaried workers in all of Argentina. They constituted over half of the country's textile, garment, and chemical workers. In 1944, before the Peronist government came into power, the first special women's agency, the Division of Labor and Assistance, was established (Navarro 1985). This agency took on the responsibility of proposing legislation affecting women. Subsequent legislation prohibited piecework in any industry, and the principle of equal pay for equal work was established in many others.

Perón's years in office were strongly influenced by his wife and political partner, Eva Perón. A dynamic and charismatic figure, Evita (as she was affectionately known throughout the country) provided a critical conduit between the people and Juan Perón. Revered by the Argentine people for her common touch, Evita was not formally part of Peron's government and never held an elected post, but nonetheless she exerted a great deal of social and political influence. She served as the president's liaison with labor, headed the Eva Perón Foundation, and presided over the Peronist Women's Party. Under her auspices centers were formed in poor and working-class districts—*unidades básicas*—party organizations which extolled Peronist ideology. They created day-care centers; provided a meeting place for women; supplied free legal and medical care; offered language skills, painting, and sewing classes; hosted lectures and conferences; and mounted annual exhibitions focusing on women's work. In time, these units were institutionalized and absorbed into the Peronist Women's Party under the banner and direct leadership of Eva Perón.

A separate party for women was a strategic political move because it provided a forum where women acquired individual political expertise and gave them a sense of involvement. Although the platform of the Peronist Women's Party rested on blind devotion, loyalty, and confidence in Perón, Evita's organization was "entirely separate from its male equivalent" (Fraser and Navarro 1980: 107). Marysa Navarro points out that by 1952 the party had 500,000 members and

3,600 headquarters. In the next elections the Peronist Women's Party increased Perón's majority, giving him 62.5 percent of the new women's vote (Fraser and Navarro 1980: 108). Of the 3,816,460 women who cast votes in this election, 2,991,558, or 63.9 percent, did so for the Peronist ticket (Navarro 1983).

To be sure, contradictions existed within the Argentine political structure, for women did not transcend their definition as the "second sex," according to Hollander (1979). Peronist ideology perpetuated the concept of women as innately different from men: more peaceful and loving—a disposition necessary for the national happiness and welfare. It was precisely for this reason that suffrage was necessary, argued the Peronists. In the elections of 1951, all elected female candidates were *Peronistas*. However, Alicia Moreau de Justo contends that, although in working-class districts of Buenos Aires a large percentage of women supported the *Peronistas,* in upper-middle-class districts the female vote favored the Liberal Radicals. Moreau opines, therefore, that women voted more from a sense of class rather than in gratitude for the suffrage law (Hollander 1979).

In Mexico, advocates of women's suffrage stressed the example of the *soldaderas* (women soldiers) and their contributions to the formation of the revolutionary state as a significant reason for granting the vote, but universal suffrage was not conceded until 1958. Women's role in the Mexican Revolution of 1910 was both central and peripheral. As they had done in previous conflicts, women participated as camp followers, journalists, propagandists, and political activists. Some also participated against their will, for it was not unusual for women to be forced into grinding corn and making tortillas for the armies. For their services some received government pensions; most did not.

The *soldaderas* were literally part of the Mexican army, yet their role was traditional by its very nature. The Mexican *soldadera*, observed John Reed, followed her man when he left home and joined the army. If he died, she became another soldier's *compañera* (Reed 1982). The *soldadera* experience emerges further in the commentary of a United States diplomat's wife:

A thick and heartbreaking book could be written upon the soldadera—the heroic woman who accompanies the army, carrying in addition to her baby, any other mortal possession, such as a kettle, basket, goat, blanket, parrot, fruit and the like. These women are the only visible commissariat for the soldiers: they accompany them in their marches; they forage for them and they cook for them; they nurse them, bury them; they receive their money when it is paid.

All this they do and keep up with the march of the army, besides
rendering any other service the male may require. (quoted in Gross
and Bingham 1985: 48)

As camp followers, their primary concern was to provide for their
men in battle, but *soldaderas,* like the famous Zapatista La Coronela,
were also known to bear arms and participate in actual fighting. Ironically, the *soldadera,* who demonstrated a traditional aspect of wom-
en's service to the nation, became an essential part of the campaign
to gain suffrage.

Between 1929, when Ecuadorean women became enfranchised,
and 1961, when suffrage was granted in Paraguay, the right to vote
was secured for women throughout Latin America and the Hispanic
Caribbean. This political victory, however, did not guarantee wom-
en's full integration, equality, or participation in the affairs of their
nations. Nine countries, including Mexico, Bolivia, and Colombia, extended the franchise in the decade of the fifties, but opposition to
women's electoral participation or running for public office remained
high. Some authoritarian heads of state, such as Rafael Trujillo of the
Dominican Republic and Manuel Odría of Peru, extended the vote in
an effort to enhance their own political image. Indeed, the general
inertia in incorporating women into the political arena, in part responsible for their limited present-day performance at the ballot box,
has also resulted in their casting the decisive vote in critical elections.
Such was the case for Perón in Argentina and Allesandri in Chile.

Socio-Cultural and Political Change

The legal and, to a lesser extent, economic status of women improved
somewhat by the mid-twentieth century as they began to use the
ballot and hold electoral or appointive office. They entered the work
force, universities, professions, and businesses in greater numbers.
Notable women were appointed to public office. Chilean Nobel Laureate Gabriela Mistral, for example, served as special ambassador to
the League of Nations and the United Nations; the Mexican writer
Rosario Castellanos and Carmen Naranjo of Costa Rica were ambas-
sadors to Israel. In some countries, Brazil and Argentina for example,
professional women outnumbered men; but in decision-making and
positions of responsibility, the ratios were reversed. In the arenas of
family relationships, divorce, the double standard, and work, progress
was less evident. For the most part, entrance into the work force did
not redefine traditional gender relations within the family and society. Throughout the continent, changes in the laws affecting women

proceeded slowly. In Argentina, for example, the *patria potestas* was not extended to women until 1985. In Mexico, as another case in point, it can still be said that "[t]he Mexican family is founded upon two fundamental propositions: (a) the unquestioned and absolute supremacy of the father and (b) the necessary and absolute self-sacrifice of the mother" (quoted in Keen and Wasserman 1984: 481). With some exceptions, this commentary describes many Latin American societies today.

However, the socialist nations of Cuba and Nicaragua have taken giant strides toward abolishing gender discrimination in law and practice. In 1960 the Federation of Cuban Women was founded as the vehicle through which women would be integrated into every facet of the revolutionary process within the general framework of the nation's developmental policies. An important outcome of the Cuban Revolution was the emphasis placed on achieving an egalitarian and collectivist society. Encouraged to move toward total integration, women's specific goals were articulated in a manner that coincided or overlapped with national priorities. Ideally, the combination of government policies and women's aspirations would produce substantive changes, but in many cases the latter's goals were out-voted. As Max Azicri observed:

> Hence rather than pursuing goals on the basis of a status achievement orientation and hard core individualism of a self-seeking feminist ideology as their counterparts in the United States would do, Cuban women are struggling, seeking full political participation and real social equality along with and within the parameters established by the government. (Azicri 1979: 3)

Inherent in this perspective was the belief that to bring about full social equality and massive political participation, all men and women were obliged to share in nation building. The rewards would accrue to themselves and, more importantly, to future generations. Although the Federation of Cuban Women originated under government mandate, it emerged as a distinct and effective organism for women's mobilization. It successfully articulated women's aspirations to the revolutionary government while simultaneously communicating state policies and programs to the nation's women. The basic tenets that defined the role of women in the state apparatus were implemented through the establishment of educational and health programs, Children's Circles, Literacy Brigades, women's militia, Women's Improvement Plan, schools for directors of Children's Circles, the Ana Betancourt School for Peasant Girls, and schools for Children's Circle Workers. Fourteen years after its inception, the Federation represented 54 percent of the total female population.

Full integration, however, was far from complete. In 1974, the year of the Federation's Second Congress, Castro addressed this issue when he said that "there remains a certain discrimination against women. It is very real, and the Revolution is fighting it . . . (it) undoubtedly will be a long struggle" (Azicri 1979: 11). In an attempt to reduce gender discrimination the Family Code was introduced in 1976. This legislation mandated the division of household labor and childcare between men and women (Randall 1981).

Yet limiting factors—a combination of external and internal social structures including a lack of jobs, boarding schools, and daycare, coupled with persistent traditional concepts and prejudices regarding women's place—continued to inhibit full integration. In the work force, men were still preferred to women. Women were thought to be unreliable because of their maternal duties, and childcare fell heavily upon female shoulders, although the Cuban Constitution stated in Article 43 that women had the same rights as men in the economic, political, and social fields as well as in the family.

Gender issues preoccupied the committees charged with institutionalizing the revolution. Those areas where sexual exploitation was most rampant, such as domestic service and prostitution, were targeted for reform through education and sound economic programs. Many women who came through these programs became productive members of the revolutionary society. They succeeded in securing employment and played active roles in community committees.

For Cuban women social change was initiated following the actual revolution, within the framework of newly created government policies. Because changes were imposed from above, Cuban society was often reluctant to accept transformation, and conflicts of interest between women's true aspirations and government ideals were not infrequent. In Nicaragua, however, women were integral to the process of social transformation from the inception of the revolution. In both rural and urban areas, women undermined Anastasio Somoza's forces by providing food and sustenance for the rebels, serving as spies, and organizing communication networks. Women assumed high-ranking positions in the rebel army and, following the Sandinista victory in 1979, were incorporated at every level of the new government. By 1988, the Office on Women shared space with that of the president. Women's organizations propelled literacy, nutrition, hygiene, and preventative medicine brigades. However, in 1990, the revolutionary political party lost to the opposing conservative coalition led, ironically, by a woman and former supporter, Violeta Barrios de Chamorro, supporting a right-wing platform that marginalized women's equality and liberation. The Chamorro government jeopardized many of the revolutionary gains. The impact of the twenty-year effort to forge a popular and revolutionary women's movement in Nicaraguan society remains to be seen. Nonetheless, Stoltz Chinchilla argues, while Nicaragua experiences a rapidly deteriorating economy, debt, and political insecurity, "the revolution has left Nicaragua with a unique political culture that continues to influence public policies and social movements" (Stoltz Chinchilla 1995: 264).

Women as Activists

By the decade of the seventies women's potential impact on both right- and left-wing political issues became apparent both through the mobilization of working- and middle-class housewives in protest of repressive or unpopular governments and through the resurgence of women as significant literary figures. Conservative women mobilized in the 1964 "Marches of the Family, with God for Liberty," a prelude to the Brazilian coup that ushered in two decades of military rule. In Chile, right-wing women's groups organized to protest the government of Salvador Allende in 1974 (Mattelart 1980). This contingent denounced disruptive economic conditions spurred by the new political order. Serious rationing and the fear that traditional values were eroding motivated women to take their concerns to the streets, the media, and the home in well-orchestrated protests. *El poder femenino* was cited by more than one scholar as a harbinger to the fall of Allende's socialist government. But Pinochet's Chile has also elicited fierce response from women, particularly in protest of the *desaparecidos*—"the disappeared" or missing persons—and the abuse of human rights. The *arpilleristas,* composed predominantly of women, formed one such venue for protest. The Catholic Church sponsored the Vicariate of Solidarity, which in turn created the *arpilleras* to aid the relatives of missing persons. Born in the spirit of resistance, the *arpilleras* are tapestry-like, artistic wall hangings in which scraps of material are adhered to a broader backing cloth. The themes of each work convey the stories of torture, missing persons, or general oppression that grip the nation (Agosín and Scott 1987).

Irma Muller, a Chilean mother who protested against the repressive government, belongs to the Association of Relatives of Detained-Missing Persons. Its activities include demanding information on the whereabouts of approximately ten thousand persons who disappeared between 1973 and 1983. She articulates her commitment: "The best memorial I can give my son is to take up his standard and fight, and in a way that is what I've done. I am an active member of the Association . . . and have been an officer in that same organization. I make *arpilleras* and use the embroideries as a method of denouncing the human-rights abuses, and this I have done practically from the moment my son disappeared" (Agosín and Scott 1987: 214).

In Brazil, Chile, Guatemala, and Argentina, groups such as Muller's monitor and bear silent witness to the abduction and terrorism directed against student protesters and other dissenters, among others. While grandmothers and the Mothers of the Plaza de Mayo keep constant vigil in gathering and disseminating vital information on the disappeared, others seek to sway public opinion through their writings.

The image of the writer as activist is well ingrained in the history and traditions of Latin America, but for women their achievements came at the cost of great energy and frustration. Works such as *The Diary of Helena Morley* and autobiographical novels such as Rachel de Queiroz's *The Three Marías* testify to the status and role of gifted women who dared to be ambitious. The former documents the nineteenth-century rural childhood of a wealthy landowner's daughter. It provides rare glimpses into the daily experiences of family life from a woman's perspective. Some writers—for example, the Peruvian Clorinda Matto de Turner (1852–1909) and the Chilean Nobel Laureate Gabriela Mistral (1889–1957)—achieved recognition beyond their national boundaries. For others the decision to write barely elicited support within their own families. Argentine publisher and writer Victoria Ocampo recalls, "My parents were as afraid for me of the road that I proposed to follow, as they would have been for a son—intent on exploring a country of cannibals" (quoted in Gross and Bingham 1985: 41).

The evolution of Latin American literature since the sixties is characterized by a move to a universal and creative language: the use of fantasy to challenge the landscape of Latin American reality, and an innovative synthesis of literary traditions. These features combine to inspire women to take their rightful place in the literary arena (Meyer and Fernández-Olmos 1983). Within this spirit of change, women write from a female perspective that includes social criticism and protest against political and gender restrictions. Relatively few reject their native countries or seek emigration as a viable solution. All view the writer as a person of grave responsibilities.

Silvina Bullrich focuses on the problems of Argentina in her novel *Reunión de directorio.* She presents the nation as an island, alienated from the rest of the world. Revolutions effect no change and serve only to perpetuate the lack of concern on the part of the people. In the very popular *Bodas de cristal,* she captures the essence of the Argentine woman's reality. Bullrich feels deeply that the obligation of the writer is to

> bear witness and in order to do this he should be present. There are people who never go to the cemetery because it is painful. They do not think that it hurts even more for those of us who do go. The same thing happens to me with Argentina. I cannot count myself among those who cross it off with the stroke of a pen. At times it seems that its air and earth run through my veins, mixed with my blood. I adore it and hate it. I judge it and rebel against it. That is the definition of love. I go away often. I always return. The day I don't return I will have renounced my vision as a writer. (quoted in Meyer and Fernández-Olmos 1983: 60)

The Mexican writer Elena Poniatowska also conveys the sense of responsibility to the nation in her writings. She chooses to focus on Mexican history, traditions, and revolutions. Her characters are often in conflict, struggling against imposed gender roles, physical handicaps, class and racial discrimination, and—severest of all—poverty. Her sense of justice is not limited to her nation, but rather encompasses all of the Latin American world.

> Although these disappeared are not writers, among the fundamental tasks of the writer is that of giving voice to those who have none, to speak for those whose rights—their rights as human beings—have been destroyed. . . . We can agree or disagree with the politics of the disappeared; what we cannot do is stop raising our voices in protest against the infamy to which they are subjected. (quoted in Meyer and Fernández-Olmos 1983: 74)

Among the contemporary writers are many who experienced repression and exile in the formation of their political consciousness. Gioconda Belli sharpened her political wit as a university student under the Somoza régime in Nicaragua. Many of her poems are revolutionary, epitaphs to the fallen heroes of the struggles.

> The time that has passed since I have seen a blue sky
> with its heavy clouds of raw cotton
> knows that the pain of exile
> has made cypresses flower in my body.

> I grieve at the memory of damp earth,
> the daily reading of the newspaper
> that says that more atrocities
> happen each day,
> that friends fall prisoners and die
> that peasants disappear
> as if swallowed by the mountain.
> (quoted in Meyer and Fernández-Olmos 1983: 8)

Isabel Allende, on the other hand, does not consider herself a political writer but admits that politics play a key role in any Latin American novel. "After all," she remarks, "we have a few hundred years of exploitation and brutality. Not one country has been left out from that exploitation—whether by the Spanish, English or American" (*New York Times*, February 4, 1988).

Others, among whom Alfonsina Storni (1892–1938) of Argentina and Julia de Burgos (1917–54) of Puerto Rico are good examples, focus on their experiences as women. Storni was born in Switzerland but raised in Argentina. A single parent, Storni maintained her career as a teacher while writing poetry. Through her work she spoke out against women's subordinate social role. Burgos was also a teacher; she began her life in Puerto Rico but died penniless and unknown in the streets of New York, a victim of the migration experience. Her verses cover a wide range of experiences, for she wrote against the social and political conventions of her day. Burgos favored independence for Puerto Rico and defended the rights of workers, blacks, and women. In her search for personal authenticity, her poetry reflects the fine line between the public and private person.

> I wanted to be like men wanted me to be;
> an attempt at life, a hide and seek game with myself.
> But I was made of todays,
> and my feet planted over the promised land
> could not stand to walk backwards,
> and went forward, forward . . .
> ("I Was My Own Path," quoted in Acosta-Belén 1986: 13)

Through their works, Storni and Burgos hoped to change the political and social landscape by articulating the sentiments and attitudes of women in a male-dominated society.

The harsh reality of daily existence produced another type of activist, whose complex, frequently urban experiences are conveyed in the testimonials. It is against this diverse hemispheric climate that testimonies emerge and serve to individualize the female condition in Latin America. In *Child of the Dark* (1962), Carolina Maria de Jesus illustrates the meaning of survival in the squatter settlements of modern-day São Paulo. Her diary, edited and published by a Brazilian journalist, describes the gnawing hunger of body and mind that circumscribes the daily existence of this mother of three. In her testimony *Let Me Speak!* (1978), Domitila Barrios de Chungara aspires to bring about substantive change in the conditions of life for the miners and peasants of Bolivia. This work bears much in common with the struggles of de Jesus and with the Guatemalan Rigoberta Menchú, winner of the 1992 Nobel Peace Prize. Finally, the political actions and awareness of the *guerrillista* Menchú (1984) point to a constellation of unresolved conflicts between Indian and non-Indian, male and female, democracy or dictatorship in the daily lives of the rural and urban poor. Works such as these demonstrate the complexity of the dynamics between the lives of ordinary people and social change in today's world. These political writings convey a vivid portrait of women's place within a Latin American reality that can no longer be ignored.

TOWARD THE MILLENNIUM

Throughout the last half of the twentieth century, governments have viewed intensive industrialization as the panacea for Latin American progress, but, more often than not, the result has been growth without development. Rising inflation, poverty, external debts, economic instability, and the stresses of being unable to meet the aspirations of a growing population have not been adequately addressed. Structural and institutional changes have not accompanied industrialization, and the gap between rich and poor has widened in spite of the steady growth of a middle class. Some nations elected to meet the challenges of modernization through repression. Dictatorships existed in three-fourths of the governments of Latin America in 1975, but renewed democratization and a move toward privatization have dominated the eighties and nineties. Both immigration, particularly to the United States, and the emergence of a transnational industry and work force in which women are heavily represented—*maquiladoras*—have become characteristic of changing trends. Family structure and gender roles have experienced striking transformations as a result of shifting income-earning strategies in a global economy. And the notion of women working outside the home is widely accepted even as male work-force participation decreases.

Along with industrialization, family planning and population control were also pursued as progressive solutions to national problems. The case of Puerto Rico, where the use of sterilization predominated as a means to control population, cannot be underestimated with regard to the incorporation of women into an international work force. "At least 35 percent of Puerto Rican women of reproductive age are sterilized, a percentage higher than in the United States where it stands at 30 percent," states Acosta-Belén (Acosta-Belén 1986: 14). Between 1950 and the late 1970s the total fertility rate in the island was reduced by 48 percent. Sterilization was sanctioned by a system that failed to promote other contraceptive means at a time when female employment shifted from the home to the factory. A relationship clearly exists between sterilization and the incorporation of working women into growing economies, between powerlessness and empowerment, between profit and exploitation.

Puerto Rico continues to serve as a good example of the effects of economic trends and policies on women's changing roles and fortunes. The plan to modernize the island in the fifties centered on the industrialization of the island's economy and incorporated women into the labor force in record numbers. Industrial development included offering tax incentives to private corporations, subsidizing space and buildings, renovating the island's infrastructure, supplying a large pool of cheap labor, and encouraging the emigration of a quarter of the island's population who could not be incorporated into the new economic order. Variations of the Puerto Rican experience, hailed as a model for development, were exported throughout Third World countries (Rios 1995). The Puerto Rican experience served as prelude to the hemispheric international division of labor as developing nations throughout the Caribbean basin, Mexico, and Central and South America are today the sites for export processing zones and multinational manufacturing—*maquilas.*

Much of the increase in the numbers of working women throughout the Caribbean and Latin America is tied to North American trends and policies that include industrial outsourcing or offshore production. Although women have limited control over resources and earn lower wages than their male counterparts, their employment—either in *maquiladoras* at the export zone, or in subcontracting industries, or as paid piece workers in the home—is critical to the expansion of transnational corporations (Bose and Acosta-Belén 1995). Through subcontracting, export processing zones employ women either directly or indirectly. Fernández Kelly argues that *maquiladoras* on the United States–Mexico border encourage the employment of young female workers. "Women's alternatives are not substantially improved because these companies offer no job security, provide minimal possibilities for advancement, and frequently expose workers to hazardous conditions" (Fernández Kelly and Sassen 1995). As companies transfer their sites of operation to more profitable regions, workers' lives are disrupted, forcing members to migrate in search of economic survival.

According to current research, the notion of women's work has also undergone transformation, for it is now conceptualized as a continuum—from formal wage labor, to informal paid workers, to household labor (Bose and Acosta-Belén 1995). As women enter the work force in greater numbers and the employment of men declines, multiple income strategies are being substituted for the single male breadwinner. Household members pool wages, cash, subsistence products, and unpaid labor. Further study of all of these issues is needed to fully understand and appreciate the varying effects of economic development in a postmodern period on all women and their interconnections with one another.

In social and political movements, women have been highly visible in the processes of democratization. Some gains have been made. In the last ten years Brazilian law facilitated divorce, provided maternity leaves, and lifted the ban on abortion. Argentina also legalized divorce and modified the *patria potestas*, giving women greater control over their children, custody issues, and family matters. In recent times women have confronted the state directly on issues that affect them or their families. Safa notes that women are forging new relations with the state, based not on subordination, control, and dependence but on rights, autonomy, and equality (1995). The issues that unite women regardless of class are many: they struggle for reproductive rights, health care, education, basic services, and transportation. More than ever before poor women are participating in social movements. Working across class lines, often with middle-class feminists, they have moved toward greater union participation, establishing day-care centers, grassroots cooperatives, and other necessities to ameliorate life in squatter settlements. An example of the strides taken by women in terms of their identity and affirmation as women appears in Safa. She translates a citation from a Brazilian woman, leader of a neighborhood organization:

> Within the women's movement, as a woman, I discovered myself as a person, as a human being. I had not discovered that the woman always was oppressed. But it never came to my mind that the woman was oppressed, although she had rights. The woman had to obey because she was a woman. It was in the women's movement that I

came to identify myself as a woman and to understand the rights I have as a woman, from which I have knowledge to pass on as well to other companions. (cited in Caldeira 1987: 95 96)

The words of this Brazilian community activist express an awakening to contemporary women's issues that may be as much a reflection of expanding global interconnections, mass media, and other channels of communication as it is of historical antecedents. Her perceived steps toward self-affirmation resonate at several levels with the experiences of those women who in the past challenged legal constraints, struggled for female education, advanced the causes of workers, and engaged in social reform and revolutionary movements. Powerless in patriarchal societies and state and religious systems that imposed subaltern status, women have fought for inclusion, for feminist and electoral rights. They have been at the forefront of countless contestations, particularly over women's and family issues. In all, while many continue to struggle, the strides taken toward gender equality have been impressive. Thus, the study of women's history in Latin America and the Caribbean provides us with a fuller understanding of changing women's roles over a broad period of time. It engenders a quest for connections and redefinitions across the Americas.

SOURCES

The list of works included here is far from comprehensive. It covers mostly Spanish and Portuguese Latin America because these are the areas where most of the new research has been centered. For those who wish to pursue further research, Ali (1995) and Stoner (1989) contain more extensive bibliographies, including many non-English sources.

An asterisk (*) indicates readings especially suitable for students.

Acevedo, Luz del Alba. 1992. "Industrialization and Employment: Postwar Changes in the Patterns of Women's Life in Puerto Rico." In Johnson-Odim and Strobel, *Expanding the Boundaries of Women's History.*

*Acosta-Belén, Edna. 1980. "Women in Twentieth-Century Puerto Rico." In Lopez, *The Puerto Ricans.*

*Acosta-Belén, Edna, ed. 1986. *The Puerto Rican Woman: Perspectives on Culture, History and Society.* New York: Praeger.

Agosín, Marjorie. 1987. "Metaphors of Female Political Ideology: The Cases of Chile and Argentina." *Women's Studies International Forum* 10, no. 6: 571–77.

*Agosín, Marjorie, and Nina M. Scott. 1987. "Írma Muller." In Beezly and Ewell, *The Human Tradition in Latin America.*

Aguero, F., ed. 1998. *Fault Lines of Democracy in Post-transition Latin America.* Coral Gables: North-South Center.

Ali, Kecia. 1995. "The Historiography of Women in Modern Latin America: An Overview and Bibliography of the Recent Literature." Duke–University of North Carolina Program in Latin American Studies Working Paper Series, no. 18. Durham, N.C.: Duke University.

Alterman Blay, Eva. 1979. "The Political Participation of Women in Brazil: Female Mayors." *Signs* 5: 42–59.

Altman, Ida. 1989. *Emigrants and Society: Extremadura and America in the Sixteenth Century.* Berkeley and Los Angeles: University of California Press.

Anton, Ferdinand. 1973. *La mujer en la América Antigua.* Mexico: Editorial Extemporaneos.

Archetti, Eduardo. 1984. "Rural Families and Demographic Behaviour: Some

Latin American Analogies." *Comparative Studies in Society and History* 25: 251–79.

Arenal, Electa, and Stacey Schlau. 1989. *Untold Sisters: Hispanic Nuns in Their Own Works.* Albuquerque: University of New Mexico Press.

*Arrom, Silvia Marina. 1978. "Marriage Patterns in Mexico City, 1811." *Journal of Family History* 3, no. 4: 376–91.

———. 1981. "Cambios en la condición jurídica de la mujer mexicana durante el siglo XIX." *Memoria del II Congreso de Historia del Derecho.* Mexico City: UNAM.

*———. 1985a. "Changes in Mexican Family Law in the Nineteenth Century: The Civil Codes of 1870 and 1884." *Journal of Family History* 10, no. 3: 306–17.

*———. 1985b. *The Women of Mexico City, 1790–1857.* Stanford, Calif.: Stanford University Press.

Aviel, JoAnn. 1974. "Changing the Political Role of Women: A Costa Rican Case Study." In Jaquette, *Women in Politics.*

Azicri, Max. 1979. "Women's Development Through Revolutionary Mobilization: A Study of the Federation of Cuban Women." *International Journal of Women's Studies* 2: 27–50.

Azize, Lourdes. 1977. "Women in the Informal Labor Sector: The Case of Mexico City." *Signs* 3, no. 1: 25–37.

Azize, Yamila. 1979. *Luchas de la mujer en Puerto Rico: 1898–1919.* San Juan, Puerto Rico: Fraficor.

Babb, Florence E. 1989. *Between Field and Cooking Pot: The Political Economy of Marketwomen in Peru.* Austin: University of Texas Press.

Bailey, Samuel L. 1980. "Marriage Patterns and Immigrant Assimilation in Buenos Aires, 1882–1923." *Hispanic American Research Review* 60, no. 1: 32–48.

Bakewell, Peter J., John J. Johnson, and Meredith D. Dodge, eds. 1985. *Readings in Latin American History.* Durham, N.C.: Duke University Press.

Balmori, Diana, and Robert Oppenheimer. 1979. "Family Clusters: Generational Nucleation in Nineteenth-Century Argentina and Chile." *Comparative Studies in Society and History* 21, no. 2: 136–58.

Balmori, Diana, Stuart Voss, and Miles Wortman. 1984. *Notable Family Networks in Latin America.* Chicago: University of Chicago Press.

Barnes, John. 1978. *Evita, First Lady: A Biography of Eva Perón.* New York: Grove Press.

*Barrios de Chungara, Domitila, and Moema Viezzer. 1978. *Let Me Speak!* New York: Monthly Review Press.

Basu, Amrita, ed., with the assistance of C. Elizabeth McGrory. 1995. *The Challenge of Local Feminisms: Women's Movements in Global Perspective.* Boulder, Colo.: Westview Press.

*Beckles, Hilary. 1989. *Natural Rebels: A Social History of Enslaved Black Women in Barbados.* New Brunswick, N.J.: Rutgers University Press.

*Beezly, William H., and Judith Ewell, eds. 1987. *The Human Tradition in Latin America: The Twentieth Century.* Wilmington, Del.: Scholarly Resources, Inc.

Beneria, Lourdes, and Martha Roldan. 1987. *The Crossroads of Class and Gender: Industrial Homework, Subcontracting, and Household Dynamics in Mexico City.* Chicago: University of Chicago Press.

Besse, Susan Kent. 1996. *Restructuring Patriarchy: The Modernization of Gender Inequality in Brazil, 1914–1940.* Chapel Hill: University of North Carolina Press.

Bethell, Leslie, ed. 1984. *The Cambridge History of Latin America*, Vol. 2. Cambridge, England: Cambridge University Press.

*Bilby, Kenneth, and Filomina Chioma Steady. 1981. "Black Women and Survival: A Maroon Case." In Steady, *The Black Woman Cross-Culturally*.

Bishop, Elizabeth, trans. and ed. 1977. *The Diary of Helena Morley*. New York: Ecco Press.

Borges, Dain. 1992. *The Family in Bahia, Brazil, 1870–1945*. Stanford, Calif.: Stanford University Press.

Bose, Christine E., and Edna Acosta-Belén, eds. 1995. *Women in the Latin American Development Process*. Philadelphia: Temple University Press.

*Bourque, Susan, and Barbara Kay Warren. 1981. *Women of the Andes*. Ann Arbor: University of Michigan Press.

Bowser, Frederick. 1974. *The African Slave in Colonial Peru, 1524–1650*. Stanford, Calif.: Stanford University Press.

Boxer, C. R. 1962. *The Golden Age of Brazil: 1695–1750*. Berkeley and Los Angeles: University of California Press.

Boyd-Bowman, Peter. 1973. *Patterns of Spanish Emigration to the New World (1493–1580)*. Buffalo, N.Y.: Special Studies Council on International Studies.

Bunster, Ximena, and Elsa Chaney. 1989. *Sellers and Servants: Working Women in Lima, Peru*. Granby, Mass.: Bergin and Garvey.

Burkett, Elinor. 1977. "In Dubious Sisterhood: Class and Sex in Spanish South America." *Latin American Perspectives* 4, no. 1/2: 18–26.

*———. 1978. "Indian Women and White Society: The Case of Sixteenth-Century Peru." In Lavrin, *Latin American Women*.

*Bush, Barbara. 1990. *Slave Women in Caribbean Society, 1650–1838*. Bloomington: Indiana University Press.

Butler Flores, Cornelia. 1984. "Socialist Feminism in Latin America." *Women and Politics* 4, no. 1: 69–93.

Caldeira, Teresa. 1987. "Mujeres, cotidianeidad y política." In Elizabeth Jelin, ed., *Ciudadanía e identidad: Las mujeres en los movimientos sociales latino-americanos*. Geneva: United Nations Research Institute for Social Development. 47–78.

Cano, Inés. 1982. "El movimiento feminista argentino en la década del '70." *Todo es Historia* 183: 84–93.

Carroll, Berenice, ed. 1976. *Liberating Women's History*. Urbana and Chicago: University of Illinois Press.

Chaney, Elsa. 1979. *Supermadre: Women in Politics in Latin America*. Austin: University of Texas Press.

Cherpak, Evelyn. 1978. "The Participation of Women in the Independence Movement in Gran Colombia, 1780–1930." In Lavrin, *Latin American Women*.

Ciria, Alberto. 1983. "Flesh and Fantasy: The Many Faces of Evita (and Juan Perón)." *Latin American Research Review* 18, no. 2: 150–65.

Clendinnen, Inga. 1982. "Yucatec Maya Women and the Spanish Conquest: Role and Ritual in Historical Reconstruction." *Journal of Social History* 15, no. 3: 427–42.

———. 1987. *Ambivalent Conquests: Maya and Spaniard in Yucatan, 1517–1570*. Cambridge: Cambridge University Press.

*———. 1991. *Aztecs: An Interpretation*. Cambridge, England: Cambridge University Press.

Conniff, Michael, ed. 1982. *Latin American Populism in Comparative Perspective*. Albuquerque: University of New Mexico Press.

Constenla, María I., and María Amelia Reynoso. 1980. "La mujer y la política." *Todo es Historia* 183: 69–79.

Cook, Alexandra Parma, and David Noble Cook. 1991. *Good Faith and Truthful Ignorance: A Case of Transatlantic Bigamy.* Durham: Duke University Press.

Corbiere, Emilio. 1982. "Entrevista con Alicia Moreau de Justo." *Todo es Historia* 183: 68–69.

Couturier, Edith B. 1978. "Women in a Noble Family: The Mexican Counts of Regla, 1750–1830." In Lavrin, *Latin American Women.*

———. 1979. "Dowries and Wills: A View of Women's Socioeconomic Role in Colonial Guadalajara and Puebla." *Hispanic American Historical Review* 59, no. 2: 280–304.

Crahan, Margaret, and Franklin W. Knight, eds. 1979. *Africa and the Caribbean.* Baltimore, Md.: Johns Hopkins University Press.

Craton, Michael. 1979. "Changing Patterns of Slave Families in the British West Indies." *Journal of Interdisciplinary History* 10, no. 1: 1–36.

Crespo, Alfonso. 1980. *Evita viva o muerta.* Barcelona, Spain: Fontalba.

Cross, Harry. 1978. "Living Standards in Rural Nineteenth-Century Mexico: Zacatecas, 1820–1880." *Journal of Latin American Studies,* Part 1: 1–19.

Davis, Darien J. 1995. *Slavery and Beyond: The African Impact on Latin America and the Caribbean.* Wilmington, Del.: Scholarly Resources, Inc.

Deere, Carmen D. 1979. "Changing Social Relations of Production and Peruvian Peasant Women's Work." In *Women in Latin America.*

*de Jesús, Carolina Maria. 1962. *Child of the Dark.* New York: New American Library.

De la Cruz, Sor Juana Inés. 1997. *Poems, Protest, and a Dream.* New York: Penguin Books.

*Delpar, Helen. 1989. "Soledad Román de Nuñez: A President's Wife." In Ewell and Beezley, *The Human Tradition.*

Demitropoulos, Libertad. 1981. *Eva Perón.* Buenos Aires: Centro Editor de América Latina.

Desanti, Dominique. 1972. *A Woman in Revolt: The Biography of Flora Tristan.* New York: Crown.

Díaz, Carlos Arturo. 1977. "Las mujeres de la independencia." *Revista de Historia* [Colombia] 1, no. 4: 33–41.

Díaz del Castillo, Bernal. 1956. *The Discovery and Conquest of Mexico.* New York: Grove Press.

Eckstein, Susan, ed. 1989. *Power and Popular Protest: Latin American Social Movements.* Berkeley: University of California Press.

*Escobar, Arturo, and Sonia E. Alvarez, eds. 1992. *The Making of Social Movements in Latin America: Identity, Strategy and Democracy.* Boulder, Colo.: Westview Press.

Etienne, Mona, and Eleanor Leacock, eds. 1980. *Women and Colonization: Anthropological Perspectives.* South Hadley, Mass.: Bergin and Garvey.

*Ewell, Judith, and William H. Beezley, eds. 1989. *The Human Tradition in Latin America: The Nineteenth Century.* Wilmington: Scholarly Resources, Inc.

Fariss, Nancy M. 1984. *Maya Society Under Colonial Rule: The Collective Enterprise of Survival.* Princeton, N.J.: Princeton University Press.

Feijóo, María del Carmen. 1982. "La mujer en la historia argentina." *Todo es Historia* 183: 8–17.

Fernández Kelly, P. A., and Saskia Sassen. 1995. "Recasting Women in the

Global Economy: Internationalization and Changing Definitions of Gender." In Bose and Acosta-Belén, *Women in the Latin American Development Process.*

Figueiredo, Mariza. 1983. "The Socioeconomic Role of Women Heads of Family in a Brazilian Fishing Village." *Feminist Issues* 3: 83–103.

Fonseca, Guido. 1982. *História da prostituição em São Paulo.* São Paulo: Editora Resenha Universitária.

Foppa, Alaíde. 1977. "The First Feminist Congress in Mexico, 1916." *Signs* 5, no. 1: 192–99.

*Fowler-Salamini, Ilcather, and Mary Kay Vaughan, eds. 1995. *Women of the Mexican Countryside, 1850–1990: Creating Spaces, Shaping Transitions.* Tucson: University of Arizona Press.

Franco, Jean. 1990. *Plotting Women: Gender and Representation in Mexico.* New York: Columbia University Press.

*Fraser, Nicholas, and Marysa Navarro. 1980. *Eva Perón.* New York: W. W. Norton.

Gallagher, Sister Miriam Ann, R.S.M. 1978. "The Indian Nuns of Mexico City's Monasterio de Corpus Christi, 1724–1821." In Lavrin, *Latin American Women.*

Garro, Elena. 1986. *Recollection of Things to Come.* Austin: University of Texas Press.

Gautier, Arlette. 1985. *Les soeurs de solitude.* Paris: Éditions Caribéennes.

Gerardo Pena, Devon. 1980. "Las Maquiladoras: Mexican Women and the Class Struggles in the Border Industries." *Aztlan* 11, no. 2: 159–229.

Graham, Maria Dundas. 1969. *Journal of a Voyage to Brazil and Residence There During Part of Three Years, 1821, 1822, 1823.* New York: Praeger.

Graham, Sandra Lauderdale. 1991. "Slavery's Impasse: Slave Prostitutes, Small-Time Mistresses, and the Brazilian Law of 1871." *Comparative Studies in Society and History* 33, no. 4: 669–94.

———. 1992. *House and Street: The Domestic World of Servants and Masters in Nineteenth-Century Rio de Janeiro.* Austin: University of Texas Press.

Greishaber, Erwin. 1979. "Hacienda-Indian Community Relations and Indian Acculturation." *Latin American Research Review* 14, no. 3: 107–28.

*Gross, Susan Hill, and Marjorie Wall Bingham, eds. 1985. *Women in Latin America,* Vols. I and II. St. Louis Park, Minn.: Glenhurst Publications.

*Gutiérrez, Ramón A. 1985. "Honor Ideology, Marriage Negotiation, and Class/gender Domination in New Mexico, 1690–1846." *Latin American Perspectives* 12, no. 1: 81–104.

———. 1991. *When Jesus Came, the Corn Mothers Went Away: Marriage, Sexuality, and Power in New Mexico, 1500–1846.* Stanford, Calif.: Stanford University Press.

Guy, Donna J. 1978. "The Rural Working Class in Nineteenth-Century Argentina: Forced Plantation Labor in Tucuman." *Latin American Research Review* 13, no. 1: 135–45.

———. 1981. "Women, Peonage, and Industrialization: Argentina, 1810–1914." *Latin American Research Review* 16, no. 3: 65–89.

———. 1985. "Lower-Class Families, Women, and the Law in Nineteenth-Century Argentina." *Journal of Family History* 10, no. 3: 318–22.

———. 1988. "White Slavery, Public Health, and the Socialist Position on Legalized Prostitution in Argentina, 1913–1936." *Latin American Research Review,* 23, no. 3: 60–80.

————. 1990. "Prostitution and Female Criminality in Buenos Aires, 1875–1937." In Lyman Johnson, *The Problem of Order in Changing Societies.* Albuquerque: University of New Mexico Press.

————. 1991. *Sex and Danger in Buenos Aires: Prostitution, Family and Nation in Argentina.* Lincoln: University of Nebraska Press.

*Hahner, June E. 1978. "The Nineteenth-Century Feminist Press and Women's Rights in Brazil." In Lavrin, *Latin American Women.*

————. 1979. *Women in Latin American History: Their Lives and Views.* Rev. ed., Los Angeles: University of California Latin American Center Publications.

————. 1980. "Feminism, Women's Rights, and the Suffrage Movement in Brazil, 1850–1932." *Latin American Research Review* 15, no. 1: 65–111.

————. 1990. *Emancipating the Female Sex: The Struggle for Women's Rights in Brazil, 1850–1940.* Durham, N.C.: Duke University Press.

Harris, Barbara J., and Joann McNamara, eds. 1984. *Women and the Structures of Society: Selected Research from the Fifth Berkshire Conference on the History of Women.* Durham, N.C.: Duke University Press.

Hemming, John. 1970. *The Conquest of the Incas.* New York: Harcourt Brace Jovanovich.

*Henderson, James, and Linda R. Henderson. 1978. *Ten Notable Women of Latin America.* Chicago: Nelson-Hall.

Henshall, Janet D. 1981. "Women and Small-Scale Farming in the Caribbean." In *Papers in Latin American Geography in Honor of Lucia C. Harrison.* Muncie: Conference of Latin Americanist Geographers.

Higman, B. W. 1979. "African and Creole Slave Family Patterns in Trinidad." In Crahan and Knight, *Africa and the Caribbean.*

Hoberman, Louisa Schell, and Susan Midgen Socolow. 1986. *Cities and Society in Colonial Latin America.* Albuquerque: University of New Mexico Press.

Hoberman, Louisa Schell, and Susan Midgen Socolow, eds. 1996. *The Countryside in Colonial Latin America.* Albuquerque: University of New Mexico Press.

Hollander, Nancy Caro. 1979. "Si Evita viviera . . ." In *Women in Latin America.*

*Hunefeldt, Christine. 1994. *Paying the Price of Freedom: Family and Labor among Lima's Slaves, 1800–1854.* Berkeley and Los Angeles: University of California Press.

Hunt, Eva. 1977. *The Transformation of the Hummingbird: Cultural Roots of a Zinatecan Mythical Poem.* Ithaca, N.Y.: Cornell University Press.

*James, Daniel, and John D. French, eds. 1997. *The Gendered Worlds of Latin American Women Workers: From Household and Factory to the Union Hall and Ballot Box.* Durham, N.C.: Duke University Press.

Jaquette, Jane. 1980. "Female Political Participation in Latin America." In Nash and Safa, *Sex and Class.*

————, ed. 1974. *Women in Politics.* New York: Wiley.

*————, ed. 1989. *The Women's Movement in Latin America: Feminism and the Transition to Democracy.* Boston: Unwin Hyman.

*————, ed. 1994. *The Women's Movement in Latin America: Participation and Democracy.* Boulder, Colo.: Westview Press.

Jelin, Elizabeth, ed. 1990. *Women and Social Change in Latin America.* Trans. J. Ann Zammit and Marilyn Thompson. London: Zed Books.

*Jiménez de Wagenheim, Olga. 1985. *Puerto Rico's Revolt for Independence: El Grito de Lares*. Boulder, Colo.: Westview Press.

*———. 1998. *Puerto Rico: An Interpretive History from Pre-Columbian Times to 1900*. Princeton: Markus Weiner Publishers.

Johnson, Ann Hagerman. 1978. "The Impact of Market Agriculture on Family and Household Structure in Nineteenth-Century Chile." *Hispanic American Historial Review* 58, no. 4: 625–48.

Johnson-Odim, Cheryl, and Margaret Strobel, eds. 1992. *Expanding the Boundaries of Women's History: Essays on Women in the Third World*. Bloomington: Indiana University Press.

Keen, Benjamin. 1986. *Latin American Civilization*. Boulder, Colo.: Westview Press.

Keen, Benjamin, and M. Wasserman. 1984. *A Short History of Latin America*. Boston: Houghton Mifflin.

Keremitsis, Dawn. 1984. "Latin American Women Workers in Transition: Sexual Division of the Labor Force in Mexico and Colombia in the Textile Industry." *The Americas* 40: 491–504.

Kerns, Virginia. 1989. *Women and the Ancestors: Black Carib Kinship and Ritual*. Urbana and Chicago: University of Illinois Press.

Kicza, John E. 1985. "The Role of the Family in Economic Development in Nineteenth-Century Latin America." *Journal of Family History* 10, no. 3: 235–46.

Klein, Herbert S. 1986. *African Slavery in Latin America and the Caribbean*. New York: Oxford University Press.

Knaster, Meri. 1977. *Women in Spanish America: An Annotated Bibliography from Pre-Conquest to Contemporary Times*. Boston: G. K. Hall.

Knight, Franklin W. 1978. *The Caribbean*. New York: Oxford University Press.

Kuznesof, Elizabeth A. 1980. "The Role of the Female-Headed Household in Brazilian Modernization: São Paulo, 1765–1836." *Journal of Social History* 13, no. 4: 589–613.

———. 1991. "Sexual Politics, Race and Bastard Rearing in Nineteenth Century Brazil: A Question of Culture or Power?" *Journal of Family History* 16, no. 3: 241–60.

———. 1995. "Race, Class, and Gender: A Conversation." *Colonial Latin American Review* 4, no. 1: 153–83.

Ladd, Doris M. 1976. *The Mexican Nobility at Independence, 1780–1826*. Austin, Tex.: Institute of Latin American Studies.

Landaburú, Argentino, Alfredo G. Kohn Loncarica, and Elena Pennini de Vega. 1982. "Cecilia Greirson y el Primer Congreso Femenino Internacional." *Todo es Historia* 183: 62–67.

Lau, Ana, and Carmen Ramos Escandón. 1993. *Mujeres y revolución, 1900–1917*. Mexico City: Instituto Nacional de Estudios Históricos de la Revolución Mexicana/INAH.

*Lavrin, Asunción. 1976. "Women in Convents: Their Economic and Social Role in Colonial Mexico." In Carroll, *Liberating Women's History*.

———. 1978. "In Search of the Colonial Woman in Mexico: The Seventeenth and Eighteenth Centuries." In Lavrin, *Latin American Women*.

*———. 1981. "Women in Latin American History." *History Teacher* 14: 387–400.

*———. 1983. "Women and Religion in Spanish America." In Ruether and Keller, *Women and Religion in America*.

114   Sources

*———. 1984. "Women in Spanish American Colonial Society." In Bethell, *Cambridge History of Latin America*.
———. 1986a. "Female Religious." In Hoberman and Socolow, *Cities and Society in Colonial Latin America*.
———. 1986b. "The Ideology of Feminism in the Southern Core, 1900–1940." Paper no. 169. Washington, D.C.: The Wilson Center Latin America Program.
*———. 1987. "Women, the Family and Social Change in Latin America." *World Affairs* 150, no. 2: 108–28.
*———. 1995. *Women, Feminism, and Social Change in Argentina, Chile, and Uruguay, 1890–1940*. Lincoln: University of Nebraska Press.
*Lavrin, Asunción, ed. 1978. *Latin American Women: Historical Perspectives*. Westport, Conn.: Greenwood Press.
*———. 1989. *Sexuality and Marriage in Colonial Latin America*. Lincoln: University of Nebraska Press.
Lavrin, Asunción, and Edith Couturier. 1979. "Dowries and Wills: A View of Women's Socioeconomic Role in Colonial Guadalajara and Puebla, 1640–1790." *Hispanic American Historical Review* 59, no. 2: 280–304.
León de Leal, Magdalena. 1977. *La mujer y el desarollo en Colombia*. Bogotá, Colombia: Asociación colombiana para el estudio de la población.
León-Portilla, Miguel, ed. 1980. *Native Mesoamerican Spirituality*. New York: Paulist Press.
*Lewis, Oscar, Ruth M. Lewis, and Susan M. Rigdon. 1978. *Four Women Living in the Revolution*. Urbana and Chicago: University of Illinois Press.
*———. 1978. *Neighbors Living the Revolution: An Oral History of Contemporary Cuba*. Urbana and Chicago: University of Illinois Press.
Liss, Peggy K. 1975. *Mexico Under Spain, 1521–1556: Society and the Origins of Nationality*. Chicago: University of Chicago Press.
Little, Cynthia. 1978. "Education, Philanthropy and Feminism: Components of Argentine Womanhood, 1860–1926." In Lavrin, *Latin American Women*.
Lockhart, James. 1968. *Spanish Peru, 1532–1560*. Madison: University of Wisconsin Press.
———. 1972. *The Men of Cajamarca*. Austin: University of Texas Press.
Lomnitz, Larissa. 1977. *Networks and Marginality*. New York: Academic Press.
Londono, Patricia. 1989. "Visual Images of Urban Colombian Women, 1800–1930." *SALALM Papers* 34: 99–114.
*Lopez, Adalberto, ed. 1980. *The Puerto Ricans: Their History, Culture, and Society*. New York: Schenkman.
Love, Edgar F. 1971. "Marriage Patterns of Persons of African Descent in a Colonial Mexico City Parish." *Hispanic American Historical Review* 51, no. 1: 79–91.
Lynch, John. 1973. *The Spanish American Revolutions*. London: Weidenfeld and Nicolson.
*Macías, Anna. 1980. "Women and the Mexican Revolution: 1910–1920." *The Americas* 37, no. 1: 53–81.
*———. 1983. *Against All Odds*. Westport, Conn.: Greenwood Press.
MacLachlan, Colin M., and Jaime Rodriguez. 1980. *The Forging of the Cosmic Race*. Berkeley and Los Angeles: University of California Press.
Mallon, Florencia E. 1986. "Gender and Class in the Transition to Capital-

ism: Household and Mode of Production in Central Peru." *Latin American Perspectives* 13, no. 1: 147–74.

Mannarelli, Maria Emma. 1993. *Pecados Públicos.* Lima: Ediciones Flora Tristán.

Marcos, Silvia. 1975. "La mujer en la sociedad prehispánica." *La mujer en México: Epoca prehispánica.* Mexico.

Mattoso de Queiroz, Katia. 1986. *To Be a Slave in Brasil.* New Brunswick, N.J.: Rutgers University Press.

*Martín, Luis. 1983. *Daughters of the Conquistadores: Women of the Viceroyalty of Peru.* Albuquerque: University of New Mexico Press.

*Martínez Alier, Verena. 1989. *Marriage, Class and Colour in Nineteenth-Century Cuba: A Study of Racial Attitudes and Sexual Values in a Slave Society.* London: Cambridge University Press, 1974; 2d edition, Ann Arbor: University of Michigan Press.

Masiello, Francine Rose. 1992. *Between Civilization and Barbarism: Women, Nation, and Literary Culture in Modern Argentina.* Lincoln: University of Nebraska Press.

Mathurin, Lucille. 1975. *The Rebel Woman in the British West Indies During Slavery.* Kingston: The Institute of Jamaica.

Matos-Rodriguez, Felix V., and Linda C. Delgado, eds. 1998. *Puerto Rican Women's History: New Perspectives.* Armonk, N.Y.: M. E. Sharpe.

Mattelart, Michelle. 1980. "Chile: The Feminine Version of the Coup d'État." In Nash and Safa, *Sex and Class.*

McCreery, David. 1986. "'This Life of Misery and Shame': Female Prostitution in Guatemala City, 1880–1920," *Journal of Latin American Studies,* 18, no. 2: 333–53.

McGee Deutsch, Sandra F. 1984. "Right-Wing Female Activists in Buenos Aires, 1900–1932." In Harris and McNamara, *Women and the Structures of Society.*

———. 1991. "The Catholic Church, Work, and Womanhood in Argentina, 1890–1930," *Gender and History,* 3, no. 3: 304–25 (reprinted in Yeager, *Confronting Change*).

*Menchú, Rigoberta. 1983. *I . . . Rigoberta Menchú.* Ed. Elizabeth Burgos-Debray. New York: Schocken Press.

*———. 1998. *Crossing Borders.* London and New York: Verso.

Mendelson, Johanna S. R. 1978. "The Feminine Press: The View of Women in the Colonial Journals of Spanish America, 1790–1810." In Lavrin, *Latin American Women.*

Metcalf, Alida C. 1991. "Searching for the Slave Family in Colonial Brazil: A Reconstruction from São Paulo." *Journal of Family History* 16, no. 3: 283–297.

———. 1992. *Family and Frontier in Colonial Brazil: Santana de Parnaíba, 1580–1822.* Berkeley and Los Angeles: University of California Press.

Meyer, Doris, and Marguerite Fernández-Olmos. 1983. *Contemporary Women Authors of Latin America,* Vols. I and II. New York: Brooklyn College Press.

Midlo Hall, Gwendolyn. 1971. *Social Control in Slave Plantation Societies: A Comparison of St. Domingue and Cuba.* Baltimore, Md.: The John Hopkins University Press.

Miller, Beth, ed. 1983. *Women in Hispanic Literature: Icons and Fallen Idols.* Berkeley and Los Angeles: University of California Press.

Mintz, Sidney W. 1959. "The Plantation in Socio-Cultural Type." In Rubin, *Plantation Systems of the New World.*

Molyneux, Maxine. 1986. "No God, No Boss, No Husband: Anarchist Feminism in Nineteenth-Century Argentina." *Latin American Perspectives* 48: 119–45.

Momsen, Janet H. 1993. *Women and Change in the Caribbean.* Bloomington: Indiana University Press.

Morrissey, Marietta. 1989. *Slave Women in the New World: Gender Stratification in the Caribbean.* Lawrence: University of Kansas Press.

Myers, Kathleen A. 1993. "A Glimpse of Family Life in Colonial Mexico: A Nun's Account." *Latin American Research Review* 28, no. 2: 63–87.

*Nash, June. 1978. "The Aztecs and the Ideology of Male Dominance." *Signs* 4, no. 2: 349–62.

*———. 1980. "Aztec Women: The Transition from Status to Class in Empire and Colony." In Étienne and Leacock, *Women and Colonization.*

———. 1986. *Women and Change in Latin America.* South Hadley, Mass.: Bergin and Garvey Publishers.

Nash, June, and Helen Safa, eds. 1980. *Sex and Class in Latin America.* South Hadley, Mass.: J. F. Bergin Publishers.

Navarro, Marysa. 1980. "Evita and the Crisis of 17 October 1945: A Case Study of Peronist and Anti-Peronist Mythology." *Journal of Latin American Studies* 12, part I: 127–38.

———. 1982. "Evita's Charismatic Leadership." In Conniff, *Latin American Populism in Comparative Perspective.*

———. 1983. "Evita and Peronism." In Turner and McGuiness, *Juan Perón.*

———. 1985. "Hidden, Silent, and Anonymous: Women Workers in the Argentine Trade Union Movement." In Soldon, *The World of Women's Trade Unionism.*

———. 1989. "The Personal is Political: Las Madres de Plaza de Mayo." In Eckstein, *Power and Popular Protest.*

Navarro, Marysa, and Susan C. Bourque. 1998. "Fault Lines of Democratic Governance: A Gender Perspective." In Aguero, *Fault Lines of Democracy.*

Nazzari, Muriel. 1991. *Disappearance of the Dowry: Women, Families and Social Change in São Paulo, Brazil (1600–1900).* Stanford: Stanford University Press.

Nelson, Barbara J., and Najma Chowdhury, eds. 1994. *Women and Politics Worldwide.* New Haven: Yale University Press.

Nizza da Silva, Maria Beatriz. 1984. *Sistema de casamento no Brasil colonial.* São Paulo: T.A. Eueiroz/EDUSP.

Paz, Octavio. 1979. "Juana Ramirez." *Signs* 5, no. 1: 80–97.

Pérez, Jr., Louis A. 1992. *Slaves, Sugar, and Colonial Society.* Wilmington, Del.: Scholarly Resources, Inc.

Pescatello, Ann. 1976. *Power and Pawn: The Female in Iberian Families, Societies, and Cultures.* Westport, Conn.: Greenwood Press.

Phillips, Lynne P. 1987. "Tomasa Muñoz de León: From Precarista to Cooperativista." In Beezley and Ewell, *The Human Tradition.*

*Picó, Isabel. 1986. "The History of Women's Struggle for Equality in Puerto Rico." In Acosta-Belén, *The Puerto Rican Woman.*

Power, Margaret. Forthcoming. *Gendered Allegiances: The Construction of a Cross-class Right-wing Women's Movement in Chile, 1964–1973.* State College: Pennsylvania State University Press.

Prescott, William H. 1936. *The History of the Conquest of Mexico.* 1843. Reprint New York: Modern Library.

Queiroz, Rachel de. 1985. *The Three Marias*. Trans. Fred P. Ellison. Austin: University of Texas Press.

*Radcliffe, Sarah A., and Sallie Westwood, eds. 1990. *'Viva': Women and Popular Protest in Latin America*. London and New York: Routledge.

Ramos, Carmen, Ma. de Jesús Rodriguez, Pilar Gonzalbo, Francois Giraud, Solange Alberro, Francois Carner, Soledad González, Pilar Iracheta, Jean Pierre Bastian, and Enriqueta Tuñon. 1987. *Presencia y transparencia: La mujer en la historia de México*. Mexico: El Colegio de México.

Ramos, Donald. 1975. "Marriage and Family in Colonial Vila-Rica." *Hispanic American Historical Review* 55, no. 2: 200–25.

———. 1978. "City and Country: The Family in Minas Gerais, 1804–1838." *Journal of Family History* 3, no. 4: 361–75.

———. 1991. "Single and Married Women in Vila Rica, Brazil, 1754–1838." *Journal of Family History* 16, no. 3: 261–82.

Randall, Margaret. 1980. *Todas estamos despiertas*. Mexico: Siglo XXI.

*———. 1981. *Women in Cuba: Twenty Years Later*. New York: Smyrna Press.

*Reddock, Rhoda E. 1985. "Women and Slavery in the Caribbean. A Feminist Perspective." *Latin American Perspectives* 12, no. 1: 63–80.

*Reed, John. 1982. *Insurgent Mexico*. New York: International Publishers.

Ríos, Palmira. 1995. "Gender, Industrialization, and Development in Puerto Rico." In Bose and Acosta-Belén, *Women in the Latin American Development Process*.

*Rivera, Marcia. 1986. "The Development of Capitalism in Puerto Rico and the Incorporation of Women into the Labor Force." In Acosta-Belén, *The Puerto Rican Woman*.

Rodríguez Villamil, Sílvia, and Graciela Sapriza. 1984. *Mujer, estado y política en el Uruguay del siglo XX*. Montevideo, Uruguay: Editora Banda Oriental.

Rubin, Vera, ed. 1959. *Plantation Systems of the New World*. Washington, D.C.: Pan American Union.

Ruether, Rosemary R., and Rosemary S. Keller, eds. 1983. *Women and Religion in America: The Colonial and Revolutionary Period*, Vol. 2. San Francisco: Harper and Row.

Ruggiero, Kristin. 1992a. "Honor, Maternity, and the Disciplining of Women: Infanticide in Late Nineteenth-Century Buenos Aires." *Hispanic American Historical Review* 72, no. 3: 353–73.

———. 1992b. "'Wives on Deposit': Internment and the Preservation of Husbands' Honor in Late Nineteenth-Century Buenos Aires," *Journal of Family History* 17, no. 3: 253–70.

*Russell-Wood, A. J. R. 1978. "Female and Family in the Economy and Society of Colonial Brazil." In Lavrin, *Latin American Women*.

*———. 1985. "Women and Society in Colonial Brazil." In Bakewell, *Readings in Latin American History*.

Safa, Helen I. 1981. "Runaway Shops and Female Employment: The Search for Cheap Labor." *Signs* 7, no. 2: 418–33.

———. 1995. "Women's Social Movements in Latin America." In Bose and Acosta-Belén, *Women in the Latin American Development Process*.

*Salas, Elizabeth. 1990. *Soldaderas in the Mexican Military: Myth and History*. Austin: University of Texas Press.

*Sánchez Korrol, Virginia. 1994. *From Colonia to Community: History of Puerto Ricans in New York City*. Berkeley: University of California Press.

Scarano, Francisco A. 1984. *Sugar and Slavery in Puerto Rico.* Madison: University of Wisconsin Press.

Schroeder, Susan, Stephanie Wood, and Robert Haskett. 1997. *Indian Women of Early Mexico.* Norman: University of Oklahoma Press.

Schwartz, Stuart B. 1985. *Sugar Plantations in the Formation of Brazilian Society: Bahia, 1550–1835.* Cambridge, England: Cambridge University Press.

———. 1995. "Colonial Identities and the Sociedad de Castas." *Colonial Latin American Review* 4, no.1: 185–201.

Seager, Joni. 1997. *The State of Women in the World Atlas.* Revised ed., New York: Penguin.

*Seed, Patricia. 1988. *To Love, Honor, and Obey in Colonial Mexico: Conflicts over Marriage Choice, 1574–1821.* Stanford, Calif.: Stanford University Press.

Seminar on Feminism and Culture in Latin America. 1990. *Women, Culture, and Politics in Latin America.* Berkeley and Los Angeles: University of California Press.

Sherman, William L. 1979. *Forced Native Labor in Sixteenth-Century Central America.* Lincoln: University of Nebraska Press.

*Silverblatt, Irene. 1980. "'The Universe has turned inside out. . . . There is no justice for us here.': Andean Women Under Spanish Rule." In Étienne and Leacock, *Women and Colonization.*

———. 1987. *Moon, Sun, and Witches: Gender Ideologies and Class in Inca and Colonial Peru.* Princeton, N.J.: Princeton University Press.

*Silvestrini, Blanca. 1986. "Women as Workers: The Experience of the Puerto Rican Woman in the 1930s." In Acosta-Belén, *The Puerto Rican Woman.*

*Smith, Michael E. 1996. *The Aztecs.* Oxford: Blackwell.

Socolow, Susan Midgen. 1985. "Women and Crime: Buenos Aires, 1757–97." In Bakewell, *Readings in Latin American History.*

———. 1987. *The Bureaucrats of Buenos Aires, 1769–1810: Amor al servicio.* Durham, N.C.: Duke University Press.

Soeiro, Susan A. 1974. "The Social and Economic Role of the Convent: Women and Nuns in Colonial Bahia, 1677–1800." *Hispanic American Historical Review* 54, no. 2: 209–32.

———. 1978. "The Feminine Orders in Colonial Bahia, Brazil: Economic, Social, and Demographic Implications, 1677–1800." In Lavrin, *Latin American Women.*

Soldon, Norbert C., ed. 1985. *The World of Women's Trade Unionism.* Westport, Conn.: Greenwood Press.

*Soto, Shirlene Ann. 1990. *Emergence of the Modern Mexican Woman: Her Participation in the Revolution and Struggle for Equality, 1910–1940.* Denver, Colo.: Arden Press.

Spalding, Karen. 1984. *Huarochiri: An Andean Society Under Inca and Spanish Rule.* Stanford, Calif.: Stanford University Press.

*Steady, Filomina Chioma, ed. 1981. *The Black Woman Cross-Culturally.* Cambridge, Mass.: Schenkman.

*Stern, Steve. 1995. *The Secret History of Gender: Women, Men, and Power in Late Colonial Mexico.* Chapel Hill: University of North Carolina Press.

Stoltz Chinchilla, Norma. 1995. "Revolutionary Popular Feminism in Nicaragua: Ideologies, Political Transitions, and the Struggle for Autonomy." In Bose and Acosta-Belén, *Women in the Latin American Development Process.*

Stone, Elizabeth, ed. 1981. *Women and the Cuban Revolution: Speeches and Documents by Fidel Castro and Vilma Espín.* New York: Pathfinder.

Stoner, K. Lynn. 1987a. "Directions in Latin American Women's History, 1977–1985." *Latin American Research Review* 22, no. 2: 101–34.

*———. 1987b. "Ofelia Domínguez Navarro: The Making of a Cuban Socialist." In Beezley and Ewell, *The Human Tradition.*

*———. 1991a. *From the House to the Streets: The Cuban Women's Movement for Legal Reform, 1898–1940.* Durham, N.C.: Duke University Press.

———. 1991b. "On Men Reforming the Right of Men: The Abrogation of the Cuban Adultery Law, 1930." *Cuban Studies* 21: 83–99.

———, ed. 1989. *Latinas of the Americas: A Source Book.* New York: Garland Press.

Sweet, David G., and Gary B. Nash, eds. 1981. *Struggle and Survival in the Colonial Americas.* Berkeley and Los Angeles: University of California Press.

Szuchman, Mark D. 1986. "Household Structure and Political Crisis: Buenos Aires, 1810–1860." *Latin American Research Review* 21: 55–93.

Taylor, Julie M. 1979. *Eva Perón: The Myth of a Woman.* Chicago: University of Chicago Press.

Taylor, William B. 1979. *Drinking, Homicide and Rebellion in Colonial Mexican Villages.* Stanford, Calif.: Stanford University Press.

Thomas, Hugh. 1993. *The Conquest of Mexico.* London: Hutchinson.

Towner, Margaret. 1979. "Monopoly Capitalism and Women's Work During the Porfiriato." In *Women in Latin America.*

Townshend, F. T. 1992. "Wildlife in Florida with a Visit to Cuba." In Pérez, *Slaves, Sugar, and Colonial Society.*

Turner, F. C., and J. J. McGuiness, eds. 1983. *Juan Perón and the Reshaping of Argentina.* Pittsburgh: University of Pittsburgh Press.

Tutino, John. 1982. "Power, Class, and Family: Men and Women in the Mexican Elite, 1750–1810." *The Americas* 39, no. 3: 359–82.

———. 1985. "Family Economies in Agrarian Mexico, 1750–1910." *Journal of Family History* 10, no. 3: 258–71.

*Valle-Ferrer, Norma. 1986. "Feminism and Its Influence on Women's Organizations in Puerto Rico." In Acosta-Belén, *The Puerto Rican Woman.*

Vasques de Miranda, Glaura. 1977. "Women's Labor Force Participation in a Developing Society: The Case of Brazil." *Signs* 3, no. 1: 261–74.

Vaughan, Mary K. 1979. "Women, Class and Education in Mexico, 1880–1928." In *Women in Latin America.*

———. 1986. "Primary Schooling in the City of Puebla, 1821–1860." Unpublished paper. University of Illinois at Chicago.

*———. 1990. "Women School Teachers in the Mexican Revolution: The Story of Reyna's Braids." *Journal of Women's History* 2, no. 1: 143–68; reprinted in Johnson-Odim and Strobel, *Expanding the Boundaries of Women's History.*

*Waldman, Gloria Feiman. 1983. "Affirmation and Resistance: Women Poets from the Caribbean." In Meyer and Fernández-Olmos, *Contemporary Women Authors.*

Wells, Allen. 1982. "Family Elites in a Boom-and-Bust Economy: The Molinas and Peons of Porfirian Yucatan." *Hispanic American Historical Review* 62, no. 2: 224–53.

Wightman, Ann M. 1990. *Indigenous Migration and Social Change: The Forasteros of Cuzco, 1570–1720.* Durham, N.C.: Duke University Press.

Wolfe, Joel. 1993. *Working Women, Working Men: São Paulo and the Rise of Brazil's Industrial Working Class, 1900–1955.* Durham, N.C.: Duke University Press.

Women in Latin America. 1979. Riverside, Calif.: Latin American Perspectives.

Yeager, Gertrude M., ed. 1994. *Confronting Change, Challenging Tradition: Women in Latin American History.* Jaguar Books on Latin America #7. Wilmington, Del.: Scholarly Resources.

*Zavala, Iris, and Rafael Rodríguez, eds. 1980. *Intellectual Roots of Independence.* New York: Monthly Review Press.

Zulawski, Ann. 1995. *They Eat from Their Labor: Work and Social Change in Colonial Bolivia.* Pittsburgh: Pittsburgh University Press.

NOTES ON CONTRIBUTORS

Kecia Ali is in Duke University's graduate program in religion. She is the author of "The Historiography of Women in Modern Latin America: An Overview and Bibliography of the Recent Literature" in the Duke–University of North Carolina Program in Latin American Studies' working paper series.

Cheryl Johnson-Odim is professor of history and chairs the Department of History at Loyola University, Chicago. She co-authored *For Women and the Nation: Funmilayo Ransome-Kuti of Nigeria* and co-edited *Expanding the Boundaries of Women's History*. She has published many articles and chapters on African women's history and on feminist theory. She is a past member of the board of directors of the African Studies Association and the American Council of Learned Societies and serves on the editorial boards of the *Journal of Women's History* and *Chicago Women, 1770–1990: A Biographical Dictionary*.

Marysa Navarro is Charles Collis Professor of History and chair of the Latin American, Latino and Caribbean Studies Program at Dartmouth College. She is the author of a biography of Eva Perón and has written on the feminist movement in Latin America, the Mothers of Plaza de Mayo, and women and democracy in Latin America.

Virginia Sánchez Korrol is professor and chair of the Department of Puerto Rican and Latino Studies, and director of the Center for Latino Studies at Brooklyn College, City University of New York. She researches women in diasporic communities and has written numerous book chapters on U.S. Latinas. She is best known for *From Colonia* *to Community: The History of Puerto Ricans in New York City.* More recently she co-edited *Recovering the U.S. Hispanic Literary Heritage, Volume III,* and will be co-editor with Vicki Ruiz of *Latinas in the United States: An Historical Encyclopedia.*

Margaret Strobel is professor of women's studies and history at the University of Illinois at Chicago. Her book *Muslim Women in Mombasa, 1890–1975* won the African Studies Association's Herskovits Award in 1980. She is author of *European Women and the Second British Empire* and co-editor of *Three Swahili Women, Life Histories from Mombasa, Kenya; Western Women and Imperialism: Complicity and Resistance;* and *Expanding the Boundaries of Women's History.* She serves on the editorial board of *Chicago Women, 1770–1990: A Biographical Dictionary,* and is working on a book about the Chicago Women's Liberation Union.

INDEX